Mike Dillon

M
MIKE'S WORLD
M

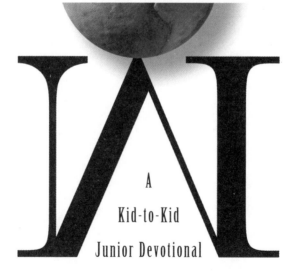

A
Kid-to-Kid
Junior Devotional

REVIEW AND HERALD® PUBLISHING ASSOCIATION
HAGERSTOWN, MD 21740

The author assumes full responsibility for the accuracy of all facts
and quotations as cited in this book.

All Bible quotations not otherwise credited are from *Holy Bible, New International
Reader's Version.* Copyright © 1995, 1996, 1998 by International Bible Society. Used by
permission of Zondervan Publishing House. All rights reserved.

Scripture quotations marked NASB are from the *New American Standard Bible,* ©
The Lockman Foundation 1960, 1962, 1963, 1968, 1971, 1972, 1973, 1975, 1977.

Texts credited to NIV are from the *Holy Bible, New International Version.* Copyright
© 1973, 1978, 1984, International Bible Society. Used by permission of Zondervan Bible
Publishers.

This book was
Edited by Gerald Wheeler
Copyedited by Eugene Lincoln and James Cavil
Designed by Willie Duke
Cover photo by Joel D. Springer
Electronic makeup by Shirley M. Bolivar
Typeset: 11/13 Veljovic

PRINTED IN U.S.A.

04 03 02 01 00 99   5 4 3 2 1

R&H Cataloging Service
Dillon, Michael Charles, 1983-
    Mike's world: a kid-to-kid devotional.

    1. Teenagers—Prayer-books and devotions—English.
2. Devotional calendars—Juvenile literature.   I. Title.

                242.6

ISBN 0-8280-1338-1

WHEN YOUR RESOLUTIONS ARE STRONGER THAN YOUR RESOLVE

Happy New Year! Here in the United States it's time for winter and snow and celebrations—and if we're lucky, a blizzard, so we can have days off from school! Baseball season is over (aw!), but basketball season is starting (yeah!). January 1 is just an all-around good day.

A lot of people use it as a time to make New Year's resolutions. A resolution is a decision you make to change something in your life. Along with a new year, people want to make a new beginning. You can put all the bad things and broken promises behind you and start over again.

A year is too long for some of us, though. Every year my mom resolves to lose weight, but by February she's forgotten her diet. I vowed to keep my room clean, but I don't want to discuss how long I was able to keep that!

One of the cool things about being a Christian is that if you've messed up, you don't have to wait till January for a new start. All you have to do is pray, and God will forgive you, and you can celebrate a clean slate all over again! So try to break your nasty habits with a New Year's resolution. But if things don't work out, start over again with God.

God, thank You for forgiveness and for being willing to wipe my slate clean and to give me a fresh start anytime. Amen.

JANUARY 1

His great love is new every morning. Lord, how faithful you are!

Lamentations 3:23.

5

SAVED BY BLOOD

One man [Adam] sinned, and death ruled because of his sin. But we are even more sure of what will happen because of what the one man, Jesus Christ, has done. Those who receive the rich supply of God's grace will rule with Christ in his kingdom. They have received God's gift and have been made right with him.

Romans 5:17.

Today is National Blood Donation Day. Thousands of people will go to schools or churches to have a pint of their blood drawn for other people who need blood transfusions.

When I was younger, I went with my dad when he donated blood. I thought I could never be a blood donor, because of the big needles they use. My dad was very brave to let them stick a needle in his arm and take his blood to give to someone he didn't even know.

It made me stop and think about Jesus, who gave His blood for me. He didn't get to give it in a blood-mobile with sterile needles and friendly people who offered Him cookies and juice when He was finished. Jesus gave His blood by being whipped, punctured by thorns, and pierced by nails. My dad's blood might save one life, but Jesus' blood can save everyone!

Jesus, thank You for giving Your blood to save me. Amen.

LET'S GET SOAKED!

JANUARY 3

But you will receive power when the Holy Spirit comes on you.... You will be my witnesses from one end of the earth to the other.

Acts 1:8.

On this day in 1991 the first Super Soaker water gun went on sale. It was a big hit— or should I say it made a big splash? Millions have been sold, several to my brother and me. My mom even joined in the fun one summer and bought 10 of them for our family reunion.

Super Soakers have been a big success, with many varieties on the market. There's nothing like getting sprayed with cool water on a hot summer day. It leaves you refreshed and full of energy to run around squirting others. When I'm in a Super Soaker water fight, I wish it would never end.

The Holy Spirit is the ultimate Super Soaker. When He gets inside of you, He refreshes and invigorates your spirit. And you'll find that it's great fun seeing other people get soaked by Him as well, especially when you are involved in the soaking process too.

Holy Spirit, please soak me today. And show me opportunities to help You soak somebody else. Amen.

JUST RIGHT

JANUARY 4

How you made me is amazing and wonderful. I praise you for that. What you have done is wonderful. I know that very well.

Psalm 139:14.

I'm not short, just vertically challenged. And so was Tom Thumb, the shortest man in history, who, coincidentally, was born today in 1838. Because of his birthday, today has been designated to honor all short people.

When Tom found a woman short enough for him to marry, a famous tall person, Abraham Lincoln, attended their reception.

Just because I'm short doesn't mean I can't do something important with my life. Zacchaeus wasn't tall enough to see over the crowd, but Jesus chose him as a dinner companion. And don't forget Knee-High-Mia (Nehemiah).

But all joking aside, short people have been important all through history. Napoleon, barely more than five feet, conquered most of Europe. I may not be very tall, but I am big enough for what God wants me to do. No matter what your height and body size, you're just right for what God hopes you will be. So don't let your size get in the way of your dreams.

God, thanks for making me just right. Amen.

AND ON THE FIFTH DAY . . .

JANUARY 5

Lord, I worship you. My God, I trust in you.

Psalm 25:1, 2.

I love fish. Not with tartar sauce, but in my aquarium. To bring fish home, however, you have to plan ahead.

You need to make sure that the tank and gravel are really clean. Any chemicals on them could hurt the fish. They need plants to hide among and play in so they don't die of boredom. Plants also help put oxygen into the water for the fish.

An aquarium needs a filter and a bubbler. The filter and the bubbler work together to keep the water clean and oxygenated. My fish love to play in the bubbles it makes.

Your fish tank will need a light, too, especially if it's not near a window. The fish need light from above so they can look up and see their food floating on the surface.

After you set up your aquarium and before you put in any fish, you need to let it sit for two days with the filter going to clean the water and warm it.

When God was setting up His giant Earth aquarium, He started with light. He added air the next day. On the third day He supplied the gravel and plants. They helped work as a filter and bubbler, too, since seaweed gives off oxygen bubbles. On the fourth day He created a huge aquarium-top light and heater we call the sun. By the fifth day the water had been filtering for two days and was ready for fish, so God created them.

Because God so carefully planned everything in His giant aquarium, I can trust Him to take care of everything I need too.

Lord, please remind me today just how trustworthy You are. Amen.

DOING ADAM'S JOBS

JANUARY 6

The Lord God put the man in the Garden of Eden. He put him there to work its ground and to take care of it.

Genesis 2:15.

In the beginning God gave Adam three jobs:
1. Naming the animals.
2. Caring for his garden home.
3. Being fruitful and multiplying.

So far I have done the first two, but I'm saving the third one for later.

I haven't named *all* the animals, although I've named all the animals in my house and some outside.

I've named my flock of parakeets (and am coming up with more names as their babies hatch), my 17 gerbils, my two turtles (Smith and Wesson), my duck (Stupid), my cats (McCavity and Magic), and my brother (although he doesn't like the names I give him).

I haven't tended many gardens, but I have taken care of three miles of road through the Adopt-a-Highway program. Four times a year my classmates and I go out dressed in silly orange vests to pick up trash along the road near our school.

I can't save all the endangered animals or stop world pollution, but I *can* make a difference to my three miles of road where I live, and care for the animals God gave me.

As for that third job, ask me again in 10 years or so!

Lord, show me how to make my little piece of earth a better place to live. Amen.

10

FOLLOW THE LEADER

O n this day in 1958 the first ant farm was sold in the United States. The next day the buyers started trying to figure out how to invent bug spray to get rid of all the ants that escaped.

I had an ant farm when I was younger and learned lots of things from it. For example, ants can't do anything without a queen. They have to have a boss or someone in charge, or else all of them will die. Also I discovered that they work much more efficiently and get a lot more done as a team.

One ant by itself can't do much. But lots of ants working together can move a mountain—or build one. If I dropped a cornflake into my ant farm, the ants didn't try to drag it all away. Instead, they broke the flake up into little pieces so that it could fit down the entrance hole.

I've found that big jobs work best that way too. King Solomon, the wisest man who ever lived, said that lazy people need to learn from the ants. I'm not lazy, but I learned a lot from my ant farm anyway. If you get an ant farm, you'll find it's tons of fun. Just remember to put the cap back on after you've put the ants in. You'll get along a lot better with your mom that way.

God, thanks for creating so many neat creatures that we can learn from. Amen.

JANUARY 7

You people who don't want to work, think about the ant! Consider its ways and be wise!

Proverbs 6:6.

JOY GERMS

A cheerful heart makes you healthy. But a broken spirit dries you up.

Proverbs 17:22.

Misery loves company. If one person starts complaining, soon everyone around them does too. But there is a germ out there even more contagious than misery. It's the joy germ. It can spread fast, infecting whole groups of people at once. The germ's side effects may include smiles, hugs, and absolute happiness. Unlike the case with such germs as typhoid, joy has no silent carriers. You can't pass it on without it infecting yourself too. And, fortunately, there is no cure! After all, none of us want to be cured of joy.

Joy germs destroy grumps, frowns, and rudeness. And joy helps the infected person to become immune to them in the future.

If you need smiles, hugs, and giggles, find someone infected with joy germs right away! Then if you see someone without a smile, give them one of yours.

Father God, thank You for giving me joy. Help me to share it with someone today. Amen.

NATIONAL PIZZA WEEK

JANUARY 9

Lord, you are everything I need. I have promised to obey your words.

Psalm 119:57.

This week is National Pizza Week, sponsored by a well-known chain of pizza restaurants. To celebrate, they want you to eat a different type of pizza each day. (It's a thankless job, but somebody has to do it!)

It is the type of celebration my mom can really get into. She thinks pizza is one of the four major food groups. In fact, she did celebrate this week when she was about my age. She and her dad were in Italy (land of the pizza). Although she wanted to eat pizza every night, her dad said she would get tired of it before the week was over.

That sounded like a challenge to her! Poor Grandpa had to eat pizza every single night. Mom didn't get sick of it, but Grandpa sure did! Every night she would have a different topping.

The idea of reading your Bible every day sounds boring to some people too. What they don't realize is that the Bible has more variety than Italy has pizzas. You can choose from poetry and proverbs, stories and letters, and my personal favorite, the maps in the back. So if you think the Bible is boring, take a look for yourself and try a different kind every day.

Lord, thank You for all the neat things You've put into the Bible for me. And please keep those surprises coming when I read it. Amen.

WHERE'S THE BEEF?

Don't let anyone look down on you because you are young. Set an example for the believers in what you say and how you live. Also set an example in how you love and in what you believe. Show the believers how to be pure.

1 Timothy 4:12.

I n 1984 a TV commercial for a hamburger chain featured a little old woman named Clara Peller asking, "Where's the beef?" She was asking where the most important part of the sandwich was. Sometimes I want to ask that at church, but not because I don't appreciate a vegetarian potluck.

For little kids, Sabbath school has to be entertaining. But I'm not a little kid anymore. As a baptized member of my church I don't want my Sabbath school to be a happy little day-care center where we sing songs and watch puppet shows.

Don't get me wrong; I like to have fun. But I'm a real Christian who wants to take part in real study, real worship, and have a real mission. I want more than just to be entertained. If you feel like this, talk to your youth leader and ask them, "Where's the beef?"

God, please give my church leaders wisdom to know Your will, courage to follow Your leading, and creativity to explain it all to me. I don't want just to play church. I want to know who You really are. Amen.

MAKING A JOYFUL NOISE

JANUARY 11

Make a joyful noise

unto the Lord.

Psalm 100:1, KJV.

My mom likes to sing. She's not very good at it, but that never bothered me. When I was a little kid, she always sang me to sleep, and I loved it. A little while ago she was in the hospital. Friday night I brought her my Walkman and some of her favorite Sabbath tapes. I knew she'd need something to do when she couldn't sleep. During the wee hours of the morning she listened to my Walkman and naturally started singing along. In a little while the nurse came to ask if Mom needed more pain medication.

"No thanks," my mother answered. "I'm fine."

"Are you sure?" the nurse questioned. "You were moaning so pitifully. It sounded like you were in a lot of pain."

Mom felt bad that her singing resembled yowls of pain. I'm really looking forward to heaven, where Mom won't ever be in the hospital again and she can sing as loud as she wants without anyone offering her pain medicine.

Jesus, I'm tired of all the pain in this world. Please come soon! Amen.

15

CLIPPING WINGS

Choose for yourselves right now whom you will serve.... But as for me and my family, we will serve the Lord.

Joshua 24:15.

I have lots of birds. My parakeets are as big as mice with wings, and our parrot is as big as a cat (with wings).

One of my jobs is to clip their wings every month. I don't actually cut their wings off. I just trim the long flight feathers so they can't fly. It doesn't hurt, but it is like getting your hair cut or cutting your fingernails.

I do this to protect them. If they flew around the house, they could crash into windows or land on the stove, or even escape right out the door. Pet birds have even been known to drown in toilets. They also leave "presents" on top of the bookcases and around the room, and Mom doesn't like that. That causes *lots* of trouble!

God doesn't "clip my wings." There are things all around me that I could get into trouble with. Since He gave me the freedom of choice, I have to choose not to get into trouble. Sometimes I think it would be easier just to have "clipped wings," but I am glad God left the choices up to me.

God, thank You for giving me choices. Help me to make good ones. Amen.

IT'S IN THE BLOOD

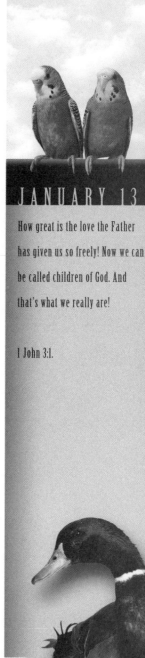

JANUARY 13

How great is the love the Father has given us so freely! Now we can be called children of God. And that's what we really are!

1 John 3:1.

When I was a little dude, my mom was the assistant vice president for nursing at a local hospital. People at the hospital treated Mom with a lot of respect.

I never thought much about it when I came to her office. Whether she was there or not, I knew to let myself in. Not even her secretary would dream of opening the drawers in her desk without permission, yet I went straight to my favorite drawer, the one where Mom kept markers and sketch pads and notebooks.

No one else in the hospital would have been comfortable doing what I did. But I always knew that I was welcome and exactly where to go to get the things I needed.

What made the rules different for me than for Mom's secretary or anyone else who worked in the hospital? It was the blood. Mom's blood runs in my veins. I was her kid. I knew she would be glad to see me.

It works that way with God too. He is the most powerful king of the universe. Everyone on the entire planet will bow the knee to Him someday and acknowledge that He is truly the victor. Yet I can barge into His office anytime, knowing that He will give me what I need and that He'll always be happy to see me. Why? Because of the blood. I'm His kid.

Jesus, thanks so much for Your blood that gives me the right to call God "Father," and to call You "Brother." Amen.

GOD AND POTLUCKS

I will never send away

anyone who comes to me.

John 6:37.

My mom has a chronic illness and is sick quite a bit. When she is, it's hard to get a home-cooked meal. That's why I really enjoy Sabbath potlucks. But the problem with potlucks is that you are expected to bring something.

I've found a really quick way to make Jell-O salad with fruit. I put frozen fruit straight from the freezer into a big bowl and pour the Jell-O over it. The cold fruit makes the Jell-O get firm, while at the same time the hot Jell-O thaws the frozen fruit.

It is the only really good thing I know how to make. The potluck women still seem happy when I show up with it, even though I've brought it to every potluck I've attended. They never complain or send me away until I learn how to make something better. Instead, they load me up with mashed potatoes and gravy, veggie meat, noodles, salad, and three kinds of dessert.

God is like a potluck woman. He always takes me however I am, and doesn't complain about why I haven't learned to be better yet. Then He loads me up with all kinds of good things and blessings, and I'm always welcome.

God, I'm glad that You don't expect too much from me and that You're patient enough to let me learn about You at my own pace, even when that seems awfully slow to me. I love You. Amen.

PART OF THE TEAM

On this day in 1892 in Springfield, Massachusetts, the official rules of basketball were published for the first time. Until then people played the game of basketball with a real basket perched on top of a pole or hanging from a wall. Everybody tried on their own to get the ball into the basket. Now suddenly it became a team sport.

No matter how great you are at b-ball, you won't be able to win unless you are part of a team. On the team different people do different things, but they're all working together for the same goal.

Dennis Rodman, who's played for the Chicago Bulls, doesn't shoot very often, and when he does, he doesn't often score. But he is one of the best basketball players anyone could ask for. His job is to get the ball back when the other team shoots. And he averages 22 rebounds per game. Pretty impressive!

Even though Michael Jordan was a great scorer, the Bulls would have lost a lot of games if all they had had were shooters. A team needs people to rebound and play defense as well.

To play on Jesus' team you don't need to have a real important church job or be a major baptism scorer. As long as you're a team player and you do what the Head Coach wants, you'll find that you too can be one of His MVPs.

Jesus, thanks for being my coach and planning a way for me to be a valuable part of Your team. Amen.

JANUARY 15

"I know the plans I have for you," announces the Lord. "I want you to enjoy success. I do not plan to harm you. I will give you hope for the years to come."

Jeremiah 29:11.

NATIONAL NOTHING DAY

Shout to the Lord with joy, everyone on earth. Worship the Lord with gladness. Come to him with songs of joy. I want you to realize that the Lord is God. He made us, and we belong to him. We are his people. We are the sheep belonging to his flock.

Psalm 100:1-3.

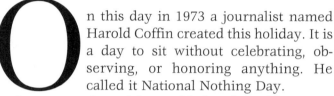

On this day in 1973 a journalist named Harold Coffin created this holiday. It is a day to sit without celebrating, observing, or honoring anything. He called it National Nothing Day.

Some people celebrate National Nothing Day about once a week. When the weekend comes, they just sit around and do nothing. They don't celebrate or do anything—they just sit.

As a Christian, I don't think that we should ever celebrate National Nothing Day, whether we're talking January 16 or the weekly Sabbath. There is so much that God has done for us around every corner or right under our noses that we should celebrate and honor Him *every* day. God does so much cool stuff for us, so let's celebrate!

God, thanks for all the neat stuff You do for us. Please forgive us when we seem ungrateful—especially when we turn Sabbath into a weekly nothing day. Amen.

THEY ARE FAMILY TOO

Oyoko Poquito Bandita was my baby parrot's real name, but she called herself "Dita," so we did too. We got her as a 3-week-old naked chick with no feathers. Until she learned to eat by herself, we had to feed her baby parrot formula with a spoon. Once she learned to feed herself, she refused to eat "parrot" food such as seeds and nuts. Instead, she insisted on eating whatever I was eating. Considering herself human and part of the family, a couple times she even tried to sleep in bed with my parents.

We also have a small flock of parakeets who live with us. They consider themselves parakeets and behave like parakeets. Since they were much smaller than Dita, she felt it was her duty to keep them all corralled. Since all their wings were clipped so they couldn't fly, Dita would waddle around the living room and chase them into a corner.

Dita had to adapt and learn that the parakeets were part of the family too. Even though they looked different, acted different, talked different, and ate different food, they were still part of the family. So Dita had to learn to get along with her "brothers and sisters" even if they were very different.

We need to learn to get along with our brothers and sisters in God's family too, even if they are a lot different than we are. Dita had to adapt. You do too.

Lord, help me to remember that people who are different from me are still Your children and part of Your family. Amen.

JANUARY 17

He came to what was his own. But his own people did not accept him. Some people did accept him. They believed in his name. He gave them the right to become children of God.

John 1:11, 12.

21

THE DAY THE SCHOOL BURNED, PART 1

JANUARY 18

Give thanks to the Lord, because
he is good.
His faithful love continues forever.
Give thanks to the greatest
God of all....
Give thanks to the most powerful
Lord of all....
Give thanks to the only one who
can do great miracles....
By his understanding he made
the heavens....
He spread out the earth
on the waters.

Psalm 136.

G o to bed," Dad said for the fifth time. "It's 10:00, and you have to get up early so you can go to school tomorrow."

"But Dad, I don't want to go to school," I pleaded. "School is boring!"

Dad looked at me sternly and replied, "Some kids in other countries don't even have a school to go to! They'd be happy to go to your school."

"They're lucky not to go to school," I replied. And with that I went to bed.

"Wake up!" My father was badgering me again.

"But Dad, I don't want to get up yet! It's only 6:00!"

"You need to get up and get dressed quickly and come with me."

"But why?"

With a serious look on his face, Dad said, "To see your school burning."

I never realized how important school was to me until that day when I saw an arsonist destroy it. For the rest of the year we felt homeless. We had to spread our school out among three buildings and the church at the local academy.

It made me really stop and think. Perhaps I should be more appreciative of the things in my life now instead of after they are gone.

Do you have something or someone that you should appreciate and don't? Develop an attitude of gratitude.

Father God, please remind me how many things I have to be thankful for. Amen.

THE DAY THE SCHOOL BURNED, PART 2

As the fire burned, Mrs. Melashenko, the first- and second-grade teacher, remembered Minnie the cat. Minnie was the class pet. The teachers and children all loved her. Mrs. Mel ran into the end of the building that wasn't burning. When we tried to stop her, she cried, "I have to save Minnie! I can't let her die."

A couple of us went in with her to look, but there was no sign of Minnie.

"She must be hiding," Mrs. Mel cried. We kept running in and out with no luck until the firefighters stopped us.

Once the fire was out, one of the firefighters found a crumpled ball of fur in the hall. Minnie had come out of hiding. He thought she was dead and started to walk on past, but then Minnie moved. Picking her up, he ran outside and placed her in Mrs. Mel's arms. Minnie died that day, but she died with someone she loved, and not alone.

If Minnie had let Mrs. Mel save her, instead of trying to save herself by hiding, she might still be alive today. But she couldn't hide from the fire, and we can't hide from the results of sin. The only way to survive is to come out of hiding and let Jesus save us.

Jesus, thank You for saving me, even though it cost You so much. Amen.

Give him the name Jesus. That is because he will save his people from their sins.

Matthew 1:21.

23

THE DAY THE SCHOOL BURNED, PART 3

JANUARY 20

You will pass through deep waters. But I will be with you. You will pass through the rivers. But their waters will not sweep over you. You will walk through fire. But you will not be burned. The flames will not harm you.

Isaiah 43:2.

The fire destroyed the fifth- and sixth-grade classroom and the kitchen. Smoke and water and the firefighters' breaking windows to let the smoke out damaged the rest of the school. But we were able to save quite a few things: all the records from the office, books from the library and those classrooms that didn't burn, some of the desks, and even our baseball equipment.

But the most amazing thing the firefighters discovered, as they shoveled out the debris left in the smoldering classroom, was that even though the desks had turned into hunks of melted plastic and twisted metal, the students' Bibles inside those desks were completely intact. On the wall was a picture of Jesus. The frame was scorched, but the canvas wasn't even singed.

After we had lost so much, the picture gave us hope. It said to us, "I am with you always, even to the end of the world."

Father God, thank You for showing us in such a real way how we can trust You to take care of us, no matter what Satan tries to do to us. Amen.

THE DAY THE SCHOOL BURNED, PART 4

Bad things don't happen only to bad people. Take Job, for instance. All of his family and everything he owned died or was taken away from him. Yet he remained faithful to God.

In the school fire all of our pets died. None of them had done anything to deserve it. Later we found out that the arsonist had burned them on purpose. A lot of the fuel he had used to set the school on fire he dumped directly on Hairy Ferret's cage. He also added extra fuel to the cages of Cocky Cockatiel, Iggy Iguana, and Timothy Turtle. The person killed our animals on purpose!

As the firefighters tossed the cage out onto the lawn with Hairy's charred little body in the bottom, I felt terrible. I felt really sick inside and angry all at the same time. If I felt that bad, imagine how the One who made them felt.

Lord, help me to remember that You cry too when someone or something You love is hurting. Teach me to recognize those who are hurting around me and to become a channel for Your love to them. Amen.

JANUARY 21

Aren't two sparrows sold for only a penny? But not one of them falls to the ground without your Father knowing it.

Matthew 10:29.

25

THE SUCKER

Anything you did for one of the least important of these [brothers and sisters] of mine, you did for me.

Matthew 25:40.

My friend Steve is a sucker. We went on a trip with the academy band to Spain and Morocco. In Morocco literally hundreds of street vendors tried to sell us overpriced tourist souvenirs. We had already bought everything we wanted when a vendor approached Steve. He was offering Steve a cushion that, when filled with stuffing, made a comfortable chair.

"My friend, I sell you this chair for special student price," he began.

"I don't want a chair, though," Steve replied.

"You know how much? Guess how much." He put his arm around my friend's shoulders.

"How much?" Steve asked irritably.

The man bent close and whispered, "Only 2,000 pesetas" (about U.S. $35).

"This is the last of my money," Steve explained. "I need it to eat. If I spend it, I won't have any food."

The man looked at him with begging eyes and said, "My friend, I too must eat."

That was enough to break Steve's heart. He not only gave the vendor the money he asked for, but 600 extra pesetas. It was all the money he had left. Steve didn't even want the thing he bought.

We all called Steve a sucker when we climbed back on the bus, but then I got to thinking. If Jesus were in Steve's position, what would He have done?

Jesus, make me willing to be a sucker for You. And give me compassion and sympathy for Your children who have less than what You have blessed me with. Amen.

26

NO PAIN, MY GAIN

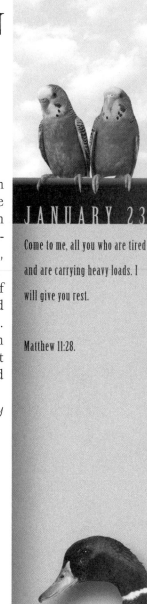

My mom had a lot of arthritis pain in her knees and ankles and joints. We had to spend a lot of money on pain medication for her. Then our doctor told us she should get a hot tub, or Jacuzzi.

She found that the hot, bubbly water felt as if somebody were massaging all the pain out of her and into the bubbles. In fact, it even took away headaches.

Jesus can be a lot like a hot tub sometimes. When you're feeling down, He can remove the pain right away, and it will just float away into the bubbles. And just like Mom's hot tub, you can use it every day.

Jesus, thanks for being the Great Pain Reliever on my down days. Amen.

JANUARY 23

Come to me, all you who are tired and are carrying heavy loads. I will give you rest.

Matthew 11:28.

God, create a pure heart in me. Give me a new spirit that is faithful to you.

Psalm 51:10.

YOU GOTTA HAVE HEART

On this day in 1964 surgeons performed the first heart transplant operation at University Hospital in Jacksonville, Florida. It was unsuccessful, and the patient died. Since then, heart transplants have come a long way, and usually the patients make it. People may need a heart transplant if their heart is worn out or damaged. God offers heart transplants to worn-out and damaged people too. And His patients always make it. But what happens next is up to them. Just like heart transplant patients, Christians have to take care of their new heart and not let it get damaged the way the first one did.

A heart transplant doesn't do any good unless you follow the doctor's post-transplant instructions. Fortunately, God made the instructions clear for us. Is your heart worn out or damaged? If it is, just ask Him for a new one and ask Him how to take care of it.

God, thanks for the new heart. Now teach me how to keep it full of You. Amen.

WHO YA GONNA CALL?

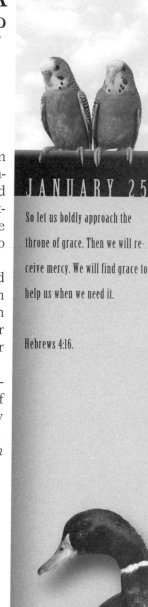

O n this day in 1915 Alexander Graham Bell placed the very first transcontinental phone call between New York and San Francisco. It was an incredibly exciting event, marveled at by the entire country. Imagine, someone in New York being able to speak to someone in San Francisco and be heard!

The year before that, no one would have dreamed such a thing possible. Yet when I was born, my dad in Illinois called my grandparents in Africa to tell them about my very undignified arrival (but that's another story). Long-distance communication is a lot easier now than it was for Alexander Graham Bell.

But for thousands of years people have been making calls from here all the way to heaven, billions of light-years away. And they didn't need any fancy equipment. All they had to do was whisper a prayer.

God, I'm glad I can always talk to You. And even more glad that You listen! Amen.

JANUARY 25

So let us boldly approach the throne of grace. Then we will receive mercy. We will find grace to help us when we need it.

Hebrews 4:16.

LIFE IS IMPORTANT

Before I was born, the Lord chose me to serve him.

Isaiah 49:1.

My mom was sick and having to take a lot of medicine when she found out that I was on the way. Her doctor worried about the effect of the drugs on me since there was a huge chance that I would be born with serious deformities and health problems. He told Mom to have an abortion and try again later when she didn't have to take so much medicine.

Upset, Mom prayed and prayed about it. She decided that I was her kid and my life was important, and that God wouldn't have given me life if He didn't have a plan for me. And that's what she told the doctor.

Mom decided she would love me and take care of me even if I had a cleft palate or was seriously disabled.

I'm so glad that she placed such value on me. I was born healthy with all of the appropriate parts, but it feels good to know that Mom would have wanted me anyway. It makes me really love my mom.

God placed an even higher value on me. He sent His only Son to die for me and would have done it even if I were the only person on earth who needed it.

Understanding how important I am to God changes the way I feel about myself. I have value, and it makes me love Him.

God, thank You so much for valuing me so highly. Teach me to recognize the value in all Your other children as well. Amen.

UGLY DUCKLINGS

Parakeets don't breed well in captivity. At least that's what my book about parakeets says. But my parakeets didn't read the book. They seem to believe "the more the merrier."

When my baby parakeets first hatch, they look like little naked ducks the size of a jelly bean. They seem to be all bulgy eyes, beak, and claws.

As their little feathers start coming in, they resemble a cross between a golf ball and a pincushion. But I love looking at them, because by studying the tint of the pins (their pinfeathers) I can tell what color they will be when they grow up.

Even though they seem really ugly to anyone else, I think they're beautiful. They are perfect as far as they've grown, looking just like a parakeet their age should. When I examine them, I don't see just the little ugly duckling awkward ball of fluff and claws, I see the beautiful swan . . . er . . . parakeet that they will become.

Sometimes I get frustrated as I try to grow to be like Jesus. I don't look much like Him yet. But when God sees me, He doesn't look just at what I am now. He focuses on what I am becoming and what I will be. And to Him, I am perfect as far as I've grown.

Father God, thanks for looking beyond my present ugly duckling stage and seeing me as complete and perfect already. Amen.

JANUARY 27

Dear friends, now we are the children of God. He still hasn't let us know what we will be. But we know that when Christ appears, we will be like him.

1 John 3:2.

CINNAMON'S BRANCH

The angel of the Lord stands guard around those who have respect for him. And he saves them.

Psalm 34:7.

My pet cockatiel, Cinnamon, was out of her cage and sitting with me and Mom in her bedroom. Cinnamon really wanted to visit the cage of our big parrot, Wamml. But Wamml is very protective of his cage and would bite her if she dared climb the sacred bars. That could be bad. (He has a huge beak and is much bigger than she is.)

Cinnamon would be much happier in life without a giant hole through her head, so I kept her with me, although she kept trying to run away.

Going outside, I got a little branch for her to play on instead. But the branch wouldn't stay up by itself. I had to hold it steady to keep Cinnamon from falling over and getting hurt.

Sometimes we are like Cinnamon, clinging to our branch for dear life. We may be having fun, but if God were to take His eyes off our branch, we could fall over and get hurt too. I'm glad I can always count on Him to watch out for me.

God, thanks for always being there to make sure my wobbly branch doesn't come toppling down. Amen.

HAPPY BIRTHDAY!

Today I grow a year older, since it's my birthday. It happens only once a year, and it's one of my favorite times.

On my thirteenth birthday I received one of the most special birthday presents anybody can ever get. My grandpa baptized me. So now, not only is this a celebration of my birthday, but today I celebrate my rebirthday. That means I'm not the only one who gets presents today. Every year on this day I give God a present. I give Him me.

God, today I commit myself to You again. Hope You like Your present! Amen.

No one can enter God's kingdom without being born through water and the Holy Spirit. People give birth to people, but the Spirit gives birth to spirit.

John 3:5, 6.

33

LESSON FROM THE SLIME PUPPIES

The Bereans were very glad to receive Paul's message. They studied the Scriptures carefully every day. They wanted to see if what Paul had said was true. So they were more noble than the Thessalonians.

Acts 17:11.

One of Mom and Dad's friends, Dr. Brauer, rescued some baby possums whose mother had been killed on the road. He brought them to our house, knowing that my brother and I specialized in baby animals.

The baby possums were making their little "k-k-k-k-k" noises and were quite dehydrated. Dr. Brauer brought us some Pedialyte, a substance that doctors give to dehydrated human babies. We fed them the Pedialyte with a tiny bottle, and the next day got some special baby mammal formula for them.

They grew quickly, and soon we were able to put them on solid food. Now, they could eat on their own out of a dish. However, they weren't interested in actually eating the food. They crawled through and rolled around in the dish. Then they would find a corner of the cage and would lick the food off each other's fur. This trick earned them the nickname "slime puppies."

My mom commented that sometimes people are like that. God provides a whole lot of spiritual food for us in the Bible, but for some reason we like to get it secondhand from each other. The little possums also got all kinds of dirt and other things. When we take our spiritual food from other people's opinions instead of straight from the Bible, it can be a little contaminated too. It is much smarter to get our food right from the dish God gave us.

God, please make us hungry for Your Word straight from You. Amen.

MY RONALD REAGAN PEN

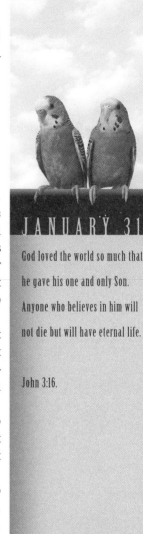

A while ago my mom went to California. While she was there, she visited the Ronald Reagan Library. It had lots of cool things there, such as expensive jewels and gifts from kings, queens, and other presidents, the bullet they took out of President Reagan's chest the time he was shot, and a huge slab of the Berlin Wall.

Mom bought lots of postcards, but she does that wherever she goes. She also brought me back a T-shirt and a pen. Ronald Reagan had used the pen to autograph his book. It is a black ballpoint pen with Reagan's signature embossed in gold on the side.

I thought it was really cool, but when I took it to school to show my friends, they didn't believe that Ronald Reagan had really used it. However, their not believing it didn't decrease the pen's value.

Some people may act like you aren't valuable to God yet just because you're a kid. Don't believe them. God has always used kids who were willing. Remember Samuel, Esther, Captain Naaman's servant girl, Timothy, and Ellen Harmon. Not believing that God uses kids doesn't change our value either!

Jesus, please use me today to show Your love to someone who needs to know You better. Amen.

JANUARY 31

God loved the world so much that he gave his one and only Son. Anyone who believes in him will not die but will have eternal life.

John 3:16.

35

ENCOURAGE SOMEBODY

FEBRUARY 1

But when the Comforter is come, whom I will send unto you from the Father, even the Spirit of truth, which proceedeth from the Father, he shall testify of me.

John 15:26, KJV.

Today is the day to encourage somebody. Liz Curtis Higgs, a Christian comedian, hilarious speaker, and author of humor books, declared it National Encouragement Day.

She often encourages others by telling about horribly embarrassing incidents that have happened to her and letting people know that they are not alone in experiencing such things. Like the time her panty hose got caught in the back. She made her husband come into a tiny ladies room to help her get them unhooked. But she forgot that she hadn't switched off her little lapel mike, and the entire auditorium got to listen to her huffing and puffing and the grunted instructions she gave her husband.

Different people need different kinds of encouragement. With some people it helps if you describe something embarrassing that happened to you. Others, like my mom, can be encouraged with just a big hug. My friend Carl gets encouraged just by somebody telling him that he's not weird. Having a clean house encourages my dad. However you may encourage somebody, just make it a point to do it today. And whenever you need encouragement, just ask God, because the Holy Spirit knows exactly how to do it.

Holy Spirit, Jesus said You would be our comforter. Thanks so much for being there when we need You. Amen.

36

THE RAINSTORM

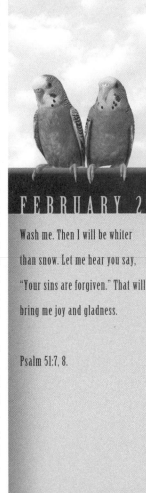

One day my brother and some of his friends were bored. And when my brother becomes bored, things can get ugly. They decided to throw toilet paper up in one of Jared's trees. They chose Jared not because they didn't like him, but because he was fun to annoy. What they didn't realize was that Jared's parents were coming home the next day. When my brother and his friends found out, they got real scared. Jared's dad could be kind of intimidating.

That night my brother, Donnie, prayed for rain like he had never prayed before. He prayed for rain, because toilet paper dissolves in water, and it would fall out of the tree before Jared's parents arrived home. The guys really didn't deserve the rain, because they had deliberately made the mess. But at 4:00 a.m. it started to sprinkle, then finally turned into a good solid rain. The rain washed away the evidence before Jared's parents reached home.

Just as the rain washed away all evidence of Donnie's mischief, God's grace can remove all traces of our sins. Grace is something that we don't deserve, but God gives it to us anyway, just because He loves us.

God, thank You for Your willingness to wash the sin from my life. Amen.

FEBRUARY 2

Wash me. Then I will be whiter than snow. Let me hear you say, "Your sins are forgiven." That will bring me joy and gladness.

Psalm 51:7, 8.

TRUST

FEBRUARY 3

He has also given us his very great and valuable promises. He did it so you could share in his nature. He also did it so you could escape from the evil in the world.

2 Peter 1:4.

On this day in 1690 the colony of Massachusetts issued the first paper money in America. They called each piece of paper a promissory note. It was a promise that the government would exchange the paper for a certain amount of gold.

When people bought and sold with this paper money, they had to have confidence that the government would keep its promise to exchange paper for gold. The paper by itself was worthless. The people had to learn to trust the government. Even today people suspicious of the government don't trust paper money.

Promissory notes from God fill the Bible—promises that He will keep. But the only way that they can be any good is if we trust in them and in the Person who gave them to us. Trust in God is just like having a wallet full of $100 bills. As long as you trust Him, you're rich.

Thank You, God, for all Your promises. Please help us to trust You more each day. Amen.

LIBERIA AND THE CONFEDERACY

On this day in 1822 the nation of Liberia formed in West Africa. It was a country for freed slaves who had returned from the United States. The American Colonization Society helped them establish it.

Since the British had outlawed slavery long before this, they tried to stop the ships carrying African slaves to North America. When they caught one, they would tow it to Liberia and free the slaves there.

Also on this day in 1861 delegates met in Montgomery, Alabama, to found the Confederate States of America. It depended on slave labor for their economy. They tried to split away from the rest of the United States in order to keep their slaves, causing the Civil War.

Isn't it ironic that two countries, based on opposite views about slavery, established themselves on the same day, only 39 years apart? One stood for freedom, the other for continued bondage.

Freedom is so important to God that He was willing to give His only Son to die so that His people could be free. Not just people of one race, but people of all races. To be His follower, I need to respect the freedom of others too.

God, thank You for giving me freedom from Satan's bondage. Help me to use it to free others who are still his slaves. Amen.

The Spirit of the Lord is on me. He has anointed me to tell the good news to poor people. He has sent me to announce freedom for prisoners. He has sent me so that the blind will see again. He wants me to free those who are beaten down.

Luke 4:18.

THE DAY THE LONGEST WAR ENDED

He who gives witness to these things says, "Yes. I am coming soon."

Revelation 22:20.

The Third Punic War started in 149 B.C. It did not officially end until more than 2,000 years later when on this day in 1895 the mayors of Rome and Carthage finally signed a treaty. (Carthage is known as Tunis today and is on the Mediterranean coast west of Egypt.) This qualifies in most books as the longest war in history, lasting 2,045 years. But I don't consider it the longest conflict.

An even more fierce and long-lasting war, one that would take more lives than all the wars on earth put together, started thousands of years ago. Fought between God and Satan, the great controversy began even before the creation of our world. It is being fought on Planet Earth because we humans were the only ones to allow Satan to set up his base here. Just by living on earth, we are in enemy territory.

Fortunately, this war will soon be over and we prisoners of war, who have been loyal to the King of the universe, will be rescued. I can't wait for the day the longest war in history *really* ends!

Please come soon, Jesus. We can't wait! Amen.

BE THE HEADPIN

I like to bowl, my mom likes to bowl, my brother likes to bowl, my mom's friends like to bowl, my friends like to bowl. In fact, I don't know many people who don't like to bowl. Although it's totally beyond me why this sport of throwing a ball at a bunch of pins is so popular, it is still fun.

The secret to bowling is not trying to knock the pins down one at a time or smash all of them at once. The ball is only so big. You can hit only so many pins at a time. So the pins you hit have to bring the rest down in order to get a strike.

When God speaks to us, He speaks only to us. But do you really think that we are the only people He's trying to touch? I think God would make a great bowler, because He knows whom to select as the headpin. If He hits the headpin, not only will He touch that person, but that person will share with other people what the Lord has done for him or her. So if the Lord chooses you as the headpin, to influence other people through you, be a headpin and not a pinhead.

Lord, thanks for being willing to use us as Your instruments to reach other people. Now make us willing to be used. Amen.

You are the light of the world. A city on a hill can't be hidden. Also, people do not light a lamp and put it under a bowl. Instead, they put it on its stand. Then it gives light to everyone in the house.

Matthew 5:14, 15.

YEAH, I'VE BEEN BAPTIZED, BUT GOD ISN'T FINISHED WITH ME YET

When I was a child, I talked like a child. I thought like a child. I had the understanding of a child.... What I know now is not complete. But someday I will know completely, just as God knows me completely.

1 Corinthians 13:11, 12.

When my mom was a teenager, she and her best friend, Hela, would argue sometimes. My mom is pretty good at arguing now and must have been then too. So when Hela would run out of other ammunition, she could always stop Mom by saying, "And you're a baptized person too." She spit out each syllable as if it tasted bad. Mom would retreat, feeling terrible that she, a baptized Christian, could have made somebody so angry.

But baptism is not qualification for sainthood. Baptism is a public admission that you need help. A public request to God to take away your old life and start a new one, it doesn't make you instantly perfect. You're a forgiven sinner who is trying to learn how to be more like Jesus every day, not a retired saint.

Hela and my mom both got older and developed more mature ideas of baptism. And in a couple years Hela chose to be baptized too. After that when Hela said the word "baptism," it didn't sound as if it tasted quite so bad.

If you haven't been baptized yet, don't wait till you are perfect. And if you have been baptized, don't expect to be perfect all at once. Baptism is a start. Perfection is a growing thing.

God, thanks for not expecting more from me than I can give. And thanks too for helping me grow. Amen.

KEEP JESUS FIRST

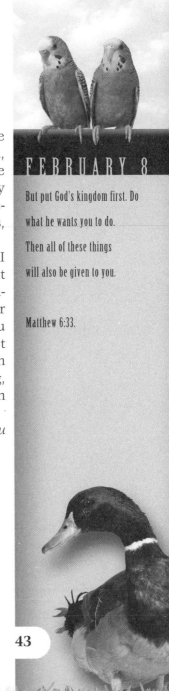

Isaac Asimov was born on this day in 1920. He has been called the father of science fiction, and so this day was named National Science Fiction Day. Today has been designated a day to honor all science fiction authors and celebrate science fiction and fantasy books, magazines, and movies.

Not everyone approves of science fiction, but I must admit that it helps exercise my imagination. But with science fiction, as with any kind of entertainment, it is important that you never let your books or magazines or movies become more important to you than Jesus Christ Himself. If that happens, it doesn't matter if you're reading science fiction books or Ellen White's books—it's idolatry. With all of your reading, remember to keep Jesus the most important thing in your life.

Lord, please help me always to remember to put You first in everything I do. Amen.

FEBRUARY 8

But put God's kingdom first. Do what he wants you to do. Then all of these things will also be given to you.

Matthew 6:33.

RUBBER SNAKES

Lord, I will sing about your
great love forever.

Psalm 89:1.

When my mother was a little girl in Nigeria, she and her sister enjoyed playing with rubber snakes colored the same as the real poisonous ones.

One day Mom left her snake outside when she went in for supper. The next morning she was horrified to see a man attacking her toy with a machete. Every time he hit the snake it would bounce into the air, seemingly unhurt. What baffled everyone was Mom running out, screaming, "That's my snake, that's my snake," grabbing it up from the ground, and racing back into the house with it. The man turned pale, shook his head, and ran the other way. The poor man had spent all his energy fighting something that wasn't even real, distracting him from other things he needed to do.

So often we as Christians spend a lot of energy fighting things that seem to me to be rubber snakes. When Bach and Beethoven wrote the beautiful music that we enjoy in church, some people considered it sacrilegious, because only Gregorian chants were properly reverent back then. Now some vigorously oppose other types of music as inappropriate for worship. Could it be that God accepts sincere worship from the people He loves, even if it doesn't appeal to everyone? Could it be that contemporary Christian music might be just a rubber snake?

God, please teach us the difference between rubber snakes and those things that are spiritually harmful. Amen.

44

TURN OFF THE TV

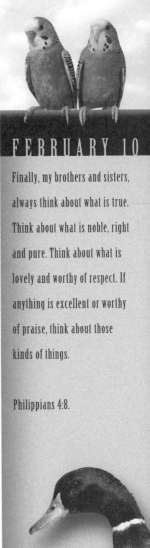

Today an organization called Morality in Media has sponsored a big protest against violence, sex, and vulgarity in network TV shows by urging people to turn off their television sets. It is called National Turn-Off-Your-TV Day. It is something that my mom practiced for almost four years.

When I was little, we didn't have a television set, which meant that I had to live without *Sesame Street*. I did lots of other fun things with my mom and brother, such as playing games and making things and reading stories, instead of watching TV.

One day some friends gave us one of their TVs. Feeling sorry for us because they thought that we couldn't afford one, they didn't realize it was a choice that Mom and Dad had made. Mom returned the TV with thanks and an explanation. Our friends had only heard of people living without a TV, but had never actually met anyone who did.

I'm not asking you to live without television for four years. Whether you turn off your TV for just today or a week, a month, or however long, it makes a statement, and it witnesses to others. And it will give you a lot of extra time to do some things for and with people you enjoy.

God, please help me to use my time wisely today. Amen.

Finally, my brothers and sisters, always think about what is true. Think about what is noble, right and pure. Think about what is lovely and worthy of respect. If anything is excellent or worthy of praise, think about those kinds of things.

Philippians 4:8.

NOW IT'S MY CHOICE

Choose for yourselves right now whom you will serve.... But as for me and my family, we will serve the Lord.

Joshua 24:15.

One day I asked my mom, "What are the benefits of being baptized?"

Instead of giving me a direct answer, she told me a story. "Michael, the night before you were born I stayed up the whole night praying for you and your whole life. As I rocked in my rocking chair and felt you moving gently inside my tummy I prayed for you and for every part of your life from the time you were little until you grew up to be a man. That night I gave you to God.

"Later when you were about a month old, we took you to church for a special dedication ceremony where we officially gave you to God. But through all of those, you had no choice. You were pretty much a captive audience the time I prayed all night for you. And as a little bundle in church being dedicated, you didn't have a lot of choice about whether you wanted to be there or not, or whether you wanted to be God's child or not. We made that choice for you.

"When you choose to be baptized, you have control. You're allowed to make the choice. Now you have reached an age at which you can take responsibility for your life and what you want to do with it.

"Do you choose to still be God's child? If you do, you can choose to be baptized. It's a way of showing God and everyone else in the church that you want to start a new life walking with Him, because you choose to be His man."

It sounded good to me.

God, please help me always to choose You. Amen.

46

HONESTY IS STILL THE BEST POLICY

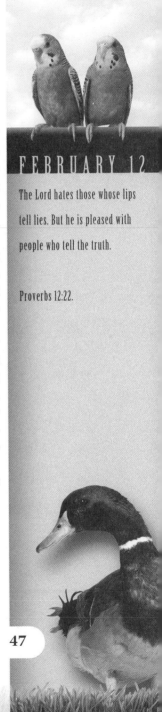

Today is the birthday of America's sixteenth, and one of the greatest, presidents. A lot of people loved him for many reasons, but one of the things that always stood out in his character was his honesty. He became known in his Illinois hometown as Honest Abe.

People told stories of someone receiving incorrect change in his store and his walking miles to return as little as six cents. His honesty especially stands out today when we consider that we usually don't remember politicians for that quality.

Honesty is something I appreciate from my friends, and so does God. Several times He reminds us of it in the Bible. Being honest doesn't mean just not telling lies, but presenting the whole truth. Sometimes this isn't easy. It landed Joseph and many others from the Bible in jail. But because it's important to God, it's important to me and should be important to you too.

Jesus, please remind me how important it is to be honest in everything that I do. Amen.

FEBRUARY 12

The Lord hates those whose lips tell lies. But he is pleased with people who tell the truth.

Proverbs 12:22.

A NEW NAME

Those who have ears should listen to what the Holy Spirit says to the churches. I will give hidden manna to those who overcome. I will also give each of them a white stone with a new name written on it. Only the one who receives that name will know what it is.

Revelation 2:17.

The Wellness Permission League in New York has named today Different Name Day. On this day if you don't like your name, you may use a different name, just for fun, of course. A lot of people in the Bible received new names too. Some took new names because they moved to different countries, and God gave others new names.

Daniel's three friends were named Hananiah, Mishael, and Azariah. But when they went to Babylon, the authorities changed Daniel's name to Belteshazzar, and his three friends became Shadrach, Meshach, and Abednego. Queen Esther's original name was Hadassah.

God changed Abram and Sarai's names to Abraham and Sarah. He altered Saul's name to Paul and Simon's to Peter. Also He renamed Jacob Israel and made him the father of the nation of Israel.

Sometimes in other countries when people become Christian, they adopt new names too. In Nigeria, where my mom lived when she was younger, people became Christians and added a Christian name to their family one. When we get to heaven, Ellen White tells us, each of us will have our own special name that only You and God will know. Don't like your name? Don't worry, God has a brand-new one planned—just for you.

God, I can't wait to find out what new name You have for me when I get to heaven. I sure hope it's soon. **48** *Amen.*

WILL YOU BE MY VALENTINE?

Today is Valentine's Day. It celebrates and honors Saint Valentine, the patron saint of lovers and romance. Many use Valentine's Day to tell people that they love them, whether it be family or friends—or even girls or guys. Some send little cards or store-bought valentines. Others make their own. Many give candy and flowers. But no matter how you do it, Valentine's Day is the day to say "I love you" to somebody.

The best valentine's gift I ever received came from my grandparents. When I was 4 I didn't get much mail. I received mail only on Valentine's, Day and I loved it. Knowing that someone somewhere in the world who knew my address and cared enough about me to send me a valentine made me feel like a grown-up. And it always had a dollar in it, which I would promptly carry around with me until I set it down somewhere, never to be found again.

The greatest valentine's gift that anybody has ever received was given to them by Someone even more awesome than my grandparents. God sent as His valentine's gift, Jesus, who came and died to show us all that He loved us.

He gave up His only Son because He couldn't bear the thought of living through eternity without me and without you and without anybody else willing to accept Jesus' sacrifice. So when you're telling people that you love them this Valentine's Day, don't forget to tell God how you feel about Him.

Jesus, we love You so much, and are so grateful that You made it possible to live forever! Amen.

FEBRUARY 14

God loved the world so much that he gave his one and only son. Anyone who believes in him will not die but will have eternal life.

John 3:16.

49

TWINS?

FEBRUARY 15

I do not look at the things people look at. Man looks at how someone appears on the outside. But I look at what is in the heart.

1 Samuel 16:7.

When I was 4 years old I had to have surgery. I had two doctors—my regular doctor, Dr. DeShay, and my surgeon, Dr. Smith. The day before surgery I had to visit both of them. Dr. DeShay is a tall Black man who looks a lot like Bill Cosby. Dr. Smith is short, stocky, bald, and White.

After my appointment with Dr. Smith, I shook his hand and said, "Thank you very much, Dr. DeShay."

My mom bent down and whispered in my ear, "This isn't Dr. DeShay. This is Dr. Smith."

I looked up at her in surprise and said, "Well, he looks just like Dr. DeShay."

Dr. Smith, his nurse, and my mom all convulsed with laughter as I stood there confused. The reason they both looked so much alike to me was because I saw them mostly from the knees down. I couldn't tell who was who. All I knew was that they both were helping me get better.

I didn't judge them by appearances, and their color didn't matter. While God *can* tell all of us apart, He doesn't judge by appearances either, and He is color-blind too!

God, thanks so much for not judging me by what's on the outside, but by what's in my heart. You know that I love You, and that's what really matters. Amen.

50

IF YOU WANT TO PLEASE HIM, DO THINGS HIS WAY

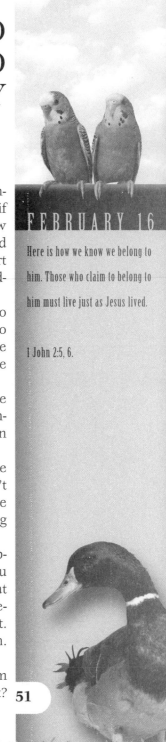

FEBRUARY 16

Here is how we know we belong to him. Those who claim to belong to him must live just as Jesus lived.

1 John 2:5, 6.

Sometimes it's hard to know exactly what others want from you. Wouldn't it be easier if they provided a detailed list so that you knew exactly what it was? Well, your Best Friend has done exactly that. God gave a four-part list, commonly known as the first four commandments, of exactly how He wants you to treat Him.

The first commandment is "Thou shalt have no other gods before me." That means that He wants to be the most important thing in your life. Because He is the God of the universe, He has to come before anyone else in your life.

The second commandment is "Thou shalt not make unto thee any graven image." He seeks to be more important than anything else in your life, whether it's an idol or TV or CD player or a book or anything.

The third commandment is "Thou shalt not take the name of the Lord thy God in vain." God doesn't want you to disrespect Him, but to worship Him. He wishes you would use His name only if you're talking to or about Him.

The fourth commandment is "Remember the sabbath day, to keep it holy." (For the long version, you may want to look in Exodus 20, but I don't have that much room on this page.) God hopes you will remember that He's there for you anytime you want. But once a week He wants you to be there for Him. It's a date.

Now you know exactly what God wishes from you. And that makes it easier to be friends, doesn't it? **51**

God, thanks for making it so clear. Amen.

BE LIKE DAD

So be perfect, just as your Father in heaven is perfect.

Matthew 5:48.

My dad was the coolest. He could say more than three words, could walk, drive a car, and read books. I wanted to do all those things so badly. The trouble was that I did all those things so badly. After all, I was a toddler.

I tried hard to talk, but my babbling was often something that only my brother could understand. He was 3. I could crawl around, but whenever I tried to stand up, I would fall and hurt either my head or the other end. Too bad my head wasn't as well padded.

Driving was something I worked hard at too. Frantically I would turn the steering wheel on my car seat, but that never seemed to change the direction the car went. I would try to read, but my appetite would always overcome my desire to read, and the books looked so tasty. It took me only six months to eat most of a set of encyclopedias.

Trying to be like Dad was very frustrating. But Dad didn't get mad at my failed attempts (except for the encyclopedia part). He could tell that I was trying to be like him, and it made him really happy. He thought I was cute.

My attempts to be like Jesus are just as frustrating and almost as successful. But He knows I'm trying to be like Him, and that makes Him happy. And if I continue, as time goes by I will become a lot more like Him, just as I'm a lot more like my dad now.

God, You know how much I want to be like You. Thanks for helping me grow just a little bit each day. Amen.

HOW TO GET ALONG

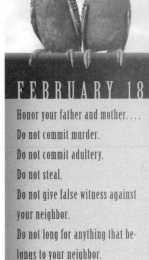

S ome people have trouble making friends. Many worry about how to please God. And still others have trouble making friends. If you have either problem, then God made a special list for you. It is commonly known as the last six commandments.

The first on this list is, as most of us have learned it, "Honour thy father and thy mother." We must respect our parents and do what they tell us, even taking out the garbage.

Number two on the list is "Thou shalt not kill." If you kill off all your friends, then whom are you going to be friends with? Following this commandment also keeps you out of jail.

Third on God's list is "Thou shalt not commit adultery." If you steal other people's husbands or wives, it leads to divorce. Also if you lure away your best friend's spouse, chances are you won't be best friends anymore.

Fourth on the list is "Thou shalt not steal." Who wants to be friends with you if you steal their things?

Fifth on the list is "Thou shalt not bear false witness." It means don't lie. If you lie, people aren't going to want to be your friend. Why? Think about it. It also keeps you from facing charges of perjury in a court of law.

The last is "Thou shalt not covet." If you want everything that your friends have, you'll never be happy with your own life, and you'll be jealous of them. But if you can be content, it won't happen.

God, thanks for making it so plain how to please You and get along with other people. Amen.

FEBRUARY 18

Honor your father and mother....
Do not commit murder.
Do not commit adultery.
Do not steal.
Do not give false witness against your neighbor.
Do not long for anything that belongs to your neighbor.

Exodus 20:12-17.

STOP THE INSANITY

FEBRUARY 19

We know that all that God created has been groaning. It is in pain as if it were giving birth to a child. The created world continues to groan even now.

Romans 8:22.

In the year 1859 a man named Dan Sickles murdered his wife's lovers. When the authorities took him to court for it, he was acquitted on grounds of temporary insanity. It was the first time temporary insanity worked as a defense in the United States. Unfortunately, even though Dan Sickles did plead temporary insanity, the consequences were still the same, and some people were still dead.

Temporary insanity can seem like a bogus plea bargain, and a lot of people don't agree with its being used at all, because they believe that if someone is insane, then they will stay insane, and that if they are not, then people need to take responsibility for their actions. I, however, can sympathize with people who plead temporary insanity because every now and then, temporarily, I become insane. But then again who doesn't? However, when I do get a little crazy, I still pay the consequences for the weird stuff I do.

Very shortly the whole world is going to need to plead temporary insanity, because everything that you know will change when Jesus comes. The very foundations of the earth will temporarily do all kinds of crazy things that they've never done before and never will again, such as El Niño and earthquakes and tornadoes in weird places where they've never happened before. But take heart. Remember that it is only temporary insanity. Help is on the way. Jesus is coming soon. And He makes all the sense in the universe.

Jesus, please come soon and save us from the insanity all around. Amen.

THERE IS A BOMB IN GILEAD

Mom," I whispered during song service, "shouldn't somebody help those people in Gilead?"

She looked at me puzzled and asked, "What are you talking about?"

"The bomb. There's a bomb in Gilead. Someone ought to help them," I said.

Mom tried her best not to laugh hysterically, since we were in church. But she wasn't very successful. Mom is prone to fits of giggling anyway. Amid dirty looks from those in the pew around us who hadn't heard what was evidently a great joke, she stopped giggling and said, "It's balm, not bomb. Balm is like ointment or something soothing that helps heal hurts and wounds."

"Oh, good," I answered. "Somebody did help them."

Now that I am a little older, I understand that God pours happiness and good things into everyone. It's just that some people have so many wounds that it all leaks out and they still feel empty inside. My job as God's follower is to be a balm and help them heal their wounds and hurts and not be a bomb and cause more injuries!

Dear God, help me to be a balm and not a bomb! Amen.

Is there no balm in Gilead? Is there no physician there? Why then is there no healing for the wound of my people?

Jeremiah 8:22, NIV.

GOD IS FAIR

FEBRUARY 21

A man named Ananias and his wife, Sapphira, sold some land. He kept part of the money for himself.... He brought the rest of it and put it down at the apostles' feet. Then Peter said, "Ananias, why did you let Satan fill your heart? He made you lie to the Holy Spirit."... When Ananias heard this, he fell down and died."

Acts 5:1-5.

When I was in kindergarten, my nemesis was Andrew Wood. He and I were always fighting about something. We also got in trouble for it a lot.

When we both faced discipline for squabbling, it didn't bother me, because I knew that we had both done something wrong. And we both deserved to stand against the wall instead of playing at recess. I knew this, so I took the responsibility for my actions. And as long as Andrew did too, I didn't mind.

What used to make me really mad were the times we got in a fight and I had to stand against the wall, but Andrew didn't. Especially since he would come by and make silly faces at me and do all kinds of unpleasant things while I was trying to stand there in peace. It particularly upset me when it was a fight that he had started, because I wouldn't have even been standing there if it hadn't been for him.

One time, when I told Mom about it, she felt my pain. But she also made me realize that a lot of times life isn't fair. And people don't always get punished fairly. Then she read me the story of Ananias and Sapphira from the book of Acts.

It comforted me to know that when two people committed a sin together, God believed they should both be punished equally and not just have one person stand against the wall. No matter how unfair things are in life, I can know that God is always fair.

God, I'm glad that I can always count on You not only to be fair but also merciful. Amen.

56

THANKSGIVING DAY?

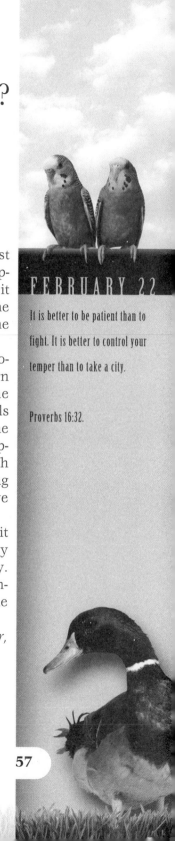

Most people think that the first American Thanksgiving Day happened in November. But actually it took place on February 22 in the Massachusetts Bay Colony when the first colonists came over in 1630.

A Native American named Quadequina introduced popcorn to the colonists when he brought corn to the first Thanksgiving celebration in the Massachusetts Bay Colony and dropped the kernels on a hot rock next to the fire. Suddenly to the colonists' alarm, they heard lots of high-pitched popping sounds. But it wasn't the Indians playing with cap guns; it was merely the kernels of corn popping into white fluffy balls of tastiness. Americans have been addicted to popcorn ever since.

People can be like popcorn sometimes. A little bit of heat under their collar and they explode—only usually the results aren't nice and white and fluffy. But with Jesus' help, we can learn not to lose our tempers when we face a little bit of heat. We can gain the ability to keep ourselves under control.

Jesus, please help me to learn to control my temper, even when people around me are getting hot. Amen.

IT DOESN'T HAVE TO HURT FOREVER

FEBRUARY 23

Sin entered the world because one man sinned. And death came because of sin. Everyone sinned so death came to all people.

Romans 5:12.

One of the worst things about sin is that a lot of the time it doesn't hurt only the sinner, but innocent people, too. In 1941 Commander Mitsuo Fucida led the Japanese air force in the bombing of Pearl Harbor. The United States retaliated by declaring war on Japan. Thousands of deaths later the United States ended the war by dropping an atomic bomb on Hiroshima and another one on Nagasaki.

Thousands of people died or vaporized instantly, and thousands of others suffered from radiation sickness and perished later. A lot of them were innocent and knew nothing about the reasons for the war. Some of the people in those cities were against the war and didn't even want to attack Pearl Harbor, but that didn't matter to the atomic bomb. It wiped out everyone.

Sin is like that. It hurts everyone around it, both the innocent and the guilty. Thank God that there's an antidote for sin and the damage that it's caused, and healing for those of us who have been injured.

Jesus, thank You for being the antidote for my sin infection. Now, please help me get rid of it altogether. Amen.

PRAY, DON'T FUSS

Moses lifted up the snake in the desert. The Son of Man must be lifted up also.

John 3:14.

My friend Poky (not his real name but what everybody calls him) has five earrings. He also goes to my church. Several not very gentle people at church have berated him for wearing them. We have some people in our church who feel that God has called them to be the jewelry police. The same people are often also the music police, the Sabbath school police, and sometimes the potluck police. Such individuals are highly critical if you ever do something that they feel is wrong.

I have often wondered what would happen if, instead of fussing at Poky for his jewelry or whomever they are picking on that week, they were to spend the same amount of time praying for my friend and going out of their way to be friendly and supportive of him. Most people are drawn to Jesus by His beautiful love and His plan for forgiving our sins, not by a list of rules. Jesus is the most effective bait when we are trying to be fishers of men and women. Perhaps we would be more successful with other people if we spent our time with Jesus learning to act like Him.

God didn't call us to point out other people's mistakes. He asks us to love each other and lift each other up, to help us all be closer to Him. Remember that God has summoned us only to be fishers of men and women. Jesus never told us to clean them.

God, please help me remember what my job is in Your plan of salvation and to love the people I meet instead of criticizing. Amen.

59

BUT I'M RIGHT!

If possible, live in peace with

everyone. Do that as much

as you can.

Romans 12:18.

What makes you think you're so right?" my dad bellowed at me. We were arguing again.

"Because God is on my side," I hollered back.

"He can't be," Dad responded. "He and I are friends."

At this point I stormed off to my bedroom to think about it. Was God on my side, or was He on Dad's?

During World War II people asked a similar question. Adolf Hitler felt that it was his Christian duty to wipe out all the Jews. He was sure that that was what God wanted him to do. Most Germans felt that God was on their side.

Both the Germans and the Americans felt that God was on their side and asked for His help throughout the war. And God did. We hear countless stories of divine intervention when God saved the lives of His people on both sides of the fighting lines.

Sometimes God doesn't take part in such conflicts. It just breaks His heart to see His people hurting each other. Just as my mom gets upset when my brother and I fight, perhaps God feels that way too. Perhaps what we do saddens and hurts Him—and He gets upset with both of us for acting that way. Perhaps He wishes we would solve our differences without violence (verbal or physical). And perhaps He loves His children on both sides of a conflict—even when I am right!

Jesus, please help me to remember to live peaceably with everyone, especially my family and school friends. Amen.

GOD IS A WRITER TOO

W hat do you think the worldwide best-selling book is? It's a book of stories sprinkled with poetry and information on the history of the nation that is central to its plot. This book has freedom fighters who kill men with their bare hands, giants, dragons, monsters, sea serpents, passionate romance, surprise endings, thrilling suspense as heroes flee their captors, and supernatural phenomena.

But it isn't a science fiction novel or even the *X Files*. Believe it or not, the bestselling book of all time is the one and only Holy Bible.

The *Guinness Book of World Records* says that there have been 2.5 billion copies of the Bible sold. And that is only between 1815 and 1975. By the end of 1993 the whole Bible had been translated into 337 languages. At least one book of the Bible has been translated into 2,062 different languages.

Bibles have been selling since 1591. The first one published by Cambridge University Press, in England, was the Geneva Version. Today we have many versions available on the market. My favorite is the NIV Student Bible. I also like the NIRV, which is the New International Reader's Version.

God must really know what people want if He can stay number one on the best-seller list for more than 400 years! He's a great writer!

God, thanks for preserving Your Word for all these years so that I can understand Your plan for me. Amen.

FEBRUARY 26

Your word is like a lamp that shows me the way. It is like a light that guides me.

Psalm 119:105.

WOUNDED FAITH

The Lord doesn't turn his back
on people forever.

Lamentations 3:31.

Sometimes it's hard to understand why God lets such horrible things happen. Eli Wiesel was a Nazi prisoner at Auschwitz during World War II. Auschwitz was a death camp in which many Jews and other prisoners perished. Eli was 6 years old when the Allies liberated his camp. He had seen horrible things, including the death of his father.

A few years ago he went back to Auschwitz and saw the death camp as it is today. All of his old memories came flooding back like a nightmare. As a result he wrote some very angry things about God.

Recently someone who read those things asked him, "Have you lost your faith in God?"

Eli answered, "No, my faith is wounded. I still have faith in God, for without Him . . . what am I?"

Sometimes, when I see footage of the brutal mass killings in Rwanda, or starving kids in Ethiopia, I wonder what God is doing about it. I don't understand. But I still have faith in Him. Someday He will explain it all to me. My faith may be wounded, but without Him, who am I?

God, sometimes I don't understand. But please help me to continue to trust You. Amen.

GOD IS NOT A VENDING MACHINE

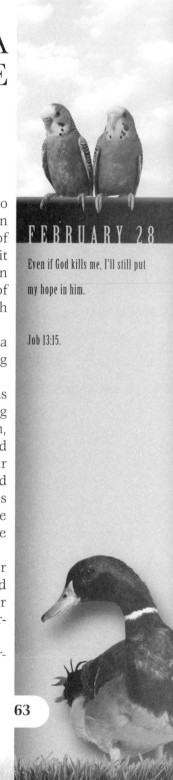

FEBRUARY 28

Even if God kills me, I'll still put my hope in him.

Job 13:15.

I have a friend named Becky. A couple years ago she had cancer. The doctor said he had seen that kind of cancer only twice before. One of those times his patient had died. I went to visit her in the hospital a lot. She was on chemotherapy for several months. It was kind of funny to see her with no hair, considering how much she was into "looking good."

Another girl in my classroom named Rachel has a brain tumor. She is on chemotherapy too. Nothing the doctors do is making it stop growing.

My mom was sick too. Her doctor told us she was going to die. She couldn't talk straight and kept falling down. A disease called lupus had spread to her brain, and her blood pressure was really high. We prayed hard for all three emergencies. And God answered our prayers for all three. For Becky, He said yes, and healed her. For Rachel, He has so far said no, and it makes us all very sad. For my mom, He said yes and no. He didn't take away her lupus, but He healed her brain. She can think and talk and walk and be Mom again.

God is not a vending machine; you don't put your prayer into the slot and get anything you ask for. God loves us all very much, but He knows what's best for us, and He has reasons that we don't always understand for everything He chooses to do.

God, help me to trust You, even when I don't understand. Amen.

READY OR NOT!

But we know where this man is from. When the Christ comes, no one will know where he is from. . . . Still, many people in the crowd put their faith in him. They said, "How will it be when the Christ comes? Will he do more miraculous signs than this man?"

John 7:27-31.

I learned about leap day and leap year when I was 4 years old. I adored my teenage cousin, Charlie, who was also 4 years old. Though he wasn't actually 4 years old, he had had only four birthdays, because his birthday was February 29. It made me feel so cool to have the same number of birthdays as Charlie had. After all, he was my role model.

Some people think that leap day is a real drag because it makes the year one day longer and it's another day that we have to wait until Jesus comes. But leap year doesn't have any effect on Jesus' second coming. He will come when nobody expects Him, whether it be tomorrow, three years from now, or 100 years from now. Leap day won't make His coming any further away. Here He comes—ready or not!

Jesus, please help me to be ready for Your coming, no matter when it happens. Amen.

MAD AS BILL

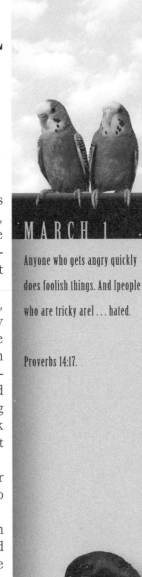

Bill has an extremely bad temper, but he's my favorite grumpy parakeet. Of course, he's my *only* grumpy parakeet, since the rest of the flock are almost always delighted with life. But Bill doesn't just get mad—he *stays* mad.

The last time I clipped his wings he was, as usual, furious. He screamed and squawked and bit my hand—as usual. When I finished, I let him go, but he returned to keep on biting my hand. I carried him back to his tree, where the rest of the flock were playing. Bill didn't hop onto the tree as the others would have. Instead, he stayed on my finger, chomping away. When I put him on a branch, he hopped back onto my hand and attacked me again. Talk about holding a grudge!

The other parakeets were playing and eating their treats while Bill continued to fuss. He missed so much fun because he was busy having a tantrum.

Staying mad like Bill can cause you to miss out on a lot of fun. It's hard to have fun when you stay mad at somebody. God's kids forgive and forget. Don't be like Bill.

God, when someone does something mean to me, help me to forgive and forget, just as You are willing to forgive and forget my sins. Amen.

MARCH 1

Anyone who gets angry quickly does foolish things. And [people who are tricky are] ... hated.

Proverbs 14:17.

65

YAWN

Come to me, all of you who are
tired and carrying heavy loads.
I will give you rest.

Matthew 11:28.

This month is National Chronic Fatigue Syndrome Awareness month. Doctors do not understand chronic fatigue syndrome, but its victims know that they are just plain tired. They feel exhausted even when they wake up in the morning. Also they ache and often have other problems. It bothers some people so badly that they can't hold a job. Sometimes chronic fatigue goes along with other illnesses such as lupus or fibromyalgia. My mom has problems with this.

Jesus had something to say for people like her. "Come to me, all of you who are tired and are carrying heavy loads," He said. "I will give you rest." But His promise isn't just for people like Mom. Toward the end of February in North America many students fall into the doldrums. It's gray and cold outside and just plain discouraging.

Then toward the end of the semester, before summer break, lots of projects come due at the same time, and test week looms just around the corner. We feel burned out and overwhelmed. Jesus' promise is for us, too.

Mom's favorite text for bad days is Isaiah 40:31: "Those who trust the Lord will receive new strength. They will fly as high as eagles. They will run and not get tired. They will walk and not grow weak." She keeps a rubber eagle on top of her computer to remind her of the verse on those kinds of days. It sounds good to me, too.

I'd write more about this, but I'm too tired . . .
Thank You, God, for rest. Amen.

PRAYING IS NOT AN ANNUAL THING

Every year on the first Friday in March, which happens to be today, women around the world unite for a day of prayer and prayerful action. Called the World Day of Prayer, it began in 1887.

A day of prayer is a good thing, but God didn't intend it to be just an annual event. He planned a world day of prayer once a week. Now He does want us to pray every day, but on Sabbath He would like to have us take part in a day of special prayer and prayerful action.

And there's another difference too. On Sabbath, instead of its being just women, God invites everyone. And while women sponsor the World Day of Prayer (two thirds of the Adventist Church are women), God summons everybody for a day of prayer, whether it be men or women or children.

God, thank You that we can talk to You anytime, and for setting aside a whole day to spend with us each week. Amen.

MARCH 3

Therefore confess your sins to each other and pray for each other so that you may be healed. The prayer of a righteous man is powerful and effective.

James 5:16, NIV.

OF AMNESTY AND LIBRARY BOOKS

MARCH 4

If we confess our sins, he is faithful and just and will forgive us our sins and purify us from all unrighteousness.

1 John 1:9, NIV.

An organization called Prevention of Cruelty to Cartoonists has dubbed this week Return the Borrowed Books Week. It urges you to bring back any borrowed books to your friends and libraries.

Any opportunity to return library books without paying a fine is important to my family. I believe that my family has single-handedly paid for the renovation and expansion of the Rockingham County Public Library just through our late fees. But this week many libraries will forgive your late fees. It's called amnesty.

God also offers amnesty, but He does it more than just a single week a year. For God every week is "Return Borrowed Lives Week." If we've messed up the life that He has given to us, then we can bring it back to Him. And He will forgive all of our mistakes and sins. God is much more gracious than our local librarian.

God, thanks for being willing to forgive us when we mess up. And help us to learn not to mess up as often in the future. Amen.

SAY NO TO DRUGS, SAY NO TO DRUGS!

The National PTA Association has named this week Drug and Alcohol Awareness Week. Parents need to educate themselves to recognize, understand, and combat drug and alcohol abuse among teenagers. My mom can really get into such programs. In fact, by the time I was 3 she had taught me to chant, "Say no to drugs, say no to drugs."

When I was 4 I had a hernia. A hernia occurs when you have a hole in the lining of your abdomen and a loop of intestine gets caught in it. It has to be surgically repaired and can be life-threatening. I almost died from my first hernia. So this one we had treated right away. The day before surgery I was lying on the examination table when Dr. Smith began to poke my tummy.

"Are you going to cut my tummy open while I'm still awake?" I asked him.

"No, we'll give you some drugs first so that you'll sleep through it," he replied.

I struggled into a sitting position and shook my finger under his nose as I chanted, "Say no to drugs."

Dumbfounded, Dr. Smith said nothing for a minute. Then he replied, "What if we just give you some medicine instead?"

Lying back down, I said, "That would be OK."

Now I'm old enough to understand the difference between medicine and addictive drugs. Also I'm old enough to recognize why it's bad to use drugs.

God, You've got so many good things for us. Please help me stay away from the bad things out there. Amen.

MARCH 5

Do you not know that your body is a temple of the Holy Spirit, who is in you, whom you have received from God? You are not your own.

1 Corinthians 6:19, NIV.

69

HATING WHAT YOU DO BEST

His mother said to the servants,
"Do whatever he tells you."

John 2:5, NIV.

I f Michelangelo were alive today, it would be his birthday. One of the greatest artists of all time, he painted the ceiling of the Sistine Chapel and sculpted David and a statue known as the Pieta. The Pieta depicts Mary holding Jesus after His crucifixion. You can see it in the Vatican today in Italy. It's the only statue with Michelangelo's name engraved on it.

He loved to sculpt. Sculpting was what he felt he was best at. When Pope Julius II asked him to paint the ceiling of the Sistine Chapel in the Vatican, he declined and felt upset that someone would ask a great sculptor like him to lower himself to painting ceilings. The pope then told him that he had to do it anyway, and Michelangelo reconsidered.

Today the Sistine Chapel ceiling is one of the most famous pieces of art. Almost everyone has seen a picture of it. And many people have formed their views of God merely on the artwork Michelangelo did on that ceiling.

Even though his most famous piece was the ceiling at the Sistine Chapel, he was a sculptor at heart, not a painter. Sometimes God asks us to do things that we feel don't match our best talents. But He knows not only what we can do the best but also what He needs us to do.

God, please make us willing to follow You, and thank You for forgiving us and loving us when we don't. Amen.

GOD LIKES BOARD GAMES

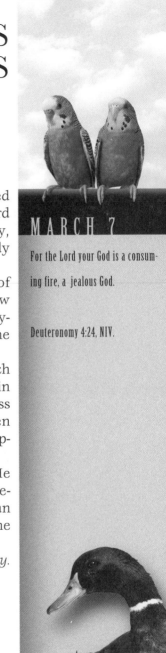

On this day in 1933 a company called Parker Brothers redefined the board game. Their new product, Monopoly, took the country by storm. Everybody played it, even my grandpa.

All the spaces in the American version of Monopoly are real places in Atlantic City, New Jersey, that you can visit today. They have everything there from Baltic Avenue to Boardwalk. The British version has places in London.

The point of Monopoly is not only to get as much property as you can, but also to buy your property in sets. For example, Boardwalk isn't much good unless you have Park Place. Once you have a whole set, then you can build houses and hotels, making your property more valuable.

God needs a monopoly of His people, too. He won't settle for just having me or just having you, because once He has a whole set of people, then He can build His house in our hearts. And we all become more valuable.

God, I want to be one of Your pieces of property today. Please show me what I can do for You today. Amen.

For the Lord your God is a consuming fire, a jealous God.

Deuteronomy 4:24, NIV.

BUT I LOVED YOU FIRST!

MARCH 8

"Sir," the woman said, "I can see that you are a prophet."

John 4:19.

Today is my Great-grandma Tadman's birthday. Grandma T. is in a nursing home now because she is old and sick. My mom writes to her every single week, and sometimes more than once a week. She watches for neat little things to send to Grandma that will make her laugh or cheer her up, or things that Grandma can show off to her other friends in the nursing home.

Grandma always seems so amazed that Mom writes to her so often. But Mom told me the reason that she does it is because when she was a little girl, she never got much mail, but Grandma T. used to write to her all the time. She would send her little cards and stickers and notes and even a dollar occasionally. Mom remembers how special she felt when Grandma would write to her as a little girl, and so it doesn't seem hard at all to write to her now and send special things to her.

She loves Great-grandma Tadman because Great-grandma first loved her. It's like that with Jesus too. We love Him because He first loved us. He created us, He made our beautiful world for us, and He even came to die for us so that we would have everything we needed, including a chance at eternal life. We can't help loving Him. He loved us first.

Jesus, I'm so grateful that You loved me first. Right back at You! Amen.

WHEN IN DANGER OR IN DOUBT, RUN IN CIRCLES, SCREAM, AND SHOUT!

The Wellness Permission League has named this day Panic Day. It is the day to run around in circles shouting, "I can't take it anymore." We all need a Panic Day because none of us can take it anymore.

My grandma Jo always used to say, "When in danger or in doubt, run in circles, scream, and shout." I'm sure she would have appreciated Panic Day. Usually she was teasing somebody else for panicking when she said that, though.

Jesus knew that we all needed a Panic Day and that we couldn't take it. And that's why He sent His Son to come and "take it" for us so that we don't have to panic and we don't have to "take it" anymore.

So the next time you feel like panicking, just remember the wonderful sacrifice that Jesus made for you. He invites you to cast all your cares upon Him, for He cares for you.

Jesus, You know that I'm afraid sometimes. Please be really close today and help me to remember to be confident in You. Thanks! Amen.

MARCH 9

Turn all your worries over to him.

He cares about you.

1 Peter 5:7

73

DON'T BE A WHINER

He who is sitting on the throne said, "I am making everything new!" Then he said, "Write this down. You can trust these words. They are true."

Revelation 21:5.

In my family we have a joke that goes like this: "How many Adventists does it take to change a lightbulb? Eleven. One to change the lightbulb and 10 to whine about how much better the old one was."

God's ancient people had this problem too. In the year 515 B.C., when they finished rebuilding the Temple of Jerusalem and all of the young people were so happy and thought it was grand, all of the old geezers remembered how much better Solomon's was. The Bible says that they cried and wailed.

It seems like whenever anything new comes, some people are always disappointed with it. People who will try their best to convince you that "change is bad."

But one new thing is guaranteed to delight everyone and that is when Jesus brings His temple back to earth from heaven. When that happens, even the cranky old people won't be able to cry about it, because it will be the most beautiful thing they have ever seen, and for once everyone will be happy and contented!

Jesus, please teach me to be content where I am and to trust You to take me to where You want me to go. Amen.

JOHNNY APPLESEED

Today has been set aside to honor Johnny Appleseed and to remember his contribution to our country. Of course, Johnny Appleseed wasn't his real name. It was actually John Chapman.

His great mission in life was to plant apple trees. He took apple seeds across the eastern United States. When he was traveling, he even used apple seeds for packing materials around his Bible the way we might do with styrofoam peanuts today.

Where I live, in the Shenandoah Valley of Virginia, apples are one of the most important products, right behind poultry. White House applesauce and apple butter come from the Shenandoah Valley. Those products use apples from orchards that Johnny Appleseed started. The people in the valley fondly remember him.

There's even a restaurant near where I live named after him. In honor of Johnny Appleseed they serve one free apple fritter to each person who eats there. It's my favorite thing to eat there. Johnny Appleseed died on March 11, 1845, but everyone still remembers him because of the unselfish things that he did.

Will people remember you 150 years after you have died? God has a special job for you, just as He did for Johnny Appleseed. And you can be just as great a blessing to the people who come after you as he was if you follow God's plan, whether or not they name a restaurant after you.

God, please use me to bless someone for You today. Amen.

MARCH 11

Trust the Lord with all your heart. Do not depend on your own understanding.

Proverbs 3:5.

THE HOLY EXPRESS

I will send the Friend to you from the Father. He is the Spirit of truth, who comes out from the Father. When the Friend comes to help you, he will give witness about me.

John 15:26.

One of the early ways to deliver mail was known as the pony express, because young men would ride across the country on horse from the state of Missouri all the way out west. Their official motto was "the mail must get through."

The pony express riders braved harsh weather conditions, attacks by Indians and wild animals, and many other dangerous things, just to bring sentimental notes and messages of encouragement from home to the people waiting for them.

God also has a pony express. We commonly refer to Him as the Holy Spirit. The reason I say that He's like the pony express is that His motto is "I must get through." And He will stop at absolutely nothing before He has penetrated your heart and delivered God's message of love and hope and encouragement to you.

Holy Spirit, please get through to me today. And use me to help You get through to somebody else. Amen.

76

BE A GOOD SAMARITAN

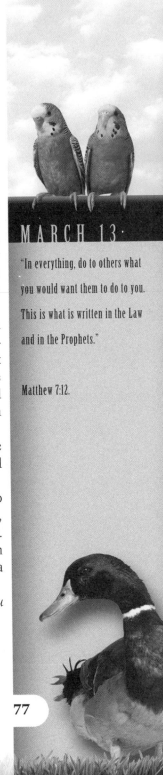

MARCH 13

"In everything, do to others what you would want them to do to you. This is what is written in the Law and in the Prophets."

Matthew 7:12.

Today has been designated Good Samaritan Involvement Day. Jesus told a story about a Samaritan who helped a Jewish man beaten up by robbers. Two supposedly good people passed by and didn't even help the poor man in Jesus' story. Unfortunately, there are still lots of people like that today.

On this day in 1964 a man stabbed to death a woman named Kitty Genovese in front of her apartment in New York. Thirty-eight neighbors saw what was happening and were horrified, but not a single one went down to help her. They just watched and listened. Not even one of them called the police. Each thought someone else would.

When Jesus finished His story, He asked who the man's neighbor was. It was the Samaritan who had helped him when he was hurt.

To be followers of Jesus we need to be willing to get involved. We can't just sit and watch and say, "Oh, how terrible," when bad things happen to people. Instead, we need to help them, as the good Samaritan did. Don't just watch and listen. Get involved. Be a good Samaritan.

Jesus, please show me someone I can help for You today. Thanks! Amen.

DO YOU HAVE THE BRAIN OF A 3-YEAR-OLD?

MARCH 14

If any of you need wisdom, ask God for it. He will give it to you. God gives freely to everyone. He doesn't find fault.

James 1:5.

We have a cockatoo named Skippy, and he bites hard. We don't allow him to do it, though, and when he does, he gets put in his cage for five minutes. By then he doesn't even remember what he's done wrong, so we usually take him back out.

Because he's mentally on the same level as a 2- or 3-year-old, he never remembers what he did wrong and so he does it again. Sometimes he can learn through his mistakes, but as for biting, he still hasn't learned. So every time he bites, we put him in his cage for five minutes. And eventually he will learn not to bite us.

When Skippy bites, it hurts not only him, but also the person he's biting. In the same way, when you do wrong things it hurts not only the person that we're doing them to, but also us.

We have to face the consequences of our misbehavior again and again until we learn not to do it anymore. If we ask God, He can give us the wisdom not to repeat our mistakes but to learn from them the first time.

Dear Lord, please help me to catch on the first time. Amen.

MY HOUSE IS UNDERWATER

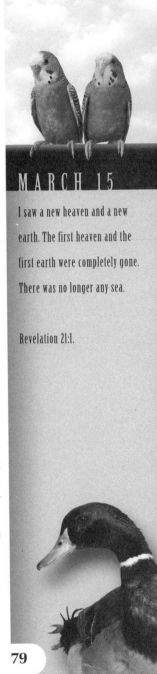

MARCH 15

I saw a new heaven and a new earth. The first heaven and the first earth were completely gone. There was no longer any sea.

Revelation 21:1.

On this day in 1960 the first Undersea National Park opened in Key Largo, Florida. It is totally underwater. The only way to get to it is by scuba diving. My brother and I are both licensed scuba divers, but my mom has no such luck.

Mom won't be a scuba diver until the Second Coming, when Jesus gives her a new body. My brother and I do a lot of talking about what life will be like then, and what kind of home we will live in in the new earth. We've imagined tree houses and space stations and underground fortresses. But Mom wants an underwater one from which she can look at fish all day. She loves all the sea creatures, whether they be fish, sea urchins, sea anemones, or octopuses. In fact, she even likes cuttlefish.

My mom's convinced that God will give her an undersea mansion, where she can study all the critters that she's never been able to dive with. We don't know what life on the new earth will be like, but we do know that it will be better than anything my brother and I could imagine.

I can hardly wait for Jesus to come, so we can see exactly what it will be like.

Please hurry back, Jesus. We miss You. Amen.

PURIM

I looked to the Lord, and he answered me. He saved me from everything I was afraid of.

Psalm 34:4.

When my brother and I were little guys, Mom did some weird things for worship with us. One day we celebrated Purim. Purim is a Jewish holiday during which the Jews remember the story of Esther and celebrate her victory over the wicked Haman, who wanted to kill her people.

Today happened to be that day in history when Esther and her uncle Mordecai told all the Jews they could fight back. Instead of a day that was supposed to be a mass genocide of all the Jews living in Persia, it was a day for them to overcome their enemies.

Mama showed us how the Jews celebrate that day. She made cookies supposedly shaped like Haman's that are known as "Hamantaschen." They looked a lot like the three-cornered patriot hats we wore when we went to Williamsburg. Also we did the Haman dance. First we wrote Haman's name on the bottoms of our tennis shoes. Then we jumped up and down until his name was completely gone.

While we as Christians don't celebrate Purim, we would probably be better off if we did remember and celebrate times when God has delivered us.

Our biggest problems seem to come when we forget how God has taken care of us in the past. And if we were to celebrate that, as the Jews do Purim, we would always remember how powerful and strong our God is, and then nothing would look frightening in the future.

God, I know that You've done a lot for me. And You've probably done more that I don't know about. Thanks. Amen.

80

KISS ME, I'M IRISH

Today is Saint Patrick's Day. Many people think it has to do with shamrocks and little leprechauns. But it's actually a day set aside to remember Saint Patrick, who died on this day in the year A.D. 461.

Pirates kidnapped Patrick from his home in England when he was a teenager. They took him to Ireland, where they made him work as a slave for several years. Patrick eventually escaped and made it back to England. There he became a Christian and later a priest. He returned to Ireland to the people who had abused and enslaved him, to tell them about Jesus.

People have lost sight of who Patrick really was, and these days the big thing on Saint Patrick's Day is to wear green. Often kids at school will pinch anyone who is not wearing green. In Ireland the Protestants wear orange on Saint Patrick's Day, and often a lot of squabbling takes place between those wearing green and those wearing orange. This is very sad.

On this day we should remember a man who was willing to forgive those who treated him cruelly when he was a teenager and who then went back to share Jesus with them. Patrick could be a role model for all of us instead of just a color choice.

Lord, please help me to learn to be gracious and loving, even to those people who don't treat me very well. Thanks. Amen.

MARCH 17

Forgive us our sins, just as we also have forgiven those who sin against us.

Matthew 6:12.

THE WAY, THE TRUTH, THE LIGHT, . . . AND BABY BIRDS

MARCH 18

How did God show his love for us?
He sent his one and only Son into
the world. He sent him so we could
receive life through him.

1 John 4:9.

Our African gray parrot, Wamml, loves to sit by the window and talk to the outside birds. He often mimics their noises and can converse quite fluently with robins, blue jays, and others.

One day we kept hearing him peep like a baby bird. When we went outside, we discovered a baby robin on the corner of the garage roof right near the window where Wamml sits. A fluffy little round ball of fuzz, it reminded me of a short, fat, bald man.

My brother and I walked around the garage and found the spot where the bird's nest was on the other side, but we couldn't figure out how to lead it back to its nest.

Suddenly we realized the solution. Wamml spoke the language. Perched on Mom's shoulder, Wamml continued to cheep, answering the baby robin. We walked slowly around the garage. Every time the robin cheeped, Wamml would cheep back, and the robin would hop along the edge of the garage to be closer to Wamml. By using Wamml, we led the little robin all the way to the other side of the garage, where the nest was and where the bird's mom flapped down and pecked it for running away.

Jesus came to earth to help us—little humans who had wandered away from the safety of the nest. Even though He was God, He spoke our language and was able to show us the way back. My parrot is awesome, but my God is even more wonderful!

God, You're awesome! Without You I'd have nothing to look forward to. But with You I can look forward to heaven and living for ever! Thank You so much! Amen.

I'LL NEVER BE LOST AGAIN

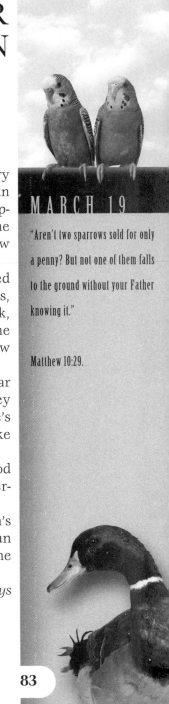

MARCH 19

"Aren't two sparrows sold for only a penny? But not one of them falls to the ground without your Father knowing it."

Matthew 10:29.

Today is Swallows Day. On this day every year the swallows return to the San Juan Capistrano Mission in California. It happens every year. No one knows how the birds know the exact date, but they show up without fail.

When my mom was a little girl, her family lived across the street from a big park in St. Albans, England. A lot of ducks lived on the pond in the park, and a few of them escaped, waddling across the street and nesting on the green in front of Mom's row of townhouses.

That fall Mom's ducks disappeared. The first year it happened, she felt just heartbroken, thinking they had been run over or had moved to someone else's yard. But every spring her ducks returned, just like the swallows at Capistrano.

Somehow God not only places maps and a good sense of direction in migratory birds, but also a perfect calendar that never fails them.

If He can do that for the swallows and Mom's ducks, we can trust Him to do that for us, too. We can rely on His direction and timing because, just like the swallows, He'll never fail us either.

God, Your timing is fantastic. Please help me always to remember to trust You more. Amen.

83

WHERE'S THE BEEF . . . EATERS?

So eat and drink and do everything else for the glory of God.

1 Corinthians 10:31.

My parents have a mixed marriage. Mom is vegetarian; Dad isn't. Today is the Great American Meat-out Day. It is a day set aside for families like mine to think about kicking the meat habit and exploring a more wholesome and less violent, plant-based diet.

More than 30 million Americans have tried a vegetarian diet. Beef consumption has dropped in this country by 30 percent and veal consumption by 70 percent. Most fast-food chains now offer salad bars, and some even provide meatless entrées like veggie burgers. Major food manufacturers are now getting into the meatless food business. Five other organizations have launched campaigns to reduce meat consumption.

For a long time the only vegetarians I knew were Seventh-day Adventists, but now it is popular among all kinds of people. I was surprised to learn that the amount of grain it takes to feed a cow in order to grow one pound of meat could feed 20 people for a whole week if they ate the grain instead of its being fed to the cow. This makes meat eating not only a health issue but also a selfishness issue.

If we stop eating meat in the United States, there would be enough grain to supply every hungry person in the world with bread. Perhaps more issues are at stake than just your body being the temple of the Holy Spirit, which in itself is an important one.

God, when You created the earth You made enough for everybody. Please help me not to want more than my share. Amen.

YOU BIRDBRAIN!

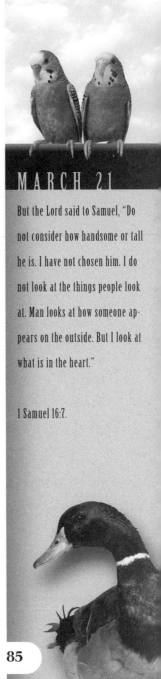

My brother used to call me a birdbrain, but that was before we had several birds join our family. We learned that birds are quite smart. Wamml knows how to change the subject when Dad is mad at him. The budgies know to go get their last drink and snack and find their perches when Dad says he's going to turn the light out in five minutes. Skippy runs screaming through the bedroom when Aunt Pat tells him he'd better be good or she's going to get Mom.

An old Spanish proverb says that "every person is a fool in somebody's opinion." Perhaps that's because most people decide their opinion by looking at each other, person or birdie, from the outside, and it isn't until you really get to know others that you understand just how smart they are.

I'm glad that when God looks at me, He sees me on the inside and doesn't judge me from the outside. Aren't you?

God, if You looked only at my outside, I'd be sunk. Thanks for reading me inside as well. Amen.

MARCH 21

But the Lord said to Samuel, "Do not consider how handsome or tall he is. I have not chosen him. I do not look at the things people look at. Man looks at how someone appears on the outside. But I look at what is in the heart."

1 Samuel 16:7.

85

MY INDIAN PEACE TREATY

MARCH 22

Love each other deeply. Honor others more than yourselves.

Romans 12:10.

The first American Indian treaty took place on this day in 1621. The Pilgrims and the Indian leader Massasoit agreed on a league of friendship. One year later the brother of another Indian chief named Powhatan led a massacre of some settlements around Jamestown, Virginia, and war began in the American colonies.

A hundred years ago my great-great-grandpa Berndt Thompson made a similar treaty with an Indian chief named Mickinock, who lived on his property. Mickinock was a leader of the Chippewa tribe. When my grandpa Berndt first moved to Minnesota, he discovered that his property was the winter campsite of Mickinock's tribe. Instead of fighting over it, Grandpa Berndt and Mickinock struck a deal. Grandpa Berndt gave Mickinock a pony in exchange for letting him live on his land. And the tribe still came back every winter.

The reason that their bargain lasted was mutual respect. Mickinock respected Grandpa Berndt because he kept his word. Grandpa Berndt respected Mickinock because he was a good provider for his tribe and a responsible leader. The treaty in the 1620s didn't work because of lack of respect. Without respect people don't keep their promises.

Mickinock and Grandpa Berndt respected each other, and our families are still friends a hundred years later. My friend, Andy Lipscomb, is a descendant of Mickinock's band.

God, I'm glad I can count on You always to keep Your promises. Amen.

86

"GIVE ME LIBERTY, OR GIVE ME DEATH!"

Today is Liberty Day. On this day in 1775 Patrick Henry spoke in favor of arming the Virginia militia against the British. At the end of his speech he said, "Give me liberty, or give me death."

Patrick Henry is my favorite patriot. I even had a three-cornered patriot hat just like his. All of the American patriots admired Patrick Henry as a great freedom fighter (though some of them considered him a hothead).

There have been many other freedom fighters through history that I admire too, such as Gideon, who fought the Moabites; Samson, who fought the Philistines; the Maccabees, who fought the Greeks; the French resistance and other heroes of World War II; those who ran the underground railroad that helped the slaves escape from the South into the North before and during the Civil War; and Martin Luther King, Jr., who reminded us that we still have a way to go for equality and freedom in our country.

But the greatest freedom fighter of them all was Jesus Christ. He didn't say, "Give Me liberty, or give Me death." Instead, He said, "Give Me death so that they can have liberty."

Thank You, Jesus, for this wonderful opportunity. Amen.

MARCH 23

The Spirit of the Lord and King is on me. The Lord has anointed me to tell the good news to poor people. He has sent me to comfort those whose hearts have been broken. He has sent me to announce freedom for those who have been captured. He wants me to set prisoners free from their dark prisons.

Isaiah 61:1.

WHEN LIFE WON'T STOP TUMBLING

My brothers and sisters, you'll face all kinds of trouble. When you do, think of it pure joy. Your faith will be put to the test. You know that when that happens, it will produce in you the strength to continue.

James 1:2-4.

One year for Christmas my grandpa bought me and my brother a rock polisher. We would find the most unattractive rocks in streambeds or on hikes, wash them, and put them into the tumbler. The tumbler had a solution in it with lots of grit. Then we turned it on and let it tumble for days and days. When it was done, we opened the tumbler and took our rocks out. Some of them had just disappeared. The tumbling had broken them into tiny pieces, and they had become part of the grit in the tumbler. But the valuable rocks were gorgeous! They were smooth and shiny and as beautiful as jewels.

It made me stop and think for a long time as I watched the rocks tumbling over and over in the barrel with the grit and the solution. It looked rough on the rocks.

Sometimes I feel like those rocks. Life can tumble us over and over and over again, bumping us against other sharp things. It's not fun. But just as my tumbler produces beautiful, smooth semiprecious stones, hard times in life can knock off some of my sharp edges and make me into a better person too.

When I feel that life is getting too hard, I look at some of my beautiful stones and thank God that He is watching over me and He thinks I'm valuable enough to polish.

God, You know that it hurts sometimes when You polish my character. Please be close to me then and help me keep focused on the goal You've set before me. Amen.

I'M GLAD
I'M NOT PREGNANT

Many Christians celebrate today as the Feast of Annunciation. It celebrates the time when the angel Gabriel announced to the virgin Mary that she was to be the mother of Christ.

MARCH 25

She is going to have a son. You must give him the name Jesus. That is because he will save his people from their sins.

Matthew 1:21.

When I was younger, it never really occurred to me what a big deal that was—until Maria moved in with us. She was 19 and pregnant. Even though she was married, a lot of people were very hard on her because she was so young. To make matters worse, her husband wasn't with her anymore.

Mary had an even harder time. She was only engaged, not married. And she was probably only about 13. In those days couples stayed engaged for a year. This made sure that the woman hadn't become pregnant with somebody else's baby during that time. If she had, people could drag her out into the public square and stone her in front of everybody. And I thought Maria had a rough time!

When Gabriel gave Mary the news, he didn't mention anything about explaining things to her parents or to Joseph. No wonder they sent her away to stay with Aunt Elizabeth.

God never forces anybody to do anything. Mary could have said no, that she didn't want to give birth to Jesus. But she took that responsibility because she loved God and trusted Him to keep her alive.

God, please help me to be willing to take on a hard assignment for You. And help me to remember that You'll take care of all the details as long as I trust You. Amen.

89

THANK GOD
FOR ERASERS

That will happen in a flash, as quickly as you can wink an eye. It will happen when the last trumpet sounds. The trumpet will sound, and the dead will be raised to live forever. And we will be changed.

1 Corinthians 15:52.

A wise little first grader once wrote, "Having a pencil without an eraser is just like having a pen."

Everyone makes mistakes, and it's easier to clean them up if you have some kind of tool that will remove them. Hyman Lipman patented the first pencil with an eraser in 1853. Since then writing has been much easier.

Some erasers are better than others. They remove mistakes cleanly, while others leave a dark streak. As erasers get old, they get hard and darker. An old eraser may just smear the marks until you have a large dark smudge instead of a small mistake. This is especially annoying when you're trying to draw a picture, although it's a problem in homework, too.

Jesus is the perfect eraser. When my eraser on the end of my pencil erases things, it may take away all of the black marks or graphite, but it still often leaves a little indentation in the paper. But when Jesus removes something from my life, it is completely gone. No traces remain, and unlike erasers, Jesus' ability does not diminish with time. His erasing abilities will always be the best there ever are. But I'm looking forward to the time when He won't need to use them anymore. When with the twinkling of an eye, I will be changed and be just like Him and live with Him forever, and there will never be any more mistakes for Him to clean up.

Jesus, thanks for making my life all spotless and clean, and for erasing all memory of my sins. Amen.

90

THAT'S *SIR* DILLON TO YOU!

O n this day in 1513 Juan Ponce de León, a Spanish explorer, sighted Florida for the first time. Recently I've discovered that he is a member of my family tree. We always knew that the Dillons came from Ireland, and because they were of noble blood, it was easy to find their family records. We followed them back to England, from where they had been exiled for helping Prince John usurp the throne.

Next we traced the family tree to France. My ancestors came over to England when the Normans invaded. That was when they became Dillons. Their name had been De Leon up until then, but that was just too French. The De Leons had been nobility in France, too, and married other royalty in Europe. That is how we found Ponce de León.

Even though I am of noble blood, my family tree has a lot of very ignoble people on it. Learning about a family tree can be discouraging and even embarrassing. I've found slave owners right up to the time of the Civil War. Also I found aristocrats who overtaxed the poor and horse thieves.

But we have to remember that everybody has some dark spots in their family tree, even Jesus. He put His family tree in Matthew for everyone to see, even though there were some real slimy characters there too. Jesus wasn't embarrassed of His ancestors, and I shouldn't have to be either, because no matter whom I descended from, God loves me.

God, I'm glad I'm part of Your family! Amen.

MARCH 27

This is the record of the family line of Jesus Christ. He is the son of David. He is also the son of Abraham.

Matthew 1:1.

91

MY TANGE'S ALL TOUNGLED, AND I CAN'T STINCT DISPEACKLY!

In the same way, the Holy Spirit helps us when we are weak. We don't know what we should pray for. But the Spirit himself prays for us. He prays with groans too deep for words.

Romans 8:26.

One summer Mom's lupus attacked her brain cells. It caused a lot of problems for her and made her very sick. It also left her confused, creating a lot of funny family stories. She would try to brush her teeth with the hairbrush, or toss her toothbrush into the toilet and flush after brushing her teeth. When she got cold, she would ask for a "leg thing," when what she really wanted was a blanket. The thing Mom would do that made my brother and me laugh the most was asking for a beer when she was thirsty. It was funny because Mom doesn't drink beer. She hasn't had a beer in more than 20 years, and even then she never liked it. Her brain knew that she was thirsty, but what came out of her mouth was "Please get me a beer."

My family soon became very good at interpreting what Mom wanted. When Mom requested a beer, we would get her a glass of water or a soda, and she would be very happy. We learned that when Mom asked for something weird, we needed to look at her and see what she actually needed. And usually if we gave her that instead, she was happy with it.

God does that. Sometimes we ask for things that aren't good for us, or things that would harm us, but God looks carefully at us and then gives us what we really need, but not always what we ask for. I'm glad He understands me so well.

God, I know I sometimes ask for things that aren't good for me. Thanks for saying no and giving me what I need. Amen.

MR. T

r. T was my Pathfinder toad. I caught him on a Pathfinder campout when he was still tiny. He lived in an aquarium in my bedroom that had gravel and plants and a little pond to play in, but no obvious source of food. But Mr. T didn't worry about food at all.

We lived in a spooky old house that year with a lot of bugs in the basement. Every evening I would take him downstairs and set him on the floor in the middle of the basement. Then I would turn on my computer and start playing my favorite computer game. The crickets and the cockroaches loved the little computer noises in the game and came running out, squeaking and answering them. Mr. T would just hop around the floor gobbling until he was so full he couldn't hop anymore. Then I would scoop him up and take him back up to his aquarium.

Even though there was no obvious sign of his next meal, Mr. T never worried about where his food was coming from. He knew that I would take care of it and that there was always plenty.

That year I learned to be a little more like Mr. T too. Even though my dad was unemployed and money was sometimes very tight, God always took care of us. Mr. T never had to worry, and neither did I.

Thank You, God, for always taking such good care of us. And help us to remember that You know where our next meal is coming from even when we don't. Amen.

MARCH 29

I tell you, do not worry. Don't worry about your life and what you will eat or drink. And don't worry about your body and what you will wear. Isn't there more to life than eating? Aren't there more important things for the body than clothes?

Matthew 6:25.

93

GOD'S INCUBATORS

God said, "Let the waters be filled with living things. Let birds fly above the earth across the huge space of the sky." So God created the great creatures of the ocean. He created every living and moving thing that fills the waters. He created all kinds of them. He created every kind of bird that flies. And God saw that it was good."

Genesis 1:20-22.

O n this day in 1843 the egg incubator was patented. I have several, but they are the kind invented long before 1843. In fact, God created them on the fifth day of earth's existence.

They are parakeets. I was so excited the first time Miss Itchy, my parakeet, laid an egg. I was excited even more when she laid the sixth and seventh eggs. And I was most delighted when one hatched. We named her Belladonna Chick, and she has gone on to make several babies of her own.

Even though we've raised dozens of baby parakeets since then, I'm still amazed when an egg, a little white ball of nothing, becomes a bird. How does God do that, and what does He do inside that little shell? When parakeets first hatch, they don't look all that different from the newborn pink gerbils that I used to raise. But after that they become mostly beak and claws before they get feathery. By about three weeks you can tell what they are. (No, it's not a toaster oven; it's a parakeet.)

The invention of the incubator was marvelous, but what is even more wonderful is the egg and the bird that comes out of it. And I know which came first.

God, You're so wonderfully creative. And thanks for being willing to re-create me as well. Amen.

RUSTY TOWERS

O n this day in 1889 the Eiffel Tower was completed. (I just can't imagine Paris without it!) They had been working on the Eiffel Tower for quite some time, but on today's date it was finally finished.

When my mom was about my age, she was lucky enough to go to Paris and see the famous tower. She went on a school trip with her French class.

When she first saw it poking up over the horizon, her heart jumped up into her nostrils. It was dawn, the sunrise was all pink and silver, and the tower was silhouetted against the morning sky.

I remember her describing to me her bitter disappointment as she, pushing and shoving, climbed off the bus at the foot of the tower and discovered that it was a big rusty cast-iron tower that made dirty streaks on your clothes if you brushed against it.

A lot of things in life are like that. They look pretty good until you see them up close. You may think that falling in love and having sex would be great. But after I spent last year sharing a bathroom with someone who was pregnant and listening to her throw up every day, sex didn't sound nearly as glamorous to me. All of a sudden all of the counsel to wait made more sense.

Whenever you face temptation, remember the Eiffel Tower, and remember it doesn't look so great up close.

God, please help me to trust and obey You all the time, even when I don't want to, because I know that You know best. Amen.

Pay attention and listen to the sayings of those who are wise. Apply your heart to the sayings I teach.

Proverbs 22:17.

APRIL FOOLS' DAY

And in the same region, there were some shepherds staying out in the fields, and keeping watch over their flock by night.

Luke 2:8, NASB.

The first day of April is April Fools' Day. It is a time for much humor and hilarity and practical jokes. People have celebrated it for a long, long time. History books tell us that April Fools' Day celebrations started in Roman times.

Some people believe that Jesus was born in April. The shepherds were out in the fields with their sheep when the angels appeared to them. April makes more sense, considering the climate that time of year in Israel. Such people even suggest that April Fools' Day could have started as a way to make fun of Christians who were celebrating Jesus' birthday. At that time only pagans had celebrations during what we now think of as Christmastime.

I don't know for sure what the real origin of April Fools' Day is, but I never want to do anything that makes fun of Christ or His people.

Dear God, help me not to do anything that seeks to make fun of You. Amen.

GREAT LOVERS

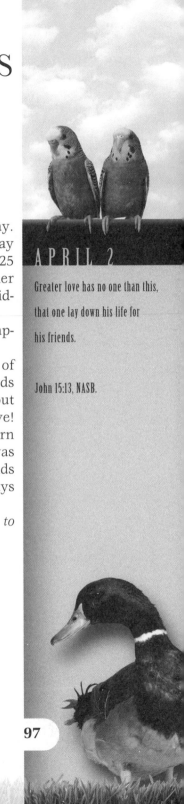

Some have called April 2 Great Lovers Day. They named it because it was the birthday of Casanova. Casanova was born in 1725 and was famous for seducing a lot of other people's wives. Many people have considered Casanova the world's greatest lover.

In 1980 the world's longest underwater kiss happened on April 2, breaking the previous record.

But when I think of great lovers, I don't think of Casanova or of kissing underwater. Ruining hundreds of other people's marriages or making out without being able to breathe sounds very little like real love!

I believe the World's Greatest Lover was born about 4 B.C. and lived only 33 years before He was crucified, trading His life for the lives of His friends and people He loved. To me, Jesus was and always will be the World's Greatest Lover.

Thank You, Jesus, for loving me. Please teach me to love other people as You do. Amen.

APRIL 2

Greater love has no one than this, that one lay down his life for his friends.

John 15:13, NASB.

97

MORE FUN THAN A BARREL OF MONKEYS

On the glorious splendor of Thy majesty, and on Thy wonderful works, I will meditate.

Psalm 145:5, NASB.

On this day in 1792 John Bill Rickett opened the first circus in the United States in Philadelphia, Pennsylvania. The circus has done well in this country ever since then.

Most of us love going to the circus. We get to see all kinds of strange sights, such as bears on bikes, elephants doing ballet, and clowns and acrobats and other things that you don't find every day.

As Christians we don't have to go to a circus for excitement. After inviting God into our lives, we just have to pay attention. Then we will notice many things that we wouldn't see every day. Instead of putting bears on bicycles, God uses His creative power to do really practical things that help both us and other people. Learning to be a Christian and a part of God's family is even more exciting than going to a circus.

Dear God, help me to remember all the neat things You do and have done. Amen.

THE ULTIMATE PARTY

Some people call this party-party day. They look for any reason for a party. Since it happens to have the same number for the month as for the day, it offers them an excuse for a party.

I enjoy parties too. And I'm looking forward to a really big one coming up soon. It's going to be held in cemeteries all across the land. I know this sounds a little strange, perhaps like a Halloween party, but it's much better than that.

Jesus is going to come to wake up all His people who have been sleeping there for so long. He will rescue all of us who love Him from Planet Earth. Those who were dead are going to rise up in the air to meet Him first, while we who are still alive will join them there. I can hardly wait!

At God's party I'm planning to meet my grandma Jo. I was only 4 years old when she died. She will be really surprised to see me a big teenager now. It's going to be the greatest party I've ever been to.

Dear God, come soon! Amen.

APRIL 4

For the Lord Himself will descend from heaven with a shout, with the voice of the archangel, and with the trumpet of God; and the dead in Christ shall rise first.

1 Thessalonians 4:16, 17, NASB.

99

MY ADOPTED FATHER

For you have not received a spirit of slavery leading to fear again, but you have received a spirit of adoption as sons by which we cry out, "Abba! Father!"

Romans 8:15, NASB.

It used to be that adopted kids never would find out who their birth parents were. Today some of the laws are changing, and many adopted people can search and find their birth parents.

My friend Mitzi was able to find her birth family. It disappointed her at first. Her birth mother really wasn't interested in a close relationship with her, and she could trace nothing of her father. However, she has become close with her brothers and sisters. Mitzi feels it was worth the search. And of course she also really loves and appreciates her adopted parents.

I've been adopted too. I was born to some very sinful birth parents. But the King of the universe adopted me and offered to make me one of His sons, which means that I can inherit all kinds of wealth. Now I'm a prince and heir to a huge kingdom.

Just like Mitzi, my birth parents are important to me, too, and I really love them, but I appreciate my Adopted Dad most of all.

Dear God, thank You for adopting me. Amen.

THE HUMAN SACRIFICE

On this day in 1896 the first of the new modern Olympic Games took place in Athens, Greece, and I'm glad they did. I love the Olympics. It's fascinating to watch people who have trained their bodies to go farther, higher, longer, and more gracefully through the various Olympic routines.

I was especially impressed watching the women's gymnastics last year. (My brother would make some rude comment here about girl watching, but please keep your mind above that stuff for a minute.)

Kerri Strug continued and finished her jump off the gymnastics horse in spite of an injured ankle, knowing that she could injure it further. She won the gold medal for the U.S. women's team by her act of unselfishness. Not only did it cost her physical pain, but it kept her from competing for any of the individual medals.

This reminds me of Jesus, who was willing to brave great physical pain to win the prize—me. By being willing to do that, He won the right to take me home with Him to live forever. What an awesome God!

Dear God, help me to be as loyal to You as Jesus is to me. Amen.

Greater love has no one than this, that one lay down his life for his friends.

John 15:13, NASB.

HAPPINESS IS . . .

In all thy ways acknowledge him, and he shall direct thy paths.

Proverbs 3:6, KJV.

Some people are better than others at reading road maps. My mom likes to study maps and see where we are. Dad prefers to just drive till he finds the place, probably something to do with his not wanting to ask for directions. This has been named National Reading a Road Map Week by the people who make road maps. Their slogan is "Happiness is knowing how to read a road map."

The Bible is kind of like a road map. God gave us directions, told us exactly how to get to where He is. But just as in the case of road maps, not everybody is interested in reading it. Worse yet, some people don't even like being given directions. They would rather just try it their own way and see if they can get there.

Like the slogan from the road map companies, I believe that happiness is knowing how to read our heavenly road map too. Without it a guy could get really lost.

Dear God, thank You for providing directions. Help me to remember to read them! Amen.

ALL IN THE FAMILY

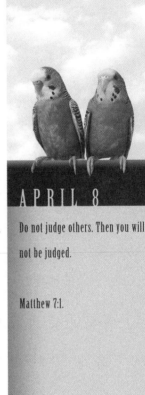

APRIL 8

Do not judge others. Then you will not be judged.

Matthew 7:1.

My friend Maria had just come to live with us. Mom had brought her home the same way she brings home little animals who need love and attention. Maria had been kicked out of school for smoking, and now she had eloped and was pregnant and homeless, too. My brother and I invited her to go to vespers with us Friday night. Just as we were sitting down, one of the church members saw her and asked her to leave. He pointed out that she was wearing earrings, had a lot of makeup on, smelled like cigarette smoke, and would be a bad influence on all the "good people."

Mom and Dad told her that it was their church too. Now that she was a part of our family, she was always welcome in our church no matter what some of the other members said. Dad went and talked to the other church member. Six months later Maria had quit smoking and dressed more modestly. She was baptized and is now a member at our church, and she brings her baby.

What would have happened if everybody had asked her to leave? If we could learn to love people who have made big mistakes instead of chasing them away, then our church would be too full for anyone to find a seat on Sabbath morning.

Dear God, thank You for making me part of Your family even before I started acting like I was. Amen.

THE SMALLEST GOOD DEED

"A man has two sons. He went to the first and said, "Son, go and work today in the vineyard." "I will not," the son answered. But later he changed his mind and went. Then the father went to the other son. He said the same thing. The son answered, "I will, sir." But he did not go.

Matthew 21:28-31.

Jesus told a parable about two sons whose father had asked both to do something. One said "Yes" and then forgot, while the other one said "No, I don't think so," but then had second thoughts and did it anyway.

Sometimes I really relate to the first son. I have a lot of good intentions. When someone asks me to do something, I often say yes. However, I'm easily distracted. It is so easy for me to walk into a room, then forget what I came there for and get busy with something else I find.

When we do things, God understands our motives behind them, but when we don't do anything, our motives really don't count. A famous quotation says, "The smallest good deed is always greater than the largest good intention." God wants His people to be a people of action, not just people who thought about doing good things. Your mother was wrong when she said it's the thought that counts. Get up and do something. Be a man or a woman of action.

Dear God, help me to be a person of action instead of just someone with lots of good intentions. Amen.

MY SMITH AND WESSON

APRIL 10

The angel of the Lord stands guard around those who have respect for him. And saves them.

Psalm 34:7.

Because my aunt Yostie lived near a prison, her husband taught her how to shoot a handgun just in case. The gun that she owned had been made by a company called Smith & Wesson. A sign hanging on their door said "This house is guarded by Smith & Wesson."

I thought that was a really cool idea for a sign, and so when I got home I named my two baby turtles Smith and Wesson. And I too wanted to get a sign on my door that said "This home guarded by Smith and Wesson."

Mom wouldn't let me. She thought it would look silly right next to the sign that said "Choose you this day whom you will serve; . . . but as for me and my house, we will serve the Lord" (Joshua 34:15).

Even though I knew the sign would be really cool, I recognized that Smith and Wesson, whether it was a gun or a pair of turtles, wouldn't compare to Jesus and a host of His angels. As long as He's on my side, I don't need Smith and Wesson, whatever they are.

Dear God, thank You for being my protection. Help me to remember that You are there and that I don't need anything else. Amen.

BRINGING DOWN THE HOUSE

The person who rests in the shadow of the Most High God will be kept safe by the Mighty One. I will say about the Lord, "He is my place of safety. He is like a fort to me. He is my God. I trust in him."

Psalm 91:1, 2.

This week has been declared National Building Safety Week. Always the second week of April, it promotes building codes so that all buildings will be safer to work in and live in.

When my mom was growing up, she lived in a tremor belt of West Africa. They never had really big earthquakes, but the ground would often shake enough to knock down some of the more carelessly constructed buildings.

She remembers being impressed with the architecture of the local American embassy, because it had been specially designed to withstand shaking ground. Mom always felt really safe there. The embassy sat on four pillars that went deep in the ground; they were attached to the building by ball joints so that the pillars could sway, but the building resting on top of the four pillars would stay level.

But even fancy high-tech antitremor architecture couldn't have helped the Philistines in their temple of Dagon. Samson grabbed two supporting pillars, asked God for extra strength, pulled them together, and brought the whole building down.

All the technology in the world cannot stand up to God and His power. Being God's kid, I feel even safer than Mom did in the American embassy.

Dear God, Your power is just awesome! Amen.

BIG WIND

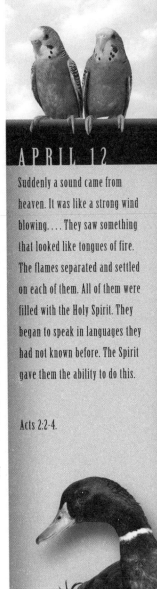

Today is known as the Anniversary of the Big Wind. On this day in 1934 the people on Mount Washington, New Hampshire, experienced the highest-velocity natural wind ever recorded. The wind reached 231 miles per hour. I can't imagine what havoc that would wreak.

Last spring a dying hurricane drifted through with winds that were 70 to 80 miles per hour. It blew branches off trees, knocked over mobile homes, and caused tremendous damage everywhere.

The kind of high-powered winds we know are very destructive. Yet Acts 2 describes the most powerful wind ever recorded when it tells us that the Holy Spirit came in like a rushing wind. The winds we experience in our weather are destructive; they hurt people and break things. The Holy Spirit blows in far more powerfully, but it is a healing force and can change the world. Which wind do you want behind your sails? You get a choice, you know.

Dear God, thank You for being willing to be the wind behind my sails and beneath my wings. Amen.

APRIL 12

Suddenly a sound came from heaven. It was like a strong wind blowing....They saw something that looked like tongues of fire. The flames separated and settled on each of them. All of them were filled with the Holy Spirit. They began to speak in languages they had not known before. The Spirit gave them the ability to do this.

Acts 2:2-4.

107

HALLELUJAH!

Sing a new song to the Lord. He has done wonderful things.

Psalm 98:1.

On this day in 1742 crowds filed expectantly into the new music hall in Dublin, Ireland. It was the premier of a new oratorio by a young composer. Crowds listened in awe, moved both by the music and the words. It was wonderful. George Frideric Handel was a big success.

Not long after that the music played for a royal audience. The oratorio crescendoed into the majestic "Hallelujah Chorus." The king jumped to his feet and stood in admiration and respect for the Messiah and the composer who honored Him.

Even today, whenever someone performs the *Messiah,* crowds always stand for the "Hallelujah Chorus." That's really great, and we *should* stand to respect and honor God. But it makes me feel a little sad to remember that when the real Messiah premiered, few people paid any attention. A few smelly shepherds were the only ones who stood by His cradle in respect for a Baby who would someday save the world.

Instead of spending a lot of time feeling bad about what they missed, though, I can make sure that I give Him all the honor and respect that I can (which is still way less than what He really deserves).

Dear God, You are my king. Hallelujah! Amen.

TAKE TIME TO LAUGH

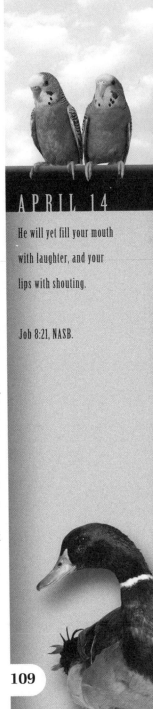

APRIL 14

He will yet fill your mouth
with laughter, and your
lips with shouting.

Job 8:21, NASB.

April has been designated as National Humor Month since 1976, probably because April Fools' Day falls during it. As I mentioned earlier, April Fools' Day is a time for lots of humor and practical jokes.

However, God has a sense of humor all year round. For a while my dad owned his own business, which meant that if his customers didn't pay their bills on time, we didn't always have enough money. One morning my mom prayed and asked the Lord to please send some checks in the mail, since things were getting a little tight.

When we went down to the mailbox and opened it up there was a small, sample-sized cereal box of Chex. Mom and I laughed and laughed. We knew God must have been just chuckling, waiting for us to go get the mail.

Mom, amid giggles, said, "Lord, these weren't the checks I had in mind!" As we pulled out the rest of the mail we found two envelopes with real money checks for Dad's business in it.

I'm so glad my God has a sense of humor. It makes me appreciate Him even more.

Dear God, I really appreciate Your sense of humor. You make my life a lot of fun! Amen.

TEENAGE MUTANT NINJA ARTISTS

APRIL 15

Give praise to the Lord, the God of Israel, for ever and ever. Amen and Amen.

Psalm 41:13.

When I was little, the hot toys were teenage mutant ninja turtles. All of my friends had them, and we played ninja turtles all day long. I thought my mom was kind of mean because she made us learn about each person the turtles were named after before we could have the toy. I was the only one who knew that Leonardo was named after Leonardo da Vinci.

I don't play ninja turtles anymore, but today is Leonardo da Vinci's birthday. Ninja turtles are now passé, but Leonardo da Vinci is still cool. He'll always be cool. Millions still flock to see his *Last Supper* and his *Mona Lisa*. Da Vinci was a great artist, inventor, military tactician, and engineer.

Some things in life are cool for a little while, but others last forever. Being a ninja turtle will be cool only until you and your friends get a little bit older or until they quit being on TV, but being a Christian will be cool for eternity.

Dear God, You will be cool forever. Amen.

110

SHARE AND SHARE ALIKE

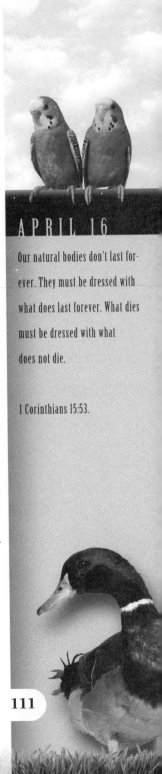

O ne of Mom's jobs was to be the organ and tissue donation coordinator at her hospital. I enjoyed this more than a lot of things Mom did, because she was always giving away cool pens and bumper stickers and buttons. My favorite one was on the back of her car. It said "Don't take your organs to heaven; heaven knows we need them here." She talked to different groups of people, encouraging them to donate their organs when they died to help other people who were still living and needed them.

It's an idea that makes good sense to me. If I die before Jesus comes, I'm planning on a whole new body with no recycled parts. And if my whole life is based on giving to others, then it makes sense to still give after I die too. Especially since we know God already has promised to return to us everything we ever lose in this battle here on earth. I'm glad I don't have to take these organs to heaven. Instead, I plan to have a much cooler body there.

Dear God, thank You for planning a new body for me. I'll need it by then! Amen.

Our natural bodies don't last forever. They must be dressed with what does last forever. What dies must be dressed with what does not die.

1 Corinthians 15:53.

RAINING ALLIGATORS

My friend Paul is a real lizard brain. I'm not saying that because he thinks like a lizard, but because he loves lizards. He has a large collection of them. His prized possession, though, is a Cayman alligator named Leviathan—Levi for short.

Levi was about seven inches long and he would swim around and eat goldfish and do all kinds of unpleasant things like that. But Paul adored him, and the alligator was a lot of fun to play with.

One day when I was holding him he bit me. It startled me because he had never done such a thing before, so I jumped a little. When I jumped, he fell off my hand and did a lovely swan dive right into the hard tile floor. He landed directly on his nose. This wasn't a good thing, considering he fell about three feet and he's only seven inches long. When he didn't move at all, I was sure that he was dead, and Paul was too.

Fortunately Levi wasn't dead, only knocked out cold. He did, however, remain unconscious for five minutes. It was one of the worst five minutes of my life. I felt guilty even though it was only an accident.

I can't even begin to imagine how bad I would feel if I had to kill a little lamb on purpose back in Bible times. I'm glad that Jesus has died for my sins so that I don't have to sacrifice animals anymore. But I'm even more glad that Jesus was willing to be that Lamb, and that because of Him, I can live forever.

Dear God, thank You for dying for me so I don't have to kill a little lamb anymore. Amen.

112

JESUS IS COMING!

One of my favorite heroes of the American Revolution was Paul Revere. Today is the anniversary of his famous ride when in 1775 he rode from Boston to Concord, shouting, "The British are coming! The British are coming!"

In school we studied the famous poem about him, and I antagonized my teacher by writing "Now, listen my children and you shall hear the midnight drive of Bob McBeer . . ." and going on to describe the exploits of a man who had had a few too many, riding through town.

Revere really fascinated me. Even though all of this happened in 1775, we still remember him for both risking his life and risking looking stupid to his friends by riding through the countryside shouting that the British were coming.

I have the opportunity of being like Paul Revere, except maybe even better. Jesus is coming soon. Instead of stumbling through and not quite getting the message right, like the sad poem of the midnight drive of Bob McBeer, I have an opportunity to be a hero and let people know that Jesus will soon be here. Not so they can organize a resistance, but so they can welcome Him.

Jesus' arrival may be as welcome to some people as the Redcoats were to Boston, but I can't wait to see Him.

Dear God, help me to let people know of Your soon coming so they can go home with You too. Amen.

APRIL 18

Enoch was the seventh man in the family line of Adam.... He said, "Look! The Lord is coming with thousands and thousands of his holy ones."

Jude 14.

113

RED AND YELLOW, BLACK AND WHITE . . .

Blessed are those who make peace.
They will be called sons of God.

Matthew 5:9.

My grandpa's grandpa was a pioneer who went out to northern Minnesota in a covered wagon and staked his claim on land there. Grandpa's grandpa (Grandpa Berndt) was responsible for making peace with the Chippewa Indians in Minnesota. He learned a lot about them. One was that, like any other group of people, you will find good people, bad people, grumpy people, and people with a sense of humor. Native Americans were no different.

Mickinock was the leader of the band of Chippewa who shared the property with Grandpa Berndt. Later one winter Grandpa's mother, baby Anna, was born. Chief Mickinock came to see the new baby. When he stood and gazed at her for a long time, it made her mama, who hated Indians, very nervous. Suddenly, he scooped up the baby in his arms and bolted out the door.

Grandpa Berndt didn't know what to do. "Take your gun," his wife shouted, but Grandpa Berndt headed after Mickinock empty-handed. He found his friend sitting on a log, cooing and playing with the baby, and laughing heartily at his practical joke.

Unlike the Indians who had given their race such a stoic reputation, Mickinock enjoyed a good laugh and had a wonderful sense of humor. Grandpa Berndt and Mickinock went on to enjoy a long friendship, and peace reigned in their part of Minnesota.

Dear God, help me to enjoy other people and not worry about the color of their skin. Amen.

SAY NO TO CELERY!

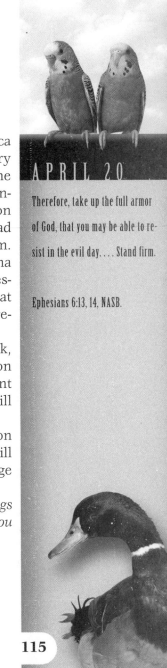

APRIL 20

Therefore, take up the full armor of God, that you may be able to resist in the evil day. . . . Stand firm.

Ephesians 6:13, 14, NASB.

The National Celery Growers of America has named April as National Celery Month. My great-uncle Dwight tells some awfully funny stories, but one of the funniest is about when my Grandpa Don first met Grandma Betty's family. Grandma Betty had brought him home because she wanted to marry him. Grammy was asking him questions, and Grandma Betty's little brothers were all hanging around eavesdropping. Then Grammy asked Grandpa Don what kind of man he was. Uncle Dwight says he still remembers Grandpa Don's response.

He said, "Well, I don't smoke, and I don't drink, and I don't eat celery." Over the years Grandpa Don has mellowed some, but not in the most important things. Grandpa Don still doesn't smoke, and he still doesn't drink, but occasionally he eats celery now.

I hope that as I go through life and mellow on some things that I used to feel strongly about, I will still stand firm on the important things, and change only on issues like eating celery.

Dear God, help me to be able to be firm on the things that are important to you and mellow only on things You don't care about. Amen.

DON'T BE STUPID

Let us not give up meeting together. Some are in the habit of doing this. Instead, let us cheer each other up with words of hope. Let us do it all the more as you see the day coming when Christ will return.

Hebrews 10:25.

One time my brother, Don, my baby-sitter, Kevin, and I were inner-tubing down the river when Kevin saw something floating over by the riverbank.

"Hey, look at what we see floating around over there," he said to me. "Go get it!"

As I got closer I heard a little "peep, peep, peep." It was a baby duck.

Sometimes adult ducks will go off perhaps 20 feet and watch the baby ducks so they will learn how to swim on their own. I thought that maybe that was what was happening. So I backed off and watched it for a little while, but no mother came out. It just kept swimming in circles, peeping away. So I brought it back to Kevin. "Look," I said, "a duck!"

"Yeah, right," he said, and shoved me off. Then I held it up to his face and it peeped at him. We took the duckling home and lovingly named it "Stupid." Stupid had not stayed with a group of other ducklings, and it was lucky that we found him before some hungry cat or other animal did. Life is hard for baby ducklings, especially when they don't stick with the group. And life can be hard for young Christians when they try to make it on their own. It's much easier if we have Christian friends to turn to when we stumble.

Dear God, help me remember to stick with Your other kids and not go off by myself as Stupid did. Amen.

STUPID IS AS STUPID DOES

O ne day later our little duck, Stupid, died. My brother discovered him early in the morning before Mom and Dad were awake. He, feeling quite grown up, took matters into his own hands and flushed Stupid down the toilet. After all, it worked for goldfish. It never occurred to my brother that a duck might affect the plumbing differently than goldfish. (My brother had a long and distinguished history of flushing inappropriate stuff down the toilet, but hadn't been in trouble for that during the past 10 years.)

When Mom found out, she had a cow. I laughed as I heard her bellow, "And you called the *duck* stupid?"

People are funny that way. We label other people stupid, when actually we sometimes are also doing really unsmart things (like flushing a duck down the toilet).

To some people, even God's instructions don't make sense, and they label Him stupid without stopping to think things through. But God has promised to give us wisdom if we ask Him. That's lucky for us, and especially for my brother.

Dear God, thank You that You are willing to help give me not only spiritual things but also things like wisdom and common sense. Amen.

APRIL 22

If any of you need wisdom, ask God for it. He will give it to you. God gives freely to everyone. He doesn't find fault.

James 1:5.

CHANGING THE SUBJECT

Lord, my Rock, I call out to you. Pay attention to me. If you remain silent, I will die. I will be like those who have gone down into the grave. Hear my cry for your favor when I call out to you for help. Hear me when I lift up my hands in prayer toward your Most Holy Room.

Psalm 28:1, 2.

O ur African gray parrot doesn't live in Africa but in our living room. In an African jungle he could chew anything wood that he liked. Unfortunately, we can't allow him to munch on all the wood in our living room. One evening, Wamml started nibbling on the window frame. He had bitten away a pretty big chunk before Dad realized what he was doing.

"No, no," he shouted. "Bad bird; don't eat the window."

"No," Wamml replied.

"That's right. No."

"No, no," Wamml repeated.

"That's right. No."

"No! No! No!" the bird shouted. Then Wamml took a few steps toward Dad, bobbed his head a couple times, and said, "So, what's up?"

My parrot didn't want to take responsibility for what he had done. He would rather change the subject and get on to something else.

How often we are just like Wamml! It's hard to take responsibility and admit that we've been wrong, and yet that's something God asks us to do. But He has promised forgiveness for us when we do. It helps us remember that only birdbrains change the subject.

Dear God, thank You for forgiving me when I've done wrong. Amen.

THE MASTER'S TOUCH

APRIL 24

Jesus touched her hand, and the fever left her. She got up and began to wait on him.

Matthew 8:15.

One of my mom's many talents is painting. But she not only loves to paint, she loves to teach other people to paint too. My cousin Jessica was at our house painting with Mom. They were creating a picture of Jesus with a nail mark in His hand, holding a lamb.

Jessie felt that her painting wasn't up to par and got rather discouraged with it. She was almost in tears, because she felt that it looked like Frankenstein holding a dog instead of Jesus with a lamb.

Mom glanced over it, said "No, it looks pretty good. Here let me help," and added two or three strokes. And poof! Magically it turned into Jesus with the lamb. All that it needed was a touch from a master (like Mom).

Sometimes we might think that our lives resemble Frankenstein with a dog. We need to remember that with a touch from the Master it can be beautiful after all. But just like my mom, He doesn't go dabbling in anyone's stuff without an invitation. He is just waiting for us to ask Him.

Dear God, please help me with my life. Amen.

COPING WITH CORRUPT LEADERS

"But suppose you don't want to serve him. Then choose for yourselves right now whom you will serve. You can choose the gods your people served east of the Euphrates River. Or you can choose the gods the Amorites serve. After all, you are living in their land. But as for me and my family, we will serve the Lord."

Joshua 24:15.

Corruption, failure, or mistakes in church leaders are especially overwhelming to those of us who look up to them. My brother and I had a pastor in Illinois we really liked. One Sabbath he wasn't in church, and all the adults were standing around in knots, talking anxiously in low voices. Our favorite pastor had run away. He had gotten a girlfriend and chosen not to be our pastor anymore.

It devastated my brother and me. Had he stopped liking us? What could we have done to keep him from going away? Why would he do such a thing? My brother didn't want to go to church anymore for a while.

The Bible shares stories about many spiritual church leaders, but it also tells some stories about some really bad ones. Eli's sons were terrible. He was the high priest responsible for taking care of the tabernacle containing the ark of the covenant. Yet his sons had no respect for it and did all kinds of terrible things.

Samuel's dad was a loyal worshiper of God, and even though the priests at the sanctuary were corrupt, he still brought his sacrifices there to worship God. Elkanah, Samuel's dad, knew that by bringing his sacrifices there, he wasn't condoning or supporting the corrupt priests. It was between him and God. Whether or not the priests were corrupt, he was going to continue to worship God.

Eventually that's what my brother and I decided too.

God, help me to remember to keep my eyes on You and not be upset by things I see human leaders do. Amen.

120

LOSING PUCK

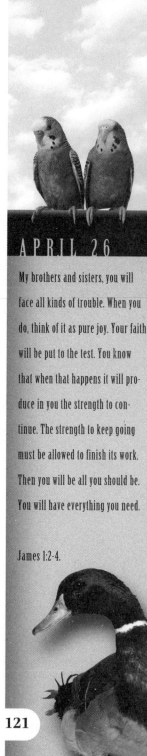

For my brother Don's first birthday he received a dog named Puck. Puck was a 6-week-old wirehaired terrier. Don and Puck fell in love and would do everything together, including share chew toys. My brother hated to see his puppy get in trouble, so when Puck would have accidents and leave "presents" around the living room, Don would pick them up and put them in Dad's shoe, where nobody would ever find them.

Puck and Don were inseparable. Later Don and Mom developed lung problems. They got sicker and sicker and didn't know what the problem was until one day they discovered that it was Puck that was making them sick. Both were allergic to dogs.

It was a sad day for everybody with tears all around when they had to take Puck away. Don couldn't understand why he had to give up something that he loved so much. And neither could Puck. But if they hadn't given him up, Don and Mom both could have gotten even sicker from him and maybe even died.

Sometimes God has to remove things that we love, and we don't always understand. But we can trust Him and know that He would never do it unless it was for our own good.

God, help me always to remember that even when I lose something I really love that Your plan is best for me. Amen.

APRIL 26

My brothers and sisters, you will face all kinds of trouble. When you do, think of it as pure joy. Your faith will be put to the test. You know that when that happens it will produce in you the strength to continue. The strength to keep going must be allowed to finish its work. Then you will be all you should be. You will have everything you need.

James 1:2-4.

UGH! ROTTEN POTATOES!

"Fathers, suppose your son asks for a fish. Which of you will give him a snake instead?"

Luke 11:11.

When I was 2, my mom would take me to her favorite restaurant, and I would order the stuff on the children's menu by pointing to what I wanted because it was all colorful and fun-looking. But I would always end up eating the au gratin potatoes that she had ordered for herself from the adult menu.

One day she decided it would be more economical just to order au gratin potatoes for both of us. When she asked the waiter for them, I began to cry.

"What is the matter, Michael?" she said to me.

Sobbing, I replied, "I don't want them rotten."

I didn't understand that she was getting me the thing that I always ate. I thought that she was going to make me eat rotten potatoes.

A lot of times we don't understand what God has planned for us. God always knows what's best for us and what we need. He will always give it to us, even though we don't always understand—and He never gives us anything "rotten."

Dear God, help me to remember You give me only good gifts and always do what is best for me—even if I don't understand it at the time. Amen.

THE CRICKET FARM

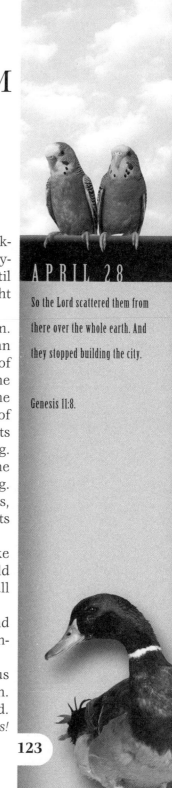

One summer we had a whole lot of crickets in our yard. My brother and I joyfully ran around catching crickets until we had a bucketful that we brought into the living room and set free.

It was fun watching Mom trying to catch them. Being the cool person that she is, Mom set up an aquarium for us to house our crickets in instead of just letting them run loose in the living room. The next morning we discovered to our horror that the crickets, even though we had given them plenty of food, had started eating each other. Many crickets were hopping around with one or more legs missing.

We were brokenhearted and felt sorry for the crickets, but we couldn't figure out what was wrong. As Mom looked up information in our nature books, she discovered that when you get too many crickets in one place, they will start attacking each other.

I guess God knew that people are a little bit like that too. And that was why in Genesis 11 He told them to spread out over the whole earth instead of all living together in one big city.

Unfortunately God is often misunderstood, and He was back then too. God had to change their language in order to get them to spread out.

We freed the crickets in the backyard. It made us sad that cooping them up in a farm had hurt them. God didn't have to learn that the hard way, as we did.

Dear God, I am glad You know everything about us! Amen.

April 28

So the Lord scattered them from there over the whole earth. And they stopped building the city.

Genesis 11:8.

123

STUCK BEHIND THE TOILET

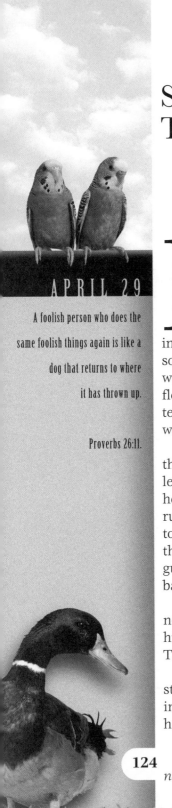

APRIL 29

A foolish person who does the
same foolish things again is like a
dog that returns to where
it has thrown up.

Proverbs 26:11.

Before I was born, my mom had an English sheepdog puppy named Napoleon. Napoleon was little at first, but he soon began growing fast. Mom and Dad lived in an apartment without any air-conditioning, and it was a hot, miserable summer. The puppy soon discovered that the coolest place in the house was the bathroom. He loved to lie on the cold tile floor. He found that the coolest place to spend the afternoon was to wiggle in behind the toilet bowl and wrap himself around it.

Unfortunately, Napoleon was bigger every day than the one before. (Puppies grow fast!) But the toilet stayed the same size. One day Napoleon realized he was stuck. He set up a howl that brought Mom running. With some tugging and pulling she managed to rescue the dog. She shut the bathroom doors, but the next time someone forgot and left it open—you guessed it! Mom heard Napoleon howling from the bathroom, stuck again. And he didn't learn, either.

Finally, one day Mom pulled and pulled and could not get him free. He started yelping, because it hurt his paws. Admitting defeat, Mom called the plumber. The plumber had to unscrew the entire toilet.

When we do things we aren't supposed to and get stuck in bad situations, God answers our pitiful howling too and rescues us. Each time, though, it becomes harder and harder to get out.

Let's learn now before it's too late.

Dear God, help me to learn from my mistakes and not keep going back over them. Amen.

124

THERE'S NOTHING LIKE FRESH FRITTERS

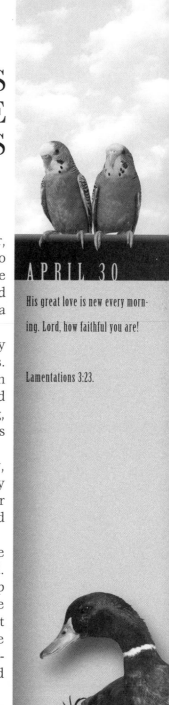

APRIL 30

His great love is new every morning. Lord, how faithful you are!

Lamentations 3:23.

My mom and I always write together, and one of our favorite places to do it is a dark little corner in a nice restaurant in New Market called Johnny Appleseed. They have a table reserved for us because we come so often.

One of the things that we like about Johnny Appleseed is the free appetizers that they give us. They're called apple fritters, and when you get them hot from the oven, they're really tender and juicy and good. But when we take them home in a doggy bag, sometimes they get a little bit old and the outside gets crusty and hard.

If you come to Johnny Appleseed every day, their apple fritters are always good. But if you buy two dozen, take them home, and try to keep them for a couple days, then the only thing that they're good for is to throw at your brother.

A life with Jesus works the same way. You have to come to Him every day to be spiritually renewed. If you go to Him just once a week and try to tank up on enough spiritual blessings to last you through the whole week, you're going to get burned out. It will get old, and you won't like it anymore. But if you come to Him every day, He will provide you with something new and fresh and warm. Not something old and crusty like a grease bomb.

Dear God, help me come to You for fresh blessings each morning instead of trying to get along with old crusty ones from yesterday. Amen.

125

A TALE OF TWO POSSUMS

Always be joyful because you belong to the Lord. I will say it again. Be joyful.

Philippians 4:4.

One day we rescued a couple baby possums. A car had killed their mother on the road in front of our house. We found one in the garage and the other in the driveway. They were still babies, but had their fur already. After putting them into a cardboard box outside, we gave them some food and water to make sure that they didn't die.

One of them we named Happy because he would run around the box and would eat the apple slices that we fed him. He drank the water and played in it, and did the kinds of things that earned him his name.

The other possum we called Grumpy because he would just sit and make rude noises in the corner of his cage. He refused the apple slices and wouldn't drink the water because it probably tasted like Happy, since the first possum had already been playing in it.

The next day when we came to check on them, both of them had fed themselves, which obviously meant that they would be OK.

People are a lot like our pet possums. When put in the same situation, some can be happy with it, and some might not. But life is what we make it. If Paul could sing in prison, it probably wouldn't hurt us to just chill out and be thankful for what we have.

Dear God, please help me to be content with whatever situation I am in. Amen.

A BEHAVIOR PROBLEM OR JUST HURT?

W e have a parakeet named Kiwi that my mom bought on sale because it would scream every time anybody would walk by its cage. The pet store people thought that it was just because it was a bad parakeet, so they were going to put the bird to sleep.

When we got it home, closer examination revealed that it had an injured wing. The underside of its wing was all skinned and torn up, and one of the bones was broken. We realized it wasn't a bad parakeet, but a hurt parakeet. We took care of the bird and put it in a cage with another baby parakeet so that it wouldn't be lonely. Eventually the wing healed.

Sometimes, when somebody is a horrible bully and really mean to people, we think that it's just because they are a bad person or a mean person. But usually it's because the individual comes from a troubled home and somebody has hurt them either physically or emotionally. We may see bad people, but God looks at them and recognizes hurting individuals. And if we could learn to see hurting people instead of bad people, the hurting people would be a lot better off. We would learn how to help them heal instead of injuring their feelings and making their problems worse. The closer we get to Jesus, the easier it is to see things His way.

Dear God, help me to look at others the way You see them instead of just judging the outside. Amen.

MAY 2

You should think in the same way Christ Jesus does.

Philippians 2:5.

127

THE UGLY PARAKEET

There is no Jew or Greek. There is no slave or free person. There is no male or female. Because you belong to Christ Jesus, you are all one.

Galatians 3:28.

When I graduated from eighth grade, my graduation present from my grandparents was a cockatiel. Now, the only kind of birds I had ever had before then were parakeets.

A cockatiel is different in some ways, but very similar in most. It's a little bit bigger and has some funny feathers on top of its head. But other than that, parakeets and cockatiels resemble each other.

I could see this, but unfortunately the parakeets couldn't. When I first put Cinnamon, my cockatiel, in the parakeets' cage, they were all mean to her until they got used to her, which took about a month. And the only reason they were mean to her was because she wasn't a parakeet and didn't fit in. She looked different and made different noises. But she was just like them in every other way. (Cinnamon was smart, though, and soon learned to speak parakeet.)

Sometimes we as Christians can do this to people too without realizing it. Just because they might not be Christian or think the same way we do, we may hurt their feelings—sometimes on purpose, other times by accident.

Luckily for us, God knows what we actually are. And if we ask Him, He can help us see other people through our Father's eyes too, and then we'll discover that we really don't look that much different.

Dear God, help me to treat others the way You would instead of the way a parakeet would. Amen.

FORGIVENESS DOESN'T KILL SPIDERS

MAY 4

Now obey me completely. Keep my covenant. If you do, then out of all of the nations, you will be my special treasure. The whole earth is mine.

Exodus 19:5.

When my mom was a little girl in Nigeria, her house had a lot of spiders in it. The lizards usually ate them, but one day a really big one climbed the wall in her bedroom. As she slipped up on it with a flyswatter, getting ready to smash it, her dad came in and said, "No, don't do it."

Quickly she brought the flyswatter down on the spider so that she could pretend that she hadn't heard what her dad had told her. Her eyes about popped out of her head when hundreds of baby spiders came crawling out of the squishy mess and spread across the bedroom.

"That's why I said not to," her dad explained. "That one we should have caught and taken outside."

My mom then ran around the room killing as many of the baby spiders as she could, but there were just too many. She should have just trusted her dad. He didn't have time to explain to her why he told her not to. She just had to have faith in him.

"Please forgive me, Daddy," she cried.

He did, but that didn't take the spiders away. Her bedroom still had hundreds of spiders, and it would take her months to get rid of them all.

Sometimes our heavenly Father tells us to do things that we don't understand, and He doesn't always explain. But if we just trust Him, we'll find out that He always knows best.

Dear God, help me to remember that repentance doesn't take away consequences and that to avoid them I need to listen to You in the beginning. Amen.

129

GOSPEL COMMISSION OR CULTURE COMMISSION?

Let us keep looking to Jesus. He is the author of faith. He also makes it perfect. He paid no attention to the shame of the cross. He suffered there because of the joy he was looking forward to. Then he sat down at the right hand of the throne of God.

Hebrews 12:2.

In a little village on the southern edge of the Sahara desert in northern Nigeria, some missionaries went to convert people to Christianity. When the women were baptized and brought to Jesus, the missionaries gave each a new set of clothing instead of the traditional tobacco leaves that they wore around their waist with nothing covering their upper body. They received blouses, skirts, and modest clothes to wear.

The problem with this was that the only people in their village who ever wore blouses and skirts and such stuff were the prostitutes. They were the only women who could afford them. So all of the good Christian women looked like prostitutes to the other villagers. Missionaries tried to make them look respectable according to their own culture. They totally forgot about the African culture in which the new Christians lived.

God didn't send us out into the world to make people exactly like us. He asked us to preach the gospel and to turn people's lives around toward Him.

And this doesn't happen only in tiny villages in northern Nigeria. It can take place in the United States, and does more often than most people realize. Sometimes we get so wrapped up trying to make people exactly like us that we forget that what we're supposed to be doing is making them more like Jesus.

Dear God, help me to remember that witnessing is supposed to help people become like You, not to become like me. Amen.

POTENTIAL VALUE

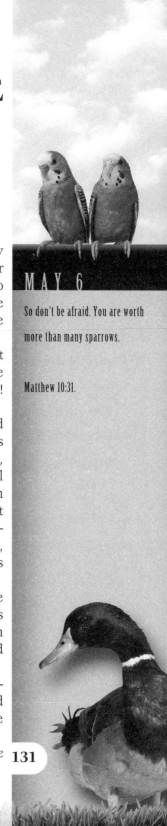

MAY 6

So don't be afraid. You are worth more than many sparrows.

Matthew 10:31.

What are you really worth? It's a law of supply and demand. Some of your personal worth depends on who loves and who wants you. And some of it involves what condition you're in and who you are and who made you.

We have several parrots. To buy a parrot in a pet store costs thousands of dollars, so relatively few people can afford them. Does that mean we're rich? Of course! But not rich enough to buy parrots from a pet store.

When Wamml came to us, he was so unhappy and had been so neglected that he had pulled most of his feathers from his chest. He was skinny and neurotic, paranoid and miserable. If anyone had tried to sell him in the pet store at that time, he would have been worth nothing. Nobody wants a feather plucker. Most of them don't live long. But Wamml was worth something to Mom. She babied him, talked to him all day, fed him little treats, and taught him how to eat fruits and vegetables instead of just seeds.

Now Wamml is fully feathered and filled out. He is a sleek and handsome African gray parrot. What is he worth now? A whole lot. But it was because Mom saw the value in him back when he was sick and scrawny and miserable.

God does that with us. We don't always seem important and valuable to other people, but when God looks at us, He sees what we could be if we were whole and loved and healed.

Dear God, thank You for loving me for what I can be someday instead of just the way I am now. Amen.

YOU CATCH MORE MICE WITH HONEY

A huge cloud of witnesses is all around us. So let us throw off everything that stands in our way. Let us throw off any sin that holds on to us so tightly. Let us keep on running the race marked out for us.

Hebrews 12:1.

Although Mom doesn't like mice in the house, she is a big marshmallow who loves all kinds of animals—even mice. One night I had been up for a late-night snack. I had left the lid off the honey jar and gone back to bed. When Mom came out to the kitchen in the morning, a poor little mouse was stuck in the honey. It had exhausted itself trying to climb out and was just lying there helplessly.

Mom felt really sorry for it. She took it outside to the deck, where it stuck. "Oh, no," she said to herself. "It could be eaten by a cat, because it can't get away." Pulling on her garden gloves, she scooped the mouse up, brought it in the house, and gave the creature a bath in the sink. Then she blew-dry the mouse so it wouldn't get pneumonia when she put it outside in the cold. By the time she finished its bath and blow-dry, the little mouse was exhausted. And so Mom fed it a snack of Cheerios.

When Mom finally felt as though the animal was able to make it on its own, she carried it outside. The mouse sat there, looking at her for a little while. Then she turned and walked back toward the house. As she opened the door, it scampered in ahead of her.

Sometimes we treat our sins the way Mom did that mouse. No wonder we can't get rid of them. If we could understand how much sin hurt God, then maybe we would regard it as the horrible thing it is and just turn away from it and get it out of our lives.

Dear God, help me to remember that sin hurts You, and not treat my sins as Mom does mice. Amen.

132

THE GREATEST ENGINEER

MAY 8

The heavens are higher than the earth. And my ways are higher than your ways. My thoughts are higher than your thoughts.

Isaiah 55:9.

When our family has great big get-togethers with lots of people around, we like to go up to New Market Gap in the mountains, where there's a big cliff, and fly balsa-wood gliders off it. We use the little cheap balsa-wood gliders that you can buy in toy stores or hardware stores, because balsa wood is biodegradable and doesn't mess up our environment.

Sometimes we have contests to see whose glider can stay in the air the longest. We put the wings and tail at different angles to get better air time, but the longest record that anybody has ever set is 22 seconds.

We were very proud of that score, but before we could get too conceited, God flew one of His gliders by. It was a golden eagle, which made a sarcastic squawk at us as it soared overhead. Then we realized that no matter what we did to our gliders, the best score we could ever get would be 22 seconds. But God designed His gliders to stay in the air for hours at a time. Our gliders must look pretty puny to Him. How much smarter He is than we could ever dream of being! What an imagination He must have! Our God is an awesome God.

Dear God, You continually amaze me with the things You've made. You are so wise and wonderful! Amen.

An honest witness tells the truth.

But a dishonest witness tells lies.

Proverbs 12:17.

MOM'S IMAGINARY COWS

One day when my mom was driving to work, she saw a herd of cows walking down the median of the freeway. Now, maybe it's just me, but I've never heard of cows strolling around in the median before. So she did a double take and looked back. And yes, there were cows on the median. She wasn't imagining things.

When she got to work and told the office secretaries about the cows, the others laughed and made fun of her. But she knew what she had seen. It couldn't have been anything else but cows in the median.

She stuck with her story despite much ridicule from her boss and coworkers, but when the news at noon came on the radio, sure enough, it had a report about some escaped cows that had wandered down the median.

After this, everyone who had been mean to her suddenly became very apologetic. They were smart to apologize, because she could fire most of them. Of course, my mother being the person that she is, nobody got fired, but they learned an important lesson.

A lot of times we'll be ridiculed and made fun of for what we know is true. That will happen to all of us before Jesus comes again. But if we stick to our guns and know that we are right, we can trust God to vindicate us in the end. So whether it be the Scriptures or cows in the median, be sure that you stick with what you know is true.

Dear God, help me have the courage to hold on to what I know is true even if others don't believe it. Amen.

SEEING KANGAROOS

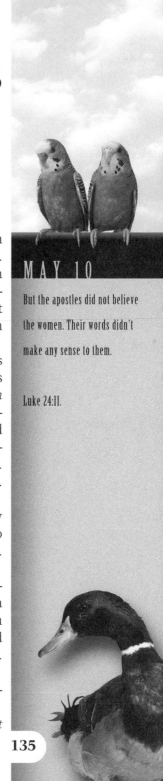

We tease my grandpa because so often he sees things that no one else does. One early morning when he lived in Abidjan, Ivory Coast, he was shaving in the bathroom and glanced out the window. He spotted something hopping through the yard. It was too large to be a rabbit.

Rubbing his eyes, he looked again. Yes, he was sure it was a kangaroo. He stopped and rubbed his eyes again, then thought, *Kangaroos don't live in Abidjan.* Sure enough, it was still nibbling on his flowers in the garden. When he ran to the door and opened it, the kangaroo hopped away into the darkness. Grandpa shook his head. Surely it couldn't be. Checking his watch, he saw it would be sunrise soon. He decided not to tell anyone about it just in case.

This must be how the women felt when they looked into the tomb in which they had expected to find Jesus' body and instead discovered it empty. People would think the women were hallucinating.

Just like Jesus' friends, though, Grandpa was vindicated. A little later that day on the news came a piece announcing that a kangaroo had escaped from the zoo in Abidjan and that anyone seeing it should report it to the authorities. Grandpa started to laugh. It was a kangaroo after all! He hadn't imagined it.

I'm sure the women felt better too after more people saw Jesus.

Dear God, help me not to be afraid to tell others what I've seen of You. Amen.

But the apostles did not believe the women. Their words didn't make any sense to them.

Luke 24:11.

135

GREEN SMOKE AND BROKEN LEGS

Turn all your worries over to him.

He cares about you.

1 Peter 5:7.

When I moved to Virginia from Maryland, I experienced severe culture shock. In Virginia fireworks were legal. But in Maryland they had been outlawed even on the Fourth of July. So within the first month that we lived here we loaded up on fireworks.

One of the things we bought was colored smoke bombs. Now, the smoke bombs did nothing but send out smoke. They weren't even hot enough to burn you. Still, Mom eyed them suspiciously and said, "They look like cherry bombs to me."

We reassured her that they weren't cherry bombs but merely colored smoke bombs.

Still worried, she said, "No, these are cherry bombs. When I was young, I saw what cherry bombs can do." So she insisted that *she* light it and then run away as fast as possible. We decided to humor her.

As we were running away Mom tripped over the edge of the deck, fell, and broke her leg.

Mom learned two important lessons. The first was that when we told her the things in the package were smoke bombs, they really were. The second was that sometimes worrying about something is actually worse than the thing itself.

Sometimes it is just safer to trust that things will be OK. It works that way trusting God too.

Help me to trust You, God, and to remember that worrying can hurt me even more than the problems I **136** *was afraid of. Amen.*

DO IT YOURSELF?

I t was mating time again for the birds on the back porch. Soon my three sets of parakeets were all sitting on eggs. Cinnamon, my cockatiel who lives with the parakeets, had finally grown up. Wanting to incubate eggs too, she tried hard to be a parakeet and do everything they do. All the female parakeets had eggs in their nesting boxes, but Cinnamon didn't have a nesting box because she didn't have a mate.

Carefully she chewed a hole in the top of a box containing Mom's punch bowl. She made a soft nest inside with the pieces of cardboard she had chewed. There she carefully laid four eggs. Cinnamon sat on her eggs faithfully for weeks and was bitterly disappointed when she finally had to crawl out of the box and go back to play with the parakeets and all their fluffy new babies. None of her eggs hatched. Cinnamon didn't realize that she couldn't make baby birds by herself.

We chuckle at Cinnamon, yet so many of us do that with God. We want to do good things for God, and we try so hard. We do exactly what we see other Christians doing. But what we don't understand is that we need a Mate. Unless we are working closely with the Holy Spirit, nothing good will come from all of our efforts either.

It's important to remember to talk things over with God, and instead of doing things for Him, do them with Him. Then your eggs will hatch too.

God, let me remember that life is not a project I can do by myself. Please help me. Amen.

MAY 12

So Jesus said, "You will lift up the Son of Man. Then you will know that I am the one I claim to be. You will also know that I do nothing on my own. I speak just what the Father has taught me."

John 8:28.

KITCHEN KLUTZ (SAY THAT FIVE TIMES FAST)

How can you say to your friend, "Let me take the bit of sawdust out of your eye"? How can you say this while there is a piece of wood in your own eye?

Matthew 7:4.

Today is Kitchen Klutzes of America Day to celebrate the not-so-accomplished cook. My mom is one (not that she makes bad food very often . . . well, only when she cooks—but she is a kitchen klutz).

One day as Don and I were bouncing a basketball around the kitchen she kept telling us to cut it out. We didn't. It was a constant "Stop." "OK." "Stop." "OK." "Stop." "OK." Mom was getting mad.

Finally she swung her arm and said, "Cut it out, or you're going to break something!" Her arm connected with a row of glasses on the counter and smashed about half the glasses that we owned. She was worried that Don and I would break something, so she tried to make us stop. But in the end it was actually she who did the damage.

A lot of times Christians are like this. Sometimes when we see something that somebody else is doing wrong, we go to them and say "You know, you have to stop that or else you're going to get hurt" or "You're going to hurt something" when actually what we are saying hurts them more than what they are doing.

That is what Jesus meant when He said, "Before you pick the speck out of your brother's eye, take the log out of your own eye." It was good advice then, and it is good advice now.

Dear God, help me to concentrate on growing more like You than on pointing out the faults of my friends. Amen.

MISGUIDED MINIATURE MISSIONARY

MAY 14

Moses lifted up the snake in the desert. The Son of Man must be lifted up also.

John 3:14.

My mom was a missionary's kid. In fact, Grandma tells stories about her wanting to be a missionary even before my grandpa and grandma went to the mission field.

When my mom was 4, she lived in Riverside, California. She played with a girl named Margie, who lived three houses down the street. Margie's family were Catholics. Mom tried to be a missionary by looking in Margie's fridge and announcing to her friend's mother that they had meat in their refrigerator, and that anyone who ate meat was going to burn up in hell with Satan and his angels.

That made Margie's mother angry, and she went storming over to yell at Grandma Betty. Right after Grandma Betty apologized and calmed everything down, Mom went witnessing again and told Margie and her mother that they were not going to be able to go to heaven because they did not attend church on Sabbath, and that only wicked people who were planning to start "the time of trouble" went to church on Sunday. Again Margie's mother went stomping down the street, and Grandma Betty apologized again.

Jesus asked us to hold Him up and let Him draw all men to Him. As we witness, let's remember to focus on Jesus and not be a missionary like Mom.

Dear God, help me to show others Your love instead of just sharing rules and punishments, so they will be drawn to You. Amen.

PARROTS ARE A GIRL'S BEST FRIEND

MAY 15

A friend loves at all times. He is there to help when trouble comes.

Proverbs 17:17.

Loyalty is something very special in a friend. Our African gray parrot, Wamml, is a very loyal friend. (He shows it only when people really need it, though.)

When my mom gets sick, Wamml climbs down off his cage and sits on her pillow. Usually Mom is too ill to notice, but Wamml perches there, guarding her carefully all day long. He doesn't let anyone near her—not even my dad—and stays there patiently. He doesn't leave for food or little drinks of water until Mom wakes up. When she opens her eyes and says hi to him, he makes his little clicking noise at her and climbs back onto his cage for a snack. Then he pretends to ignore her as long as she looks like she is doing all right. He plays on his cage and helps Mom read her magazines by chewing up all the advertising postcards that fall out of the middle. But when Mom falls back asleep, Wamml is back down on her pillow, guarding her again.

God's love for us is even greater than Wamml's love for Mom. And when we sleep or are in danger, He guards us gently and carefully, protecting us from everyone until we feel better again and are awake and safe. What a loyal Friend He is!

Dear God, may I remember that You are an even more loyal friend than a dog or a parrot. Thank You for Your friendship. Amen.

BLESSED ARE THOSE WHO DON'T GET MY JOKES

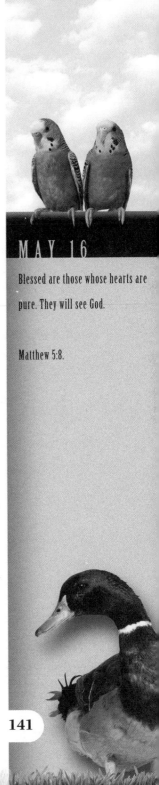

MAY 16

Blessed are those whose hearts are pure. They will see God.

Matthew 5:8.

Our family has an ongoing joke that if you want to make Grandma Betty laugh on Friday, tell her a joke on Wednesday. But we never tell her a joke on Thursday, because then she'll burst out laughing in the middle of church.

My grandmother does catch on to jokes more slowly than some people. And some jokes completely escape her. Grandma doesn't just keep from telling shady jokes—she doesn't even get them! She is very embarrassed about this and feels bad when we tease her about it, but I think it's kind of cool. Grandma Betty doesn't ever tell jokes (that I know of), and she never makes fun of other people. This is because my grandma is pure in heart.

God had a special beatitude for people like my grandma. He said, "Blessed are the pure in heart: for they shall see God" (KJV). I know that God really appreciates Grandma's pure heart and respects her for it, and so do I. And I truly believe Grandma Betty is going to see God. He promised.

Dear God, please help me to have a pure heart too. I want to see You, and soon! Amen.

HOPPING MAD

MAY 17

It is better to be patient than to fight. It is better to control your temper than to take a city.

Proverbs 16:32.

Although I remember making Grandpa really mad at me only once, I've seen him get upset with my cousin Andrew many times. My little cousin is extremely strong-willed and marches to the beat of a different drummer. He gets in all kinds of trouble and is best known for "bungee jumping" off the top of his swing set with the dog's leash tied around him.

Yet even despite Andrew's adventures, I have never seen my grandpa Don completely lose his temper. However, it makes me giggle when people use the expression "hopping mad," because it describes my grandpa when he is really upset. Grandpa doesn't exactly hop, but he does push his hands in and out of his pockets and pace back and forth in jerky motions until he settles down. While it amuses us and we make jokes about Grandpa being "hopping mad," I really respect him. He's the only person I know who never ever loses his temper.

I hope that as God lives in me and teaches me to be more like Him, I can learn to be "hopping mad" like Grandpa without ever actually losing my temper and embarrassing myself and my God.

Dear God, please help me learn to control my temper. Amen.

142

NOT NECESSARILY
A WAKE-UP CALL

I have a friend named Pokey (his mother calls him Joshua, but I'm *sure* it's really Pokey). Recently Pokey had tickets to a concert by Jars of Clay, a contemporary Christian musical group. On his way home, Pokey was in a terrible accident. His head was hit very hard and his scalp split open. Several days later he showed up with his head in stitches and bandages.

When Pokey went to church the next week, the members responded in various ways. A few, like my mom, just ran over and hugged him and got all teary and told him they were glad he was OK. Unfortunately, more of them came up to him and told him that perhaps the accident had been a wake-up call. God was teaching him something, and if Pokey didn't learn it, He might have to repeat the lesson. They greatly discouraged Pokey and made me angry.

I am not sure if I was more upset with them for discouraging Pokey (who was already hurt and discouraged) or because they were misrepresenting the way God feels about Pokey (and the rest of us). Apparently Job's friends are still alive.

My God would not take a child who loved Him and fling him into a concrete overpass, splitting his head open and leaving him with a fuzzy brain and balance problems. The God I worship knows that bad things happen to good people, but when they do, He cries along with them and holds them close to His chest as He comforts them. My God loves Pokey, and my God loves me.

Thank You, God. I love You too. Amen.

MAY 18

Family of Jacob, the Lord created you. People of Israel, he formed you. He says, "Do not be afraid. I will set you free. I will send for you by name. You belong to me."

Isaiah 43:1.

143

WITH LIBERTY AND SEPARATE NOISES FOR ALL

MAY 19

My sheep listen to my voice. I know them, and they follow me.

John 10:27.

My parrot, Wamml, recognizes that each family member is different, and he relates to each one in a different way. He blows kisses when Mom enters the room. Mom taught him that. She is the one who convinced him that he was loved when he first came to live with our family.

We always know when Dad is coming home. Wamml has a loud noise we call the "Bruce alarm" that he makes when Dad drives in the driveway or comes up the stairs. Dad will never be able to sneak up on anyone here!

When the phone rings, Wamml will shout, "Get the phone!" He loves to yell at me, hollering my name with many different inflections from delight to disgust. Often he shouts, "Michael, pick that up!" The bird shows remarkable insight by making disgusting intestinal noises at my brother whenever he is around.

Wamml speaks to each of us differently, yet we all hear him and recognize his voice, and all of us know that he loves us. God is like that (except without the rude noises). He doesn't approach every person exactly the same way. Recognizing that each of us is different and individual, He wants a separate relationship with each person. And just like Wamml, He wants to speak to us in our own language about things we are interested in, things we'll understand. Not only is He King of the universe, but He is a very intimate, personal friend. What a God!

144

Dear God, thank You for treating me as an individual. Amen.

BECAUSE SHE FIRST FED ME

Shortly before the end of the school year Mom became very sick again and spent a long time in the hospital. How were we going to take care of her? My brother and I discussed it. Dad was working at his computer job. He couldn't take time off. My brother had had his own job for a year and could make more money than I could. So I was the one who got to take care of Mom for the summer.

At first it really bothered me. I had wanted to go to work with my friends and have some extra money. Instead, I was stuck getting drinks of water for Mom, fixing her lunch, and helping her put her shoes and socks on. One day as I was slipping her socks on her feet, she chuckled and said, "You've done that for me almost as many times as I did it for you." I looked up surprised, never having thought of it that way before. Of course, Mom had done all of these things for me when I was a little guy.

Suddenly it didn't seem like such a pain. Mom never complained about putting my shoes and socks on, or feeding me, or taking me places. I was just doing for her a little bit of what she had done for me. And I had it easy. All I had to do was get things for her, fix her lunch, and help her with her shoes and socks—just doing for her a little bit of what she had done for me.

Sometimes working for God is like that. We can get focused on the work and sometimes find it irritating, but if we sit back and think about all the things He's done for us, then it's no big deal to do whatever we do for Him. It's still much less than He did for us.

Dear God, remembering that You loved me first makes it easy to love You back. Amen. **145**

MAY 20

We love because he loved us first.

1 John 4:19.

NO SPARE PARTS

Dear friend, I know that your spiritual life is going well. I pray that you also may enjoy good health. And I pray that everything else may go well with you.

3 John 2.

On this day in 1881 Clara Barton founded the American Red Cross. One of the things they do that I am most familiar with is their community health education program. My mom taught classes for them when I was younger.

Mom presented classes on baby-sitting, parenting, heart health, and the "Lowdown on High Blood Pressure" course. But my favorite course was CPR. I used to love it when she would bring the manikins home and strip them down, unsnap their chests, and remove their lungs. Then we would wash all the reusable parts and put them back together again.

I used to imagine her doing this for her patients in the hospital. After all, she did work in intensive care. Not until I was older did I realize that humans don't come apart and get fixed quite as easily as manikins. You can't just pop in a new set of disposable lungs on people who have ruined theirs by years of smoking and not taking care of their bodies.

The important thing Mom taught was that we need to take care of our bodies *now*. Don't wait until you are old and falling apart to be serious about getting healthy. Eat right. Exercise. Breathe fresh air. Get outdoors every day. Don't smoke. Get enough rest. Don't worry. Trust God. This way your parts will last, and you may never need my mom's buddies in ICU or the Red Cross.

Dear God, You are an awesome designer. Thank You for instructions on taking care of my parts. Amen.

SPIRITUAL CANES AND CRUTCHES

Mom was doing better and had gone from hobbling around with her walker to getting along fairly well with a cane, though she still couldn't keep her balance without a little help of some kind. We took her to church one Sabbath, proud that she was back on her feet. A helpful church woman rushed over and said, "Oh, it's so sad to see you having to walk with that cane. Can't you get rid of it or something?"

Mom laughed. "I could, but then I would fall down."

"I just hate to see you walking with that. Couldn't the boys carry you or something?"

Mom just looked at her. It seemed so stupid to us. And yet as church people, I believe we often do that to people spiritually. Many people have spiritual canes, things that help them stay on their feet when they aren't able to walk spiritually. And so often as a church, we tell them to get rid of the cane without focusing on helping them do the healing they must have before they can let it go.

No one is that fond of their cane. They're using it only to survive and stay on their feet. Perhaps we need to move our focus from their canes and crutches to the healing that they require. And as we focus on the healing and its source, we won't even notice their canes and crutches. And after a while they won't need them anymore either.

Dear God, help me to be a part of the healing You bring to those with spiritual crutches instead of making their way harder. Amen.

But here is what will happen for you who have respect for me. The sun that brings life will rise. Its rays will bring healing to my people. You will go out and leap like calves that have just been let out of the barn.

Malachi 4:2.

147

"BAD BIRD! BAD BIRD!"

How can you say to your friend, "Let me take the bit of sawdust out of your eye"? How can you say this while there is a piece of wood in your own eye? You pretender! First take the piece of wood out of your own eye. Then you will be able to see clearly to take the bit of sawdust out of your friend's eye.

Luke 6:42.

Wamml, my African gray parrot, has a wary relationship with Puff, my 42-inch iguana, who lives on top of the bookcase near Wamml's climbing tree. Puff doesn't always stay on top of the bookcase. That's just where he sleeps. Often he climbs down and roams around the upstairs part of the house and has even climbed onto Wamml's cage to drink his water and taste his apple slices.

One day Puff was down wandering on the floor. He crawled underneath Wamml's climbing tree. The parrot peered down at him. "What are you doing?" he shrieked. It scared Puff, and he jumped up onto a low bookcase, scrambling and grabbing for a foothold as books flew everywhere. Wamml shook his head in disgust. "Bad bird!" he said. "Bad bird!"

My brother and I laughed and laughed. But it made me think. The rules are different for Wamml and Puff. We won't allow Wamml to throw things out of the bookcase, because he likes to do it for fun. When Puff was frightened and just scrambling for a foothold, that was different. And Puff isn't a bird.

Sometimes we act like Wamml. God gave us 10 rules that are the same for everyone. Beyond those 10, though, He deals with each of us on an individual basis. God understands perfectly why others do certain things, and He doesn't think they're bad at all.

Jesus gently told us to mind our own business when He said to pick the log out of our own eye before we complain about the speck in someone else's.

Dear God, help me to mind my own business. Amen.

148

A TALE OF
TEMPTATION

Mom used to have a Garfield cartoon that said, "I can resist anything but temptation." We laughed about it, but how hard temptation really is to resist! Wamml's climbing tree is very close to the bookcase Puff likes to sleep on top of. Usually Puff dangles his tail off one end or the other, but occasionally he crawls around so that his tail hangs down the front of the bookcase, right in front of Wamml. It presents a severe temptation for a mischievous parrot.

Mom was sitting in the living room, working on one of her manuscripts and watching the bird. He would look at her carefully to make sure that she was busy and then start to lean toward Puff's tail.

"Don't even think of it," Mom said when she noticed him doing it. Wamml would put his head down. Then he would shake it as if to say, "I wasn't thinking of it," and climb to another branch and start playing with his toys. But he kept scooting back to the branch closest to Puff's tail until Mom reprimanded him again.

Mom got busy with a phone call. Wamml decided that if she was talking on the telephone, she couldn't possibly see what he was doing. He leaned out farther and almost grabbed Puff's tail in his beak—and then fell out of his tree.

How much like me sometimes! I guess Wamml and I both need some divine help in dealing with temptation. Thank God, it's available.

Dear God, thank You for Your help in resisting temptation. I need it! Amen.

So the Lord knows how to keep godly people safe in times of testing. He also knows how to keep ungodly people under guard until the day they will be judged. In the meantime, he continues to punish them.

2 Peter 2:9.

149

LABELS AND REPUTATIONS

So we are Christ's official messengers. It is as if God is making his appeal through us. Here is what Christ wants us to beg you to do. Come back to God!

2 Corinthians 5:20.

My mom keeps bringing people and animals home that need a mother. For a while a guy named Greg and a girl named Maria were a part of our family. Greg had some legal problems, so Mom and Maria spent many days sitting in court with him and waiting for him at the courthouse. Maria worried about whether or not the judge would be fair to Greg.

I had bought Mom a key ring for Christmas that said "WWJD?" It stood for "What Would Jesus Do?" Mom attached it to her purse and carries it all the time. She says that it reminds her to make decisions as Jesus would.

While Mom and Maria were sitting in court and Greg stood before the judge, the judge lifted his hand to tap his wooden gavel hammer on the table. The sleeve of his big black robe fell back, and Maria caught her breath as she saw a little black canvas bracelet on his wrist that said "WWJD."

She leaned over to Mom and whispered, "Look, Mrs. Dillon, he has your key ring on his hand." Mom smiled and nodded. "I know he'll be fair to Greg."

Maria trusted the judge because he wore the same label as my mother, and Mom had always been fair to Maria. When we take the name Christian, we are taking Jesus' name. People will trust Jesus if they can trust us, just as Maria trusted the judge because she could trust Mom.

God help me to wear Your name properly and never give You a bad reputation by anything that I do or say. Amen.

150

MOCKINGBIRDS AND MIRRORS

My pet African gray parrot, Wamml, used to sit next to the sliding glass door in Mom's bedroom and talk to a mockingbird who would perch on the deck rail just outside the window. Wamml would make a noise, and the mockingbird would copy it. Then the mockingbird would make a sound and Wamml would repeat it. They would do this for hours, entertaining each other and amusing the rest of us immensely. But the habit Wamml's mockingbird friend had that made us laugh the most was his obsession with looking at himself in the mirror.

Mom parked her van right outside the window. The mockingbird would perch on her side mirrors and hang upside-down, peering at himself until he got dizzy and fell off.

If anyone ever left the windows down in the van, Wamml's mockingbird friend would go inside and hang from the rearview mirror, again staring at himself until he fell off. We could always tell that he had been in the van because, as Dad said, he must want to buy the van because he kept leaving deposits.

Some people are like Wamml's mockingbird friend. They are so busy looking at themselves that they eventually get dizzy and fall. On our road to heaven, we need to keep our eyes on Jesus, not on ourselves, or we will look just as silly as that mockingbird. And we will fall too. So don't be a birdbrain. Keep your eyes on Jesus.

Dear God, help me to keep my priorities straight and my eyes on You. Amen.

Let us keep looking to Jesus. He is the author of our faith. He also makes it perfect. He paid no attention to the shame of the cross. He suffered there because of the joy he was looking forward to. Then he sat down at the right hand of the throne of God.

Hebrews 12:2.

LIZARDS AND LIMITS

MAY 27

Lord, I will give you honor. You brought me out of deep trouble. You didn't give my enemies the joy of seeing me die. Lord my God, I called out to you for help. And you healed me.

Psalm 30:1, 2.

When we found Puff out on Grandpa's woodpile, he was skinny, yellow, and sick. And he had two big dog bites on his side. He obviously hadn't done well outdoors in Maryland.

Puff has a lot of freedom in our house. We let him wander wherever he wants to inside. But he is fascinated with the out-of-doors. He will frequently sunbathe in the window, on the back of the couch, or hang on the screens with his sharp claws, watching the outdoor critters for hours on end. He looks longingly out at the green grass and blue sky.

We think that Puff's greatest desire would probably be to go outdoors again. It makes Mom feel sad, because she wants Puff to feel happy. And even though she lets him go anywhere he wants to in the house, he isn't content with that.

Often people are like that. God rescued us from terrible situations and put us in a safe environment. He gives us lots of freedom and lets us go anywhere we want to and do anything we want to within safe limits. And yet so many people stare out at the places God has limited them from going, wishing they could do the things they can't do instead of appreciating their safe and happy life and the protection and blessings God has given them.

So don't be a lizardbrain. Appreciate the things God has given you. And perhaps someday you'll even learn to appreciate His limits.

Dear God, help me remember that the limits You give me keep me safe. Amen.

WAR AND RELIGION

I read on the Internet that more people have been killed over religious disputes than for any other reason in the history of our world. That is sad. I believe it is true, though. Many wars in history have been fought between peoples of different religions. It has been that way since Bible times, and it continues today. The Protestants and Catholics continue to have conflicts in Ireland, the Jews and the Arabs war with each other in the Middle East. And in Bosnia, Christians and Muslims still have unrest.

All of them believe God is on their side. People who claim to serve Him and worship Him commit terrible atrocities in His name. Because of that, it makes other people cynical. After a while they don't believe He's on anyone's side.

It also desensitizes people to the real war going on—the great controversy, the conflict between good and evil, that has been going on between Christ and Satan since the very dawn of earthly time. It rages on in the background while we let human wars in the foreground distract us.

We need to be aware of the great controversy and how everything we do and every choice we make is a part of it. Often we forget that we are in the middle of a battle and that God is on our side. Someday it will be over, and He will win. No matter how rough things get, remember, we are on the winning side.

Dear God, in this war I'm glad You are my commander in chief. Amen.

MAY 28

The Lord says to you, "Do not be afraid. Do not lose hope because of this huge army. The battle is not yours. It is mine."

2 Chronicles 20:15.

JUMPING TO CONCLUSIONS

MAY 29

Do not judge others. Then you will not be judged.

Matthew 7:1.

Many of you have heard of and probably participated in DARE, Drug Abuse Resistance Education. My brother participated in it when he was your age. One day after a lesson in narcotics and steroids and how they were bad for us, my brother piped up and said, "That's not always true. My mom is on narcotics and steroids."

The narcotics officer looked at him and said, "I don't believe you. You're making this up."

When Don insisted that it was true, the teacher sent him to the principal's office, where he carefully explained (again) that it was true and that his mother was on narcotics and steroids.

What the DARE officer didn't understand was that Mom had a prescription for the narcotics and steroids. The narcotics were pain medication. Without them she would have to spend every day lying in bed moaning and groaning. And the steroids kept her from going into kidney failure.

The DARE officer's problem was that he jumped to conclusions before he understood the entire situation. Sometimes we Christians are a lot like him. When we hear any little thing wrong about people, we immediately conclude that they are bad persons.

God didn't give us this responsibility. We can't make judgments about people, because we aren't God, and just like Donnie's DARE officer, we don't know all the details.

Dear God, help me to trust You to take care of things and not to jump to conclusions. Amen.

154

MRS. MELKERSEN'S MISTAKE

Michael Dillon!" Mrs. Melkersen said firmly. "You ought to know better than to throw water on people. Wouldn't your mother be upset if she knew you threw water indoors?"

My friend Jazz and I had been having a water fight in the classroom when Mrs. Melkersen suddenly walked in. She didn't want to join in. I giggled at her angry face. "Actually," I replied, "my mom throws water indoors too."

I smiled to myself as I remembered how just last night I had tickled her feet unmercifully and she had dumped a whole glass of water over my head. Mom uses the ammunition at hand since she can't jump out of her chair and wrestle me to the floor since she's disabled. (Don't feel too sorry for her. She defends herself just fine.)

Mrs. Melkersen was pronouncing what my mother would and wouldn't do, though she didn't know her very well. I, however, happen to know her better than almost anybody, and I know what she would approve of.

People do that a lot with God. One time a woman told me that God wouldn't love me if I wasn't good in Sabbath school. I knew that wasn't true, so it didn't bother me. But not everybody knows that it isn't true, so we need to be careful about what we say about God. And before we say anything, we need to ask ourselves, "Do we really know Him?"

Dear God, help me to get to know You even better. Amen.

MAY 30

Jesus answered, "Don't you know me, Phillip? I have been among you such a long time! Anyone who has seen me has seen the Father. So how can you say, 'Show us the Father'?"

John 14:9.

RIGHT UNDER OUR NOSES

So answer me if you can. Prepare
yourself to face me.

Job 33:5.

Our iguana, Puff the Magic Dragon, is not too bright, but he's a lot of fun to watch. He likes to have his head and neck scratched, but he plays favorites. If you're not his favorite, he will bite your arm off. (Not really, but he bit my brother's lip once.)

Because he isn't too intelligent, Mom can't always put his food on top of the bookcase where he lives. She has to place it close to wherever he is right then, because he doesn't think to go back to the bookcase to get food. If he's running around and not staying put up on top of the bookcase, then he'll go for days without eating unless Mom sets his food right under his little green nose.

Luckily for the iguana species, God realized that they weren't very intelligent, so He placed them in a habitat where food is always right under their nose whether they want it there or not.

And luckily for the human species, He realized that when it comes to spiritual things, we aren't always geniuses either. So He put things right under our nose that would remind us of Him. All we have to do is look for them. Like Puff, for example. He reminds us of how smart our Creator is.

Dear God, thank You for putting evidence of Your love for us right under our noses. Help us not to miss it! Amen.

EMPOWERING US

M y brother and his friends go camping a lot. They like to sneak up on each other in the dark. One day Don came home and told Mom, "I'd really like a big medieval cloak—you know, a full-length dark one that comes all the way to the floor with a hood that would cover my head. Then I could sneak around in the dark, and no one would ever see me."

Mom smiled. "How badly do you want one?"

Donnie shrugged. Mom had been stuck in her chair for almost a year now and wasn't able to do very many things. "I don't know," he said. "I suppose it's out of the question."

"No, it's not," she said. She helped him design a pattern, then showed him how to calculate how much material he would need. Directing him from her chair, she helped Don lay out his material and cut out his cloak. Then she explained which side needed to be seamed and helped him pin the material. Finally she taught him how to use her sewing machine.

Not only did Don have his cloak, but he felt really good about himself.

Sometimes when your little brother or sister asks you for help with something, it's appropriate to assist them. Other times, if you teach them how to do it themselves, you will help them much more.

When we needed help, Jesus aided us. But He didn't just forgive us for our sins. He also empowered us to live like Him.

God, thank You for giving me what I need and also for teaching me what I need to know. Amen.

Some people did accept him. They believed in his name. He gave them the right to become children of God.

John 1:12.

157

A NEW LANGUAGE?

Let the words of my mouth, and the meditation of my heart, be acceptable in thy sight, O Lord, my strength, and my redeemer.

Psalm 19:14, KJV.

I heard this story from my grandfather.

My great-grandfather was one of the Swedish pioneers who settled Minnesota, so he spoke Swedish whenever he was with friends. When he spoke English, he pronounced his J's as Y's and W's were always V's.

One day my grandpa went with his father to the blacksmith shop to have two pieces of iron welded together. As the blacksmith tapped the metal with his hammer it broke. The blacksmith taught my grandpa a whole new language that day. He called upon God to curse the broken pieces of iron. It seemed to work, because the next time he welded it, it stayed welded.

On the way home Grandpa used some of the new words he had learned to describe those pieces of iron. His father almost ran the car right off the road! He informed Grandpa that it was not necessary to repeat everything he heard adults say. Also, he explained that the second weld probably would have worked even without that new language.

God, help me to learn to use Your name only in ways that make You happy. Amen.

PAT THE PAINTER

I love to read now, but I couldn't always read very well. One of my teachers even wanted me to get tested for a learning disability. Then Mom took me to meet a famous artist who lives near us. Her name is Pat Buckley Moss. She too had trouble reading when she was in school. At first her teachers thought she was mentally challenged. Then they decided she was just unintelligent. People didn't understand learning disabilities when she was a little girl.

And it wasn't just teachers that didn't understand her. When Pat would bring home a bad report card, her mother would tell her she must not be her child and to pack her clothes so her dad could take her to the orphanage. And even worse, Pat believed her every time and packed all her things and waited to be taken away.

We looked through her museum. I was floored by how much her paintings cost! Finally we found a print of a painting that was inexpensive (great art is never cheap) enough for us to afford. And Pat was having an open house that day, so we got her to autograph it for us.

I learned that she always says God gave everybody special talents. Some people are talented in schoolwork. And some people have other talents. But everybody has something special. Pat's talent is painting. And she taught me that I was special too!

God, thank You for making me special and for the talents You gave me. Please teach me to use them for You. Amen.

How you made me is amazing and wonderful. I praise you for that. What you have done is wonderful. I know that very well. None of my bones was hidden from you when you made me inside my mother's body.... When you were putting me together there, your eyes saw my body even before it was formed.

Psalm 139:14, 15.

"BITE MOMMY! BITE MOMMY!"

But here is how God has shown his love for us. While we were still sinners, Christ died for us.

Romans 5:8.

When Wamml first came to our house, he swung upside down in his cage, making eye contact with no one, and stopping only to pull out feathers from his chest. We named him Wamml because that was the only thing he knew how to say, and he said it a lot. The parrot seemed to like it when Mom talked to him. He would stop swinging and just hang there, listening. But anytime she touched the cage to give him food or water, he would try to bite her.

The bird bit Mom every couple of days and would make her bleed. Each time she would firmly say, "No, no, Wamml, don't bite Mommy."

"Bite Mommy! Bite Mommy!" Wamml would shout.

One day my brother noticed the scars on Mom's fingers. "Wow!" Don said, "I hope Wamml sees those scars on your hands and realizes what a horrible bird he's been."

"No," Mom replied, "I hope that if he ever notices the scars on my hand, he sees how much I love him."

Just then Wamml turned around and looked at Mom. He slowly climbed up to the top of her chair and made a loud kissing noise. We all burst out laughing.

Suddenly it all made sense. I understood why God didn't just get rid of us and start over again. He just couldn't bear to let us go. And just like Mom, He has the marks on His hands to prove it.

Thank You so much, Jesus, for not giving up on us and for giving us a chance to spend eternity with You. Amen.

TOO YOUNG?

O n this day in 1994 Michael Kearney, age 10, graduated from the University of South Alabama with a bachelor's degree in anthropology. He's the youngest person ever to graduate from college. His ambition at the time he graduated was to become a TV talk show host. Never heard of him? Well, that's because he never got a job. Who would give a job as a talk show host to someone who's 10 years old?

When I won the award for youngest published author at a writer's conference, everybody was really surprised, because I was only 12. (I had been published in *Guide* and the *Columbia Union Visitor*.) Most of the people were really happy for me. But some of the other people, who had wanted to be writers all their lives and never really sent anything in, were a little spiteful. They thought that the award should have gone to somebody a little older and that I wasn't a *real* writer. Those individuals had an especially hard time when I went on to win a contest in which we had to write in 50 words or less what our inspiration was. And then they were downright cranky when I won another prize for putting in 25 words or less why I need wisdom.

God doesn't assign people talents depending on their age. He also doesn't give them jobs depending on their age. King David was only our age when he killed Goliath. And all through history young people have played a major role. So when God gives you a job to do, don't think, *Umm, I'm probably too young for that.* Just do it.

Dear God, please help me not to be intimidated around people who are older than I am. Amen.

JUNE 5

Don't let anyone look down on you because you are young. Set an example for the believers in what you say and how you live. Also set an example in how you love and in what you believe. Show the believers how to be pure.

1 Timothy 4:12.

161

AND ALL I HAD WAS A BAG OF AIRLINE PEANUTS

My God will meet all your needs. He will meet them in keeping with his wonderful riches that come to you because you belong to Christ Jesus.

Philippians 4:19.

I'm a people watcher. Airports are one of my favorite places for observing them, and today was no exception. I was taking a plane trip and was sitting across from a very young father with two kids, about ages 2 and 3. They were cute, and I was watching them for lack of anything better to do at the time.

After takeoff, they started whining, "Daddy, I'm hungry." "Daddy, it's time for supper." "Daddy, when are we going to eat?"

Their father leaned forward and pulled his briefcase out from under the seat in front of him. I thought, *What a jerk, getting out his briefcase when his little kids are hungry. He could at least answer them.*

The man opened his briefcase. Inside was a steaming hot pizza he must have bought in the airport. He gave a piece on a paper towel to each child. This guy came equipped! The kids ate quietly. He knew what they liked, and he knew exactly what they needed.

Sniffing the pizza and looking at my generous serving of airline peanuts, I thought about how God plans ahead. He gives me not only the things I need, but often those I like. (Even when it looks like He's not listening.) Now, whenever I smell pizza, I feel loved.

Do you feel as if God isn't seeing your needs or hearing your requests? Cheer up; He's got the pizza with Him, and it's almost time to eat!

Thank You, God, for taking care of everything I need and for planning ahead, knowing I will have needs later. Amen.

THE HURRICANE

JUNE 7

I will say about the Lord, "He is my place of safety. He is like a fort to me. He is my God. I trust in him."

Psalm 91:2.

My family had looked forward to a camping trip on Virginia's Assateague Island for weeks. When the day came, we joyfully packed our camping equipment and headed for the beach. Nobody took the time to listen to the weather forecast. Why should we? It looked great outside.

During the night a horrible storm struck. The wind was so strong the tent shook and rattled. Stakes started coming out of the ground and part of the tent collapsed. Mom, who isn't a camper anyway, had had it. "I am going to a motel," she said. "You guys can come or stay, whichever you choose." Now it started raining hard. We went with Mom.

As we checked into the motel, the manager explained to us that a hurricane warning had gone out and that it had been a good idea to take shelter. He had special hurricane coverings on the windows. The next morning we went back out to our campsite.

The tent was tossing in the waves on the beach. The wind had strewn our camping gear for a half mile, and the Assateague ponies were pawing at our picnic items. We were thankful that we had been able to take shelter during the storm even though we couldn't take our stuff with us.

Jesus offers us shelter no matter what terrible storms we encounter in life. Like the motel, He doesn't always let us take our stuff with us, but He does provide us a safe place to hide until the storm is over.

Thank You, God, for being my shelter. You make me feel safe no matter what. Amen.

163

PAJAMAS WITHOUT FEET

He himself carried our sins on his body on the cross. He did it so that we would die as far as sins are concerned. Then we would lead godly lives. His wounds have made you whole.

1 Peter 2:24.

Kids hate getting clothes for Christmas. After all, it's not much fun playing with a new sweater! So you can imagine how my grandpa felt when he was 4 or 5 and opened an exciting pair of flannel pajamas instead of the truck he wanted. And to make matters worse, the pajamas had feet!

Although he tried to refuse to wear them, he was the youngest of 10 children, and there were too many bosses at home to let him get away with that. Every night he would go to bed complaining loudly, even though his feet stayed warm in the cold Minnesota winter.

Well, one day his complaining paid off. Those horrid pajamas came back from the laundry with the feet cut off. His toes were free again! Now, in northern Minnesota the temperature would drop to $-40°$ F or lower. And since they heated the house with a woodstove, the house and Grandpa's feet got pretty cold before morning. But that didn't matter. His toes were free!

You've also got to understand that in the home of a widower farmer with 10 children (Grandpa's mother died when he was about 2) bed space was at a premium. And as the baby of the family, Grandpa shared a bed with his father. So when his toes got too cold, he put his feet on his father's back. His daddy used his own body to warm Grandpa's icy toes.

It reminds me of how Jesus used His own body to help us out of a jam as well.

Thank You so much, Jesus, for giving Your own body so we can experience the warmth of Your love. Amen.

TEMPER, TEMPER!

Today is Donald Duck's birthday. Donald Duck was born on June 9, 1934. Walt Disney was his proud father. My brother was a great Donald Duck fan, and my mom used to buy things for me and Don that had Donald Duck and Mickey Mouse designs and logos on them. (Yes, whenever she would buy us matching things, he got the duck stuff, while I was stuck with the rodent memorabilia.) We had matching items from toothbrushes to T-shirts. This worked only until I started growing into some of his Donald sweatshirts. After that it was confusing for Mom.

One of the things that made Donald Duck famous was his horrible temper. Whenever his three nephews, Huey, Dewey, and Louie, would get into mischief, he would blow up and do incredibly silly things that were totally irrational while stamping and sputtering the whole time.

Sometimes people with temper problems think that if somebody has wronged them, then it's OK to throw a tantrum. But that's not the case. That is giving the person who made you angry control over your behavior. Speaking for myself, I would much rather be a person than a puppet. So don't act like a duck. You can choose to keep your temper. All you need to do is ask God to help you.

God, please help me keep my temper. Thank You. Amen.

JUNE 9

Anyone who is patient has great understanding. But anyone who gets angry quickly shows how foolish he is.

Proverbs 14:29.

BIG-TIME POWER

And Jesus came and spake unto them saying, All power is given unto me in heaven and in earth.

Matthew 28:18, KJV.

When my brother was 2 he stuck a fork into an electric outlet to see what would happen. He landed with a thud on his little padded seat but didn't cry—just looked around to find out if Mom had seen what had happened. He knew he had just committed a no-no. Mom did see but was so busy being glad he wasn't hurt that he didn't get into too much trouble. The reason he wasn't hurt is that there are only 110 volts in a standard home electrical outlet. We can thank the Federal Power Commission for that fact.

On this day in 1920 the Water Power Act created the Federal Power Commission. It would regulate power plants. The reason that we needed a Federal Power Commission was because power plants are far too powerful for humans to operate without having somebody to regulate them and to determine who gets the power where.

But our universe has an even greater power. One that could blow away any nuclear power plant. It's God. God is so powerful that He made our entire universe just by telling it to be. But He doesn't need a Federal Power Commission, because He has all His power under control. He can help whoever needs it and knows how much help to give each person. Commissions may become corrupt someday, but our God is fair and will be fair forever. Aren't you glad!

God, Your power is awesome, and I worship You!
166 *Amen.*

NO CAMELS
ALLOWED

I spent a lot of time in the seat of a grocery cart when I was little. Mom usually kept the cart in the middle of the aisle so I couldn't fill it up behind her back, but the checkout line was another story. It had so many interesting things within reach. Being a fan of all animals, one day I grabbed a little box with a picture of a camel on the front. Boy, did Mom have a cow when she saw that I had a Camel!

"No, Michael!" she said. "Those are cigarettes! Yucky! Those are nasty! We don't want any of those in our house!"

A few months later it was Christmas. I was sitting in Sabbath school, and the leader started talking about Baby Jesus. She told the story of Joseph and Mary and how the inn had no room for them. Now, I'm a hospitable guy, so I jumped up and shouted, "He could come to my house! I would let Him sleep in my bedroom, and Joseph and Mary could come too, and . . . and . . . and even the shepherds and Wise Men could come. But the Wise Men can't bring their camels in the house, because Mommy says camels are nasty!"

No point. Just a chuckle for today.

God, I'm glad You appreciate funny stories too. Amen.

JUNE 11

There is a time for everything. There's a time for everything that is done on earth.... There is a time to cry. And there's a time to laugh. There is a time to be sad. And there's a time to dance.

Ecclesiastes 3:1-4.

CAUTION! SICK SINNERS INSIDE

Jesus heard that. So he said, "Those who are healthy don't need a doctor. Sick people do."

Matthew 9:12.

Movie mogul Sam Goldwyn (of Metro-Goldwyn-Mayer) once said, "A hospital is no place to be sick." My mom would probably agree with him. She hates being in the hospital and won't go unless she is pretty bad off, but she loved working there. Actually, a hospital is a good place for really sick people. They can get the help they need so they can return home and live healthy lives.

Sam Goldwyn was as confused about hospitals as some people are about church. Such people believe that really "bad" people have no place in a nice respectable church. That is as silly as saying that sick people don't belong in a hospital until they are a little less unhealthy! A church is not a place for people with no faults, though they will develop less and less all the time by hanging out there.

Churches should be hospitals for sick sinners, not retirement centers for perfect saints. The point of being in church is to heal and rehabilitate people hurt and injured by sin. Churches should comfort them from the pain and trauma sin has caused in their lives, and help them get back on their spiritual feet.

Because of this, it is important that when you become a part of a church, you should not look to the other patients for an example. The Bible reminds us to watch Jesus, who started and finished our therapy. That way we won't get discouraged and have a relapse.

Dear God, help me keep my eyes on You only. Amen.

ANDREW AND BECKY

My aunt Janice had been praying about a dog. Their rottweiler, Sarah, who had been with them for seven years, quietly died one night, and the whole family was grieving. My cousins wanted a big dog they could play with without hurting it.

Several hours' drive away a woman named Sylvia found that she was dying from stomach cancer. She was praying about a home for her two rottweilers, Becky and Danny. She ran an ad in the local newspaper, but none of the replies seemed right.

Aunt Janice's father-in-law saw the ad and mentioned it when the family was in the area for a visit. By then the paper was quite old, and the dogs would probably be gone. Still Janice called the number.

On the way to Sylvia's home, Janice and Uncle Del agreed they didn't want two dogs. But as the door opened, Becky and Danny bounded out to meet them. The boys were delighted. And by the end of the afternoon Janice and Del had adopted both dogs.

Janice kept in contact with Sylvia, knowing how lonely she would be.

God didn't miss a single detail. The first night in their new home, Becky and Danny stood in the hall for a moment. Then Danny headed into my cousin Eric's room, and Becky bounded in and plopped onto my other cousin's bed. Andrew was delighted!

God sent Janice her dog and Sylvia comfort and a friend during her final lonely days. God sent a loving home to Becky and Danny.

Dear God, You are so good! I love You. Amen.

JUNE 13

God is able to do far more than we could ever ask or imagine. He does everything by his power that is working in us.

Ephesians 3:20.

169

THANK GOD FOR CAR WRECKS

Always give thanks to God the Father for everything. Give thanks to him in the name of our Lord Jesus Christ.

Ephesians 5:20.

Mom turned on her left blinker and slowed the car to a stop. With a crash and a crunch of twisting metal, a little black sports car plowed into the back of her van, violently jolting her. "Oh, thank You, God!" Mom screamed.

The night before my mother had such a terrible nightmare that she woke Dad up. "I had this awful dream," she said. "It seemed so real."

She had dreamed that a carful of teenagers tried to pass her and hit another car head-on instead. "I was right down in front of the house, waiting to turn left into the driveway. The kids' car was a little sports car with a T-top, and during the head-on collision the driver was decapitated."

As she was signaling to turn into the driveway later that day, she saw the little black sports car from her dream pulling up behind her. It drifted over into the left lane to pass. Sure enough, another car was coming from the other direction.

"No, God," she screamed, "don't let those kids be killed. They're just kids." God answered her prayer. The little black sports car pulled back into her lane and smashed into her van at 50 miles an hour.

If we saw what God was saving us from when bad things happen, we would be thankful instead of grumbling to Him and asking, "Why, God, why?"

Thank You, God, for everything. Please help me to remember to keep saying that. Amen.

ROBIN HOOD AND THE MAGNA CARTA

JUNE 15

You have come to Jesus. He is the go-between of the new covenant. You have come to the sprinkled blood. It promises better things than the blood of Abel.

Hebrews 12:24.

One of my favorite movies when I was a little guy was Disney's *Robin Hood.* Everybody knows the story of Robin Hood. While Robin Hood might have been a fictional character, we know for sure that Prince John was not. He really did usurp the throne from King Richard and treated his people with the same greed and dishonesty as he did his brother Richard. King Richard died without children, and Prince John came out of exile to assume the throne.

He wasn't much better as a king than he was a prince. So all the noblemen got together and wrote up a document called the Magna Carta, which gave the people some rights and freedoms. More than 500 years later the Magna Carta was the basis for American democratic thought.

After I saw the movie *Robin Hood,* my mom took me to Washington, D.C., and the National Archives to see the Magna Carta, or at least one of the several official copies of it. The paper was falling apart, and the old English script was hard to read with all the thees and thous and f's instead of s's and v's instead of u's.

Jesus' death on the cross was our Magna Carta. He didn't have to sign anything or put anything on paper. And no one had to force Him to do it. He died on the cross to ensure our freedoms and our liberties out of His own free will. While the Magna Carta in Washington, D.C., may be a national treasure, Jesus' Magna Carta is the intergalactic treasure.

Dear God, thank You for making Your covenant with us. Amen.

171

FLUFFY, THE LONELY FISH

The Lord God said, "It is not good for the man to be alone. I will make a helper who is just right for him."

Genesis 2:18.

Fluffy is Mom's goldfish. His tank is not very big, and though he had live plants to munch on, a couple tiny snails to keep it clean, and a bubbler to play in, he was lonely. But we didn't realize this at first. We thought perhaps the tank was too small for two fish. Fluffy was very sedate, spending a lot of time lying on his side in the bottom of the tank looking dead. He used to do this to scare Mom, but as soon as she tried to fish him out, he would swim away laughing—at least I was sure he was.

One day Mom and I decided to get a friend for Fluffy. When we dropped the second fish into the water, he was delighted. No more lying on the bottom. The only other thing Fluffy had enjoyed doing was eating, and soon he was so fat he looked like a marble with fins. Fluffy and his friend still enjoyed eating, but Fluffy's sedentary behavior ended. Now he was active, swimming and playing, arguing over who was going to nibble on which leaf and who was going to bump the strange goldfish off the side of the tank.

God is a lot smarter than Mom and I. He knew right from the beginning that it was not good for goldfish to be alone. The Bible tells us He provided a mate for everyone. He knows we get lonely too. If God was so smart and knew this from the very beginning, then we don't need to worry about ever being alone. He will always provide us friends and companions and stick with us.

Dear God, thank You for understanding us so well. Amen.

172

"FREE! THIS STUFF IS FREE!"

Last year my school band made a trip to Spain and Morocco. Morocco was unlike anywhere I have ever been before. (For one thing, all the band members except me got food poisoning there.) People selling souvenirs crowded around the bus and mobbed us as we climbed off, all shouting for our attention at once. After we had bought a few souvenirs, we lost interest, but not the sellers. They continued to follow us from place to place (even when we returned to the bus and drove to the next site) shouting, "Buy my spoons, buy my rugs. Genuine antiquities! Very good prices! Beautiful jewelry! Look! Look!"

Then one seller had a great idea. He shouted, "Free, this stuff is free!" It immediately caught my attention. As I turned around and looked he said, "Well, *almost* free. My prices are very good."

It was like Dad says: "Anything that sounds too good to be true usually is." But there is one thing in life that sounds too good to be true, but really is. When Jesus stretched out His arms and died for me, He said, "Michael, this is free." And it is. Not almost free like the fellows in Morocco who would then try to get your money, but totally free. How could I turn away from love like that?

Dear God, thank You for Your love. I can't help loving You, too! Amen.

God's gift is different from Adam's sin. Many people died because of the sin of that one man. But it was even more sure that God's grace would also come through one man. That man is Jesus Christ. God's gift of grace was more than enough for the whole world.

Romans 5:15.

173

MR. TASSELHOFF

JUNE 18

Even though you are evil, you know how to give good gifts to your children. How much more will your Father which is in heaven give the Holy Spirit to those who ask him!

Luke 11:13.

One day as one of our baby parakeets waddled around the little card table with its nesting boxes and the climbing trees to sit on, he lost his balance and fell to the floor. We have a ladder going from the floor up to the card table, because our parakeets often like to fly down and snack on tidbits they dropped off their table. Then they waddle back up the ladder.

The baby had not learned to climb yet. His mama was in the nesting box, sitting on some of the smaller chicks, since baby parakeets hatch many days apart. Hearing his little squeaks of distress, Mr. Tasselhoff flew down to the floor. Mr. Tasselhoff is a good daddy. Unfortunately, baby parakeets grow quite fast. The baby was as big as his dad, yet not as smart and not as coordinated.

Mr. Tasselhoff stayed on the floor with the baby, gently herding him toward the ladder and pecking him. Then he ran up and down the first two steps, trying to show him how to climb up. Mr. Tasselhoff stayed with the baby until one of us came and rescued the chick.

Mr. Tasselhoff reminds me of the Holy Spirit. The Holy Spirit does not keep us from falling. He lets us make our own mistakes, but He stays with us, gently nudging us in the right direction and showing us how to get out of our predicament. And He never leaves us alone.

As I watched Mr. Tasselhoff with his babies and smiled at how sweet he is, it made me appreciate the Holy Spirit too. And for the first time, I smiled and thought of the Holy Spirit as Someone sweet.

Thank You, God, for Your sweet Holy Spirit. Amen.

IT WON'T WORK VERY WELL UNLESS YOU PLUG IT IN

"**T**his stupid computer," Mom hissed. "What a worthless piece of junk! It's always crashing on me."

It sounded like Mom was having problems, so I went to investigate. My mom is really smart and she's good at a lot of things, but knowing her way around computers and other electronic devices is not her strongest point.

"What's the matter?" I asked.

"This stupid computer is misbehaving again," she said.

"Do you have it plugged in?"

She glared at me. I was really only kidding, but I did bend over to check. Sure enough, Mom did have it plugged into a power strip behind her desk. The problem was that the power strip wasn't plugged into the wall. She had plugged it into itself. I pulled it out from behind the desk and showed her. Mom looked really embarrassed.

"You gotta plug it into the wall, Mom, or nothing's going to work," I said.

It's a lot of fun to tease Mom about things and laugh at her mistakes. But I got to wondering how often I do similar things myself. Not with the computer, perhaps, but how often am I plugged into myself, trying to do things in my own strength and my own energy instead of plugging into Jesus? It's really not that different.

Dear God, help me always to remember to plug into You before I try to do anything. Amen.

When Peter saw this, he said, "Men of Israel, why does this surprise you? Why do you stare at us? We haven't made this man walk by our own power or godliness."

Acts 3:12.

175

THE FAMOUS BLANK FAX

When you pray, go into your room. Close the door and pray to your Father, who can't be seen. He will reward you. Your Father sees what is done secretly.

Matthew 6:6.

"May I use your fax machine?" my mom's friend asked.

Mom lets people use her fax machine, and she doesn't charge them $3 like the place down the road does. So such a request is not an unusual occurrence at our house. What was unusual was the way the woman did her fax. Three minutes later the phone rang. "We keep getting a fax from this number," a voice said, "but it just keeps coming through blank. We don't see anything."

I went in to see if I could help. "They say your fax isn't coming through," I said.

"Really?" the woman asked. "I wonder why not."

"Show me what you were doing," I suggested. She had carefully folded the document she was faxing in half before running it through the machine.

"Oh," I said, "no wonder it isn't going through. You have it folded in half. They can't see what it's saying unless you open it up."

"Well," she said, "this fax is a confidential one. I don't want just anybody reading it at the other end."

Mom thanked me for waiting until the woman left before I burst out laughing. It doesn't matter whether it's confidential or not—you have to have your paper open, or the machine can't transmit anything.

Fortunately, prayer isn't like that. When I pray, I don't even have to pray out loud. I can just think it in my head, and God will still hear me and understand everything I mean—even if it's folded in half.

176

Dear God, thank You for understanding what I am thinking and thank You for keeping my secrets. Amen.

WAMML'S MEDLEY

My parrot, Wamml, likes to sing. In fact, he likes singing a whole lot better than he does talking. He's always whistling and singing and making other little noises. Wamml sings many things, but his favorites are "La Cucaracha," "Jesus Loves Me," and "The Battle Hymn of the Republic." The bird is not picky about which song he is singing, and often he mixes them. After breaking into a rousing chorus of "Jesus Loves Me," halfway through he bursts into "La Cucaracha."

He hasn't learned the difference between secular and spiritual music and sings both with great joy no matter what day of the week it is. Most Adventists do draw a line between the two, singing secular music during the week and only spiritual music on Sabbath. While this was probably a good idea in the beginning, helping Christians focus their minds on Jesus during the Sabbath hours, it seems like an artificial separation that has ended up restricting Christian songs to Sabbaths.

As Christians, if Jesus is really the most important thing in our lives, it would make more sense if we sang to Him every day of the week, even if we did end up mixing our songs like Wamml. I'm sure Jesus would much rather be a part of our everyday lives than relegated to just one day of the week, even if it did mean an occasional chorus of "La Cucaracha" in the middle of "Jesus Loves Me."

Dear God, help me to include You in everything. Amen.

Shout to God with joy, everyone on earth! Sing about the glory of his name! Give him glorious praise!

Psalm 66:1, 2.

WHEN PUFF GOT STUCK

God, save me by your power. Set me free by your might.

Psalm 54:1.

Occasionally my iguana Puff can be a little hard to find. He hides in the closet and has been known to startle people in the bathroom as he peers down at them from the shower curtain.

A couple times we have been unable to find him for several days, so Mom gets worried, and we all go on a major Puff search. It's usually not to hard to locate him, since he forgets that he has a two-and-a-half-foot-long tail that hangs out of most of his hiding places. Often we find him lurking in the bookcase.

One day, though, we couldn't find him at all. It was a hectic time. Mom had been in the hospital for a week, and still we couldn't locate Puff. When Mom came home, we fixed her up in her comfy chair in the living room, where she immediately asked for Puff. We had to tell her.

Mom sat there quietly all afternoon. When Don and I arrived home from school, she pointed and said, "I think Puff is behind the small bookcase over there. He must have fallen down behind it, because I heard a little scratching."

Sure enough, when Don and I moved the bookcase, we pulled out a skinny, grumpy Puff.

Sometimes we act like Puff. Even though we are stuck and need rescuing because of our own stupidity, we still try to blame other people and lash out at them when they attempt to help us. Part of growing up as a Christian is learning to admit when you've made a mistake, and when you need help, and then being willing to accept it.

178

Dear God, I need help with that one. Please teach me responsibility. Amen.

STUPID CRIMINAL TRICKS

JUNE 23

Those who aren't faithful will be paid back for what they've done. And good men will receive rewards for how they've lived.

Proverbs 14:14.

Any of us who have ever been bullied at school often appreciate seeing the bullies get a taste of their own medicine. I guess that is why "stupid criminal stories" are so popular and so much fun to read.

I read a story on the Internet of a terrorist who received a taste of his own medicine. A man named Khayrahnajet built letter bombs. Apparently he had made one and sent it to an address in another country. Mr. Khayrahnajet apparently knew a lot about building bombs but was not as familiar with postage rates. His letter came back with "return to sender" stamped on it, because he had not put enough stamps for it to get to its destination. Forgetting that it was a bomb, he opened it and was blown to bits.

While it is never right for us to be happy when someone is killed, this story certainly had a ring of justice to it. The Bible says that those who live by the sword will die by the sword. Eventually there will be justice for everyone, often before they ever expect it. While it is probably not the best reason to keep the golden rule, it certainly makes God's way look a lot better. Jesus asked us to love one another as He loved us. It's a wise choice. Love will never hurt you if it backfires and splashes some on you.

Dear God, I choose Your way. Please help me do it. Amen.

179

THE PIGS DIDN'T CARE

His servant grew up like a tender young plant. He grew like a root coming up out of dry ground. He didn't have any beauty or majesty that made us notice him. There wasn't anything special about the way he looked that drew us to him. Men looked down on him."

Isaiah 53:2, 3.

I read a most ironic story on the Internet. In Bonn, Germany, animal rights advocates picketed a slaughterhouse. They were protesting the cruelty of sending pigs to a slaughterhouse for food. During the protest, some of the pigs knocked down part of the fence. It started a major stampede in the group, and 2,000 of them pounded their way through the fence, trampling the animal rights supporters. Two of them died, killed by the pigs they were trying to save.

My first thought was that they were stupid pigs. But it made me think. The Son of God came to earth to try to save us from the slaughter Satan has planned for us. And yet the very people He sought to save killed Him instead.

Leaving a palatial existence as King of the universe, He joined a poverty-stricken family in a smelly cave filled with animals, and then lived a life unappreciated by the very creatures He had made such a sacrifice to rescue.

I guess a herd of humans is not that much smarter than a herd of pigs. But you and I do have a choice. We can honor the King who was willing to give His life for us, or we can trample Him like a herd of pigs, ignoring the value of His sacrifice. Don't be a pig.

Dear God, help me to appreciate the sacrifice You made for me. You are so good. Amen.

THE MARTHA STEWART LIFE

He knows what we are made of. He remembers that we are dust.

Psalm 103:14.

Martha Stewart, popularized as a domestic goddess and a lifestyle expert, seems to do everything perfectly. If you watch her interviews, she makes it appear that she does everything herself and wouldn't think of using anything preprepared or store-bought. She froze juice that she made from fruit that she grew herself out in the yard, served food on china that she hand-painted, and used napkins that she stamped the designs on with natural inks that she made from berries that she planted along her hand-painted fence in the backyard.

A favorite quote from her that makes my brother and me howl with laughter is: "I catnap now and then, . . . but I think while I nap, so it's not a waste of time." To take Martha Stewart as your role model is never to be able to do quite enough. No matter how much you do, you probably should have done a little more and done it a little better.

God does not want us to live a Martha Stewart life. It was never His plan for us to go through life feeling perpetually inadequate. When He said, "Be still, and know that I am God," He also wanted us to be still and know that we are not. I need to understand that I'm not the smartest person in the world, that I'm not perfect. Most of all, I must recognize that He alone is God and then act on that belief. I must worship Him, accept myself for what I am, and just be myself.

Dear God, help me to be content with being just who You made me to be. Amen.

DONNIE THE TRANSLATOR

Always give thanks to God the Father for everything. Give thanks to him in the name of our Lord Jesus Christ.

Ephesians 5:20.

The Bible tells us to give thanks in all things. Sometimes it has been hard to do that when my mom has been real sick, especially when we were afraid she wasn't going to get well.

But even my mom's being sick has given Don and me some gifts that other kids have not had. I've had Mom around, available to talk to me, a lot more than some kids' moms have been.

My brother has another skill that he attributes to Mom's illness. When Mom had some problems with her brain one summer, she had a very hard time communicating with us. But we learned to figure out what she really meant.

When my brother's boss had a stroke, it left her unable to talk anymore. Lots of the students who worked for her have visited her, but many of them get frustrated because they can't understand her. My brother sits there and carries on a conversation with her, just as if nothing has changed. He understands what she is trying to say, because he has been used to interpreting Mom for so long. It has made a very special friendship between my brother and Mrs. Strickland, and even though he doesn't see her as often as he would like to, they have a close bond.

Without Mom's sickness over the years, Donnie would have never developed that skill. I guess even in that we need to give God thanks.

Even though You are hard to understand sometimes, thank You, God. I do trust You. Amen.

HOUSE RULES

I lay on the couch watching my pets play. Wamml sat in his tree playing with his toys and suspiciously watching Puff, my iguana, who was sunbathing in a pool of light on the carpet. As the sun went behind the cloud Puff started to crawl toward Wamml's corner of the room. Even though Wamml was perched high in his climbing tree, he was very territorial about all his space clear to the papers on the floor. As Puff stepped on the edge of his newspapers, Wamml swung upside down on his branch and shouted, "What are you doing?"

Puff jumped and scrambled over to the bookcase, clawing wildly at books and magazines. Finally he crawled up to a place he thought was safe as everything tumbled to the floor. Wamml was pretty certain that throwing books and magazines on the floor was a bad thing. We had reprimanded him for that before, so he continued to berate Puff. "Look what you did! Bad bird, bad bird," he shouted.

As much as we laugh at Wamml for his blanket application of household rules, we act like that to other people at church sometimes. God has a basic set of rules that we all need to stick to. We call that the Ten Commandments. Beyond that, He has different expectations for different people. Yet we like to apply all of the rules and standards in exactly the same way to everyone. Perhaps to God we look as foolish as Wamml berating Puff and calling him a bad bird.

Dear God, I may be misjudged by some people sometimes, but I am so glad I can always count on You to judge me fairly, because You understand me. Amen.

JUNE 27

But the Lord said to Samuel, "Do not consider how handsome or tall he is. I have not chosen him. I do not look at the things people look at. Man looks at how someone appears on the outside. But I look on what is in the heart."

1 Samuel 16:7.

DON'T DON'T USE USE DOUBLE DOUBLE SPEAK SPEAK

I prayed, "You are my God. I'm filled with shame and dishonor. I can hardly look to you and pray. That's because our sins are piled up above our heads. Our guilt reaches all the way to the heavens."

Ezra 9:6.

Ezra was in midconfession when he said this. He recognized that he and his people had sinned, and he was not afraid to call it sin and to ask God for forgiveness.

The 365 Stupidest Things Ever Said, by Ross and Kathryn Petras, is one of the funniest books that I have read this year. Several of the statements it quotes have been by people who were just unwilling to call something by its right name.

The governor of a prison in Derek, England, as quoted in the *Hutter's Field Daily Examiner,* said, "There was not a breach of security as such. It was a case of someone cutting a hole from the outside and facilitating the escape of three of our inmates." If three prisoners escaping is not a breach of security, I don't know what is.

It seems to be a common human problem, being unwilling to call sin by its right name. Yet in order for us to have the mind of Christ Jesus, as He asked us to, we need to be willing to recognize that sin is sin, no matter how we define it. We need to be able to call it by its right name and to recognize how hurtful it is to God. As long as we are making excuses for our behavior and pretending it's not what it is, we will never be able to abandon it and stop doing the things that hurt Jesus and ourselves.

As Christians, we need to quit the "double speak." We must call a sin a sin and keep our eyes on Jesus and be willing to turn our backs on all of it.

Dear God, help me to be straightforward and honest with myself and with You. Amen.

184

SOME OF GOD'S REAL LIVE SHEEP

And He will say unto Gerald White, "I was a teenager, and feeling like skipping church, and you phoned me and invited me to bring some friends and come to your house on Sabbath afternoon, knowing that sometimes a guy needs to hang out with people besides his family. And you said unto me, 'See you on Sabbath,' and I did."

And He will say unto Gail Melkersen, "I was in your class at school, and I was belligerent one day when I felt you had punished me unfairly. The principal spake unto me saying, 'Apologize,' and I refused, and I was suspended until I did. And my mother spake unto me saying, 'You will have to go to public school if you don't apologize and cooperate.' And yet I refused. And you called me on the phone, and apologized for not allowing me to explain my side of the story. And my stubborn heart melted and I forgot my rebellious attitude."

And He will say unto Rick Greve, "My mother was in the hospital, and my father and big brother were working, and I was alone and afraid, and showed it by misbehaving in school. And you came unto me and were my friend, and even took me out golfing and for ice cream with you and your young son. And I felt cared about, and that everything would be all right."

And He will say unto you, "Inasmuch as you have done it unto the smallest and most insignificant kids in the church, you have done it unto Me."

Dear God, don't let me forget this. Amen.

JUNE 29

When the Son of man shall come in his glory, and all the holy angels with him, then shall he sit upon the throne of his glory: and before him shall be gathered all nations: and he shall separate them one from another as a shepherd divideth the sheep from the goats; and he shall set the sheep on his right hand, but the goats on his left. Then shall the King say unto them on his right hand, Come, ye blessed of my Father, inherit the kingdom prepared for you."

Matthew 25:31-34, KJV.

185

FAT BILL

Lord, you have seen what is in my heart. You know all about me.

Psalm 139:1.

I'll admit it; I love Fat Bill. But someone I can't stand is a woman at church who is such a busybody and fusses all of the time. I dread seeing her coming. But she doesn't seem to bother Mom, and when I asked her about it, she just said, "Sometimes, once you get to know somebody and you find out why they're the way they are, you're able to like them just as they are."

Yeah, right. I would never be able to stand this woman. But Fat Bill was another matter. He was the crabbiest parakeet we ever met. One day I asked his former owner about Bill. I mentioned that he didn't fly very well and didn't climb very well, either. "Oh," said Rachel, "he's been like that ever since he got hurt."

"Hurt?" I asked. "Whatever happened to him?"

"About three years ago," she said, "a cat got him. He was injured really badly, and we thought that he was going to die. When he did get better, his legs took a long time to heal."

"Oh," I said, suddenly understanding. Fat Bill wasn't fat because he was lazy. He was fat because he had been hurt and couldn't exercise as easily as the other birds. I felt sorry for him now.

Suddenly I understood what Mom meant about her friend Miss Fussbudget. Loving Bill taught me a lot about getting along with other people at church. Now, whenever I see her, I just think of Bill, and it makes me smile. She isn't so annoying after all.

Dear God, help me to see people through Your eyes instead. Amen.

186

THEY BEAT UP HARPY!

I ran out to the back porch at the sound of all of the screeching and flapping. There lay one of the baby parakeets on the floor, bleeding from four little wounds on his head and several places on his back and his wings. Someone had pulled him out of the nesting box and beaten him up.

After I brought him into the kitchen, Mom and I fed him baby parrot formula and dabbed antiseptic on his bites. "What will we do with him?" I asked.

"Well, we have to keep him warm," Mom replied, "and we can't put him back in his nesting box until we find out who beat him up."

Changing into a shirt with a big pocket in the front, I dropped the baby into it. He needed a safe place to hide—at least until he grew more feathers. I named him Harpy. Harpy rode around in my pocket for a week and slept in a little container on top of the heating pad at night.

Because I adopted Harpy and rescued him when he was little, he considers himself a citizen of both worlds. He believes he is part human and part bird.

God rescued us when we were in trouble too. Just like Harpy, we can live in this world with the other people who look like us, but we are free to go in to His presence at any time and hang out with Him. We can be just as comfortable as Harpy, because we're part of His family too.

Jesus, thanks for rescuing me when all Satan was interested in was beating me up. Amen.

JULY 1

You didn't receive a spirit that makes you a slave to fear once again. Instead you received the Holy Spirit, who makes you God's child. By the Spirit's power we call God *"Abba." Abba* means Father.

Romans 8:15.

187

OOPS!

My brother and I enjoy collecting sports bloopers. One day while covering a Royals game in Kansas City, Missouri, the sportscaster, Jerry Coleman, said, "The sky is so clear today you can see all the way to Missouri." It took a while for it to sink in, and then we laughed. Kansas City is in Missouri, so even in thick pea-soup fog, as long as he could see his toes, he would have been able to see Missouri. Just because you're in Kansas City doesn't mean you are in Kansas.

But while we may laugh at Jerry Coleman, some of us use equally faulty logic when we look at our spiritual life. Sitting in church doesn't make us a Christian any more than sitting in a garage makes you a car. It's not enough just to be sitting in the right place. That is why, when God was talking to the Laodicean church in Revelation, He said, "Ask me for eyesalve so that I can help you see." We need God to help us see where we really are. Not only will He open our eyes to where we are, but then He will help us to get where He wants us to go.

I don't want my Christianity to be a big blooper. Do you?

Jesus, I need Your eyesalve to help me see and appreciate all that You have done for me. May I please have some today? Thanks. Amen.

BUSTER THE THREE-LEGGED DOG

JULY 3

Make me pure by sprinkling me with hyssop plant. Then I will be clean. Wash me. Then I will be whiter than snow.

Psalm 51:7.

My friend Becky has an awesome dog. His name is Buster. Buster is a golden retriever. When he was a puppy, he fell off the couch and broke his leg. Even though he made several trips to the vet, the leg never healed right, and he was in constant pain. Finally the vet suggested that they amputate. The idea horrified Buster's family. It seemed extreme, but watching their puppy suffer was just too hard. The vet removed Buster's leg.

After his surgery, Buster did much better. Soon his stump healed, and he was running around on three legs, keeping up with the other family dogs who had four. Buster is 3 years old now and doing just fine, and he doesn't even know that he is any different than the others.

Sometimes things in our lives really hurt us, but we are attached to them like Buster and his crippled leg. God wants to take them away, though it may seem a terrible decision. Just like Buster, we can trust Him and know that anything God does for us will be for the best. Letting God take whatever in our lives injures us may hurt at the time, but we will heal much faster after letting God do surgery on our lives than by hanging onto our pain.

Go ahead, trust Him. Just remember Buster.

God, help me to trust You even when You have to take away something that I'm really attached to. Amen.

189

WIGGLY JELLY BEANS

I saw a new heaven and a new earth. The first heaven and the first earth were completely gone. There was no longer any sea.

Revelation 21:1.

I cannot comprehend how anyone who has ever raised baby parakeets could be an atheist.

My parakeets lay eggs the size of jelly beans. It takes about a month of the mother bird sitting on them for them to hatch. The babies look more like tiny frogs than birds when they first appear. They just have little bulges where their eyes should be. And they are so tiny and weak they can't even pick their little heads up off the floor of the nesting box. They're totally helpless.

The mother birds push them over on their backs and poke burped-up food into their little beaks. In 24 hours they double in size, and then double again. After only three or four short weeks they are the size of their parents, just lacking as many feathers as adult birds have and still not being very coordinated. Even though they are the same size as the adults, they still have to learn how to walk, climb, fly, and eat by themselves. At about six weeks of age they start leaving the nesting boxes and start perching in the branches of their little climbing tree. The parents still have to come and feed them beak-to-beak.

So far I have raised 13 clutches of baby parakeets, and it still excites and amazes me each time as I watch the tiny, helpless little things turn into beautiful birds. As excited as I am just watching my babies hatch, I can't imagine how cool it's going to be for us to watch God create our world the second time.

Jesus, I just can't wait to see You wipe away all the bad and make everything new and perfect again. Please make it soon. Amen.

DIFFERENT STROKES FOR DIFFERENT FOLKS

My parrot, Wamml, thinks he's a family member. He has a different relationship with each person in the family and is very rigid about what he allows each person to do. Wamml's favorite person is Dad. The parrot will play with Dad, ride around on his shoulder, and let Dad scratch his neck and pet him.

Wamml loves Mom—when Dad isn't around. She's the one who feeds him every day, and his cage is next to her side of the bed at night. Every night when Mom goes to bed, Wamml climbs down on the side of his cage, grabs her pillowcase, and shakes it until she stops talking to Dad and pays attention to him. Some nights he will come over and tap his beak on her cheek, giving her a good-night kiss.

Wamml treats me differently than either Mom or Dad. He likes to yell at me. He has learned to shout "Michael" in several different tones of voice, all disapproving.

However, I am special. He never calls my brother by name. When Don enters the room, Wamml blows rude gastrointestinal noises. Don taught him how to do it. And he always announces Donnie's entrance that way.

Wamml loves each of us in his own individual way. While God and Wamml don't have many things in common, this is something they do have. The Lord wants to have a distinct and special relationship with each person, something individual.

God, it's so neat that You love me differently than everyone else. I love You too. Amen.

Before I formed you in your mother's body I chose you. Before you were born I set you apart to serve me. I appointed you to be a prophet to the nations.

Jeremiah 1:5.

191

IS IT BACK TO THE FUTURE OR AHEAD TO THE PAST?

JULY 6

It is written, "No eye has seen, no ear has heard, no mind has known what God has prepared for those who love him."

1 Corinthians 2:9.

My grandpa Don had a college professor who liked to complain, "They just don't make things the way they used too," then with a twinkle he would add, "And they never did!" Grandpa got a honk out of that, and he used to repeat it often, especially when he had car trouble.

It reminds me of a quote from Yogi Berra, a great baseball player. He said, "The future isn't what it used to be," and it isn't. That's because this used to be the future."

The prophet Daniel, who foresaw the way things are today, would probably think these were awesome times in which to live. He would probably also believe that we didn't have much future left. Daniel talks about the end of time as if when that happens, time as we know it would cease to exist. We even sing about it in the song called "When the Roll Is Called Up Yonder." The first line goes: "When the trumpet of the Lord shall sound, and time shall be no more." Can you imagine what life would be like without time? We have such linear brains that trying to contemplate life without time as we know it can give us brain cramps.

Some things are just too hard to imagine, yet we know that someday it will all make sense, and that things will be more wonderful than anything we could have ever come up with on our own. The future won't be what it used to be. Aren't you glad?

God, thanks for planning a future for me. And thanks for making it better than I can even imagine! Amen.

192

TOO COOL

Miss Cinnamon is one of the great loves of my life. A gift from my parents, she came into my life at my eighth-grade graduation. She was a baby cinnamon cockatiel, and it was love at first sight.

All summer Miss Cinnamon lived in my bedroom with me. She kept me company in everything I did. At night when I went to bed, she would sit on the top of my book and peer down at what I was reading. When school started in the fall, I figured Miss Cinnamon would be lonely in my bedroom by herself all day, so she went to daycare upstairs in the sunroom with Mom's parakeets.

The trouble was, though, that when Miss Cinnamon was with her friends the parakeets, she soon realized that the other birds considered themselves much too independent to sit on anybody's shoulder or finger. Suddenly Miss Cinnamon wouldn't do it either. But whenever I catch Miss Cinnamon and we leave the parakeet room, we are suddenly back to our old relationship. But as soon as she's back in front of her other friends, she pretends she doesn't know me.

Sometimes I treat God the same way. When we're alone together, we get along so well, but sometimes when I'm with my friends, He kind of has to chase me down to get my attention. Does it hurt His feelings?

God, You're so consistent in how You relate to me. Forgive me when I pretend I'm too cool to express how much I love You. Amen.

JULY 7

That's why I'm suffering the way I am. But I am not ashamed. I know the One I have believed in. I am sure he is able to take care of what I have given him. I can trust him with it until the day he returns as judge.

2 Timothy 1:12.

193

DO YOU KNOW WHO I AM?

JULY 8

Then the Lord said to Moses, "Reach your hand out. Take the snake by the tail." So he reached out and grabbed hold of the snake. It turned back into a staff in his hand.

Exodus 4:4.

My mom met a lot of famous people during her career as a critical-care nurse. One night her patient was extremely ill. The doctors wondered whether he would make it through the night. They certainly did not expect him to last through the weekend. Mom checked the family phone number on the chart and called his son. Gently she informed him that his dad was in critical condition and probably wouldn't survive the weekend.

The patient's son happened to be a well-known senator. He shouted back into the phone, "You need to keep him around till Monday. I can't make it till Monday."

"I don't think I can," Mom replied. "He's very ill."

"Do you know who I am?" the senator bellowed into the phone.

Mom replied coolly, "Yes, I do, but apparently you don't know who I am. I'm not God; I'm just the nurse taking care of your father. Your father would get the same care from me whether he was very important or some street bum dragged 'in by the paramedics. And no matter how important you are, your father is still very ill and will probably not live through the weekend. I just called to give you a choice."

I was proud of my mom.

Mom knows who she is, and very few people intimidate her. I would like to be like that. Knowing who I am in Jesus makes me able to face anyone calmly and quietly.

God, I don't understand how You would ever decide that I was worth the life of Your Son. But I'm glad I am. Amen.

194

THE VULTURE AND THE HUMMINGBIRD

I get depressed more easily than some people in my family. My mom is just the opposite. She's a chronic Pollyanna and has to be really sick before she gets discouraged. One day I was telling her all the things wrong with my life. Then she shared something she learned when she was a little girl.

Mom grew up in West Africa, and because she was of a naturalist bent like me, all the wildlife, especially the birds, fascinated her. She told me this: A hummingbird and a vulture can both fly over the same piece of ground. The hummingbird looks for flowers, and any flash of color will bring it zooming down to check it out. Vultures fly for miles searching for dead and dying animals. When they find them, they swoop down and devour them.

Everyone has a choice in life what kind of bird they want to be. You can focus on beautiful things, or you can concentrate on the ugly. Hummingbirds and vultures live in the same places, yet if they were to describe their surroundings, each one's perspective would be unrecognizable to the other. Having thought about that a lot, I think Mom's right. It is not only practical but biblical to be a hummingbird.

God, please help me to be a hummingbird and look for the flashes of color You provide in my life. Amen.

JULY 9

Finally, my brothers and sisters, always think about what is true. Think about what is noble, right and pure. Think about what is lovely and worthy of respect. If anything is excellent or worthy of praise, think about those kinds of things.

Philippians 4:8.

195

OF SHRIVELED APPLES AND MUMMIFIED CHEESE SANDWICHES

My God will meet all your needs. He will meet them in keeping with His wonderful riches that come to you because you belong to Christ Jesus.

Philippians 4:19.

One of the most difficult years my family faced happened when I was 3. My dad was unemployed the whole year. We were taking care of his grandma at that time. She often told my brother and me, "If your dad doesn't find a job soon, I don't know what we'll do. We won't know where our next meal is coming from."

When Mom heard her say it one time, she whisked my brother and me upstairs and tried to reassure us that she and Dad would always make sure Donnie and I ate. But we were worried. Soon we were stashing food in our bedroom so that when the time came, we would have something to eat.

While what I did as a 3-year-old sounds funny, a lot of adults do exactly the same thing. My friend's dad is stashing all kinds of things in his basement for the time of trouble, as well as investing in gold bullion. Just like my mom and dad did then, Jesus has promised to take care of us. He has promised that our bread and water will be sure and that we will be OK. It must hurt His feelings just as it did Mom's to see us constantly trying to provide for our own needs, just in case He's not able to.

Don and I never went without anything we required that whole year. I never needed to worry, but it took me a long time to learn that. Now, I'm determined not to spend years worrying about the time of trouble. God has promised that He'll take care of me, and even more than my parents, His word is good.

God, thanks for always taking really good care of me. Amen.

IF YOU WERE RIGHT, I'D AGREE WITH YOU

You need to respect him because he's your teacher," Mom repeated. "Just because he's your teacher, if you can't think of any other reasons."

Respecting people in authority is sometimes a problem for me. It's easy when the person in authority over me is doing everything the way I think it should be. When it becomes difficult is when my opinion and theirs are different, or when I feel they're not making good decisions.

As I have been writing this book, I have heard a lot of discussion on TV and elsewhere about the American president. He has had a problem with some of his decisions. Some well-known Christians have spoken extremely disrespectfully of the president in public. It has really made me think that if God puts authority figures in our lives for a reason and expects us to respect them for their position, whether or not we like their choices, then it seems that we should extend that same courtesy to the president.

It's kind of comforting to know that adults struggle with this issue just as I do. We all need God's help, whether we're little kids, teenagers, or adults. All of us need Jesus.

God, You know my struggles with those in authority. Please help me to recognize how You are leading them, too. Amen.

JULY 11

Pray for kings. Pray for all who are in authority. Pray that we will live peaceful and quiet lives. And pray that we will be godly and holy.

1 Timothy 2:2.

197

JOY

Do not try to get even. Do not hold anything against one of your people. Instead, love your neighbor as yourself. I am the Lord.

Leviticus 19:18.

Ever since I was a little guy I remember being taught in Sabbath school and in church school that joy means putting Jesus and others before yourself. But I think that we aren't really helping people by teaching them that.

It is good to put Jesus first and to make Him our highest priority, and it is good to treat others well and with respect. The problem is that we don't teach most kids much about treating themselves well. The Bible devotes a lot of time to telling us how to treat ourselves well—how to eat only the best foods for our bodies, how to avoid illness, how to have the best physical and spiritual health and happiness.

It seems to me that if we really understood the value that God places on us, then we would place higher values on ourselves. We would respect ourselves so much that we wouldn't want to do things that could either temporarily or permanently hurt our beautiful bodies God has given us. Nor would we want to do things that would degrade us and devalue our lives. And we wouldn't do that to other people either. Thus it seems to me that the joy-ranking system should be a pyramid, with Jesus at the top and others and ourselves on an equal footing at the base. Love God. Love your neighbor. Love yourself.

God, help me to remember how valuable I am and not to do anything to make myself less valuable. Amen.

ROLL OVER, BEETHOVEN

My brother's favorite composer is Beethoven. When Don was 3 years old, Mom and Dad realized he was deaf. Good at lipreading, Don seemed to understand other people pretty well as long as they faced him while they talked. He still went to preschool and did all the things that little guys do.

JULY 13

Blessed is the man whose sin the Lord never counts against him.

Romans 4:8.

Mom took the time to find out about other famous people who had been deaf. Soon Donnie knew all about them. He liked to listen to Beethoven, especially after Mom explained to him that the man who wrote the music couldn't hear either. She would turn the volume and Donnie would sit next to the speaker with his leg against the side of it. Even though his ears couldn't hear, he could feel the vibrations, and he loved it.

Later Donnie had surgery. His ears work fine now. The doctors were able to repair all of the problems, and the tumors blocking the sound didn't come back. But he still has a soft spot for people who are hard-of-hearing, and he still loves Beethoven.

God has healed us from sin, but we still need to carry a soft spot for other people who are hurting and broken. It's important for us never to forget that we were once like that. The greatest comfort during a hard time comes from someone else who has been through it and is OK now.

God, help me always to remember that You're my sin-healer, and help me to be kind and understanding of others who haven't been healed yet. Amen.

199

RED AND YELLOW, BLACK AND WHITE, ALL ARE PRECIOUS IN HIS SIGHT

JULY 14

Then Peter began to speak. "I now realize how true it is that God treats everyone the same," he said.

Acts 10:34.

Some time ago the news had a horrible report about two bomb blasts in American embassies over in Africa. The newscaster said that more than 120 died, but only 10 of them were Americans. Mom, who isn't above talking to the television, sputtered, "What difference does *that* make?" And she's right.

While people may be curious to know if some of those killed in the bomb blasts were from here and were people they knew, it did not make the tragedy any more terrible that 10 Americans perished, or any less terrible that only 10 were killed. The tragedy was the loss of human life, whether or not the people were Americans. They had parents, brothers and sisters, wives, families, pets. All of them had lives, and now they don't.

I can't picture God announcing on the heavenly news, "Today 144,000 saints from earth were translated to heaven without dying. Oh, and 93 of them were Americans." They're all people to Him. The bombing would be just as great a tragedy to God if no Americans were in the rubble.

God, help me to remember that You love all people equally, even the ones who are different from me. Amen.

ARE YOU LOSING YOUR BALANCE?

JULY 15

So eat and drink and do everything else for the glory of God.

1 Corinthians 10:31.

When Wamml first came to live with us, he wasn't well. He had many problems, one of them being his diet. Wamml ate only peanuts or sunflower seeds. He was suspicious of anything else. Little by little Mom managed to tempt him with slices of apple, waffles, blueberries, and corn on the cob. At first Wamml ignored anything she put in his food dish that didn't look like peanuts or seeds. But once she got him to try a few things, he came to love them. Now Wamml gobbles grapes, apples, oranges, macaroni, and many other things. He is more balanced.

Sometimes in my life I really get into something. Right now it is skateboarding, but in the past it has been my music, or the books I was reading, or biking with my friend Carl. Whatever it is that I'm into, I tend to do it a lot, like Wamml and his peanuts. Yet I need to remember that no matter how good each activity is, I need balance in my life too. I still need some spiritual input and some intellectual input as well as the physical input I receive from skateboarding. I believe this is part of the Christian life and that to take care of my body and my mind I need to learn balance in everything, just as Wamml did.

Lord, please help me to remember the need for balance in my life and not to get so focused on one thing that I forget all the other neat stuff You've put here for me. Amen.

201

ONE SIZE DOES *NOT* FIT ALL

How terrible it will be for anyone who argues with his Maker! He is like a broken piece of pottery lying on the ground. Does clay say to a potter, "What are you making?" Does a pot say, "You don't have any skill"?

Isaiah 45:9.

Sometimes when I look around at other people and their families, it makes me wonder why God treats us all so differently.

I don't know, but I do recognize that I treat my birds differently. When Wamml came to us, he had arthritis in his feet from sitting on a one-size perch in his cage all the time. We made a climbing tree for Wamml with a metal tray underneath to catch all the stuff he throws on the floor. And he can climb and swing and play and chew to his little heart's content.

Skippy (my cockatoo) has bad feet too, but they were deformed at birth. We made him an extra-large perch and then attached several toys to it in places he could play, but we made sure that the perch was big enough for him to get a good hold so he wouldn't fall and hurt himself. Then we put his tray only six inches below his perch, so that if he did fall it wouldn't be very far. Next, he needed a ladder to climb up and down from his perch to his tray so that he could get to all of his toys. At first glance, other people might think that I play favorites with my parrots because of Wamml's big playland and Skippy's smaller horizontal one. But I have to treat each parrot according to what his needs are and what he's able to do. I guess I need to trust that God does that with us, treating each of us differently according to our needs and what we are able to do, and that someday I'll understand all of the things that don't make sense right now.

God, I'm glad that You're creative enough to have a plan designed just for me. Amen.

MOM'S UNIQUE WAY OF SWEEPING THE KITCHEN

JULY 17

Turn my eyes away from things that are worthless. Keep me alive as you have promised.

Psalm 119:37.

My mom has neuropathy in her feet. This means that the nerves that tell Mom what her feet are feeling on the bottoms have been damaged or have died, so she has no sensation there. At first I thought that would be really cool. Imagine nothing ever hurting the bottoms of your feet! That would be awesome. But I soon learned that it's not.

My brother and I keep reminding Mom to wear her shoes whenever she's up and around. If she has been in the kitchen before someone has put her shoes on her, we have her sit down and check her feet. Often we find a bean or a lentil, a penny, or shells from Wamml and Skippy's nuts, all embedded in the bottoms of her feet. Having no sense of pain means that Mom can't tell when something is hurting her so she can remove it.

That is the biggest problem that people with leprosy have. They have such severe neuropathy everywhere that they can't tell when they are being burned or hurt or even bitten by rats. Slowly their injuries become so many and so infected that they lose whole parts, such as fingers or toes or an ear. They just don't notice, because the areas are numb.

Sinning can do that to us too after a while. Some people have spiritual neuropathy. Their consciences are so deadened that they can't tell when something is hurting them spiritually.

God, please keep my conscience sensitive, not because I want to hurt, but because I want to know when I am doing something harmful and be able to stop. Amen.

203

CHECK THE PLUG

Praise the Lord for the glory that belongs to him. Worship the Lord because of his beauty and holiness.

Psalm 29:2.

One night as she sat in front of her computer screens in the coronary-care unit, watching her patients' heart rhythms, her friend Pat leaned up against the other side of the counter above the computer screens. As Pat scribbled in the chart she was working on, her elbow bumped a set of calipers attached to a chain on the counter. (Nurses use them to measure the heart rhythms that they print out in strips to put on the patient's chart.)

Suddenly one computer screen after another flashed, popped, and went black, dark smoke billowing out the back. Mom rushed to help Pat hook the most critical patients up to temporary monitors until the guys from biomedical engineering arrived.

The computer bank had been only partially plugged into the wall. But part of the prongs in the plug were exposed, and as the chain with the calipers fell down behind the counter, it connected with the metal pins and shorted out the computer bank.

Mom handled the ensuing jokes fairly well. However, after that she was always careful to check the electrical connections in her monitors and computers at the beginning of her shift.

Sometimes people aren't very careful how they plug in to their power source either. People treat electricity with great respect. With how much more respect should we approach God?

God, when I think about how powerful You are, I feel pretty small. Thanks for loving me. Amen.

GNIKLAW SDRAWKCAB

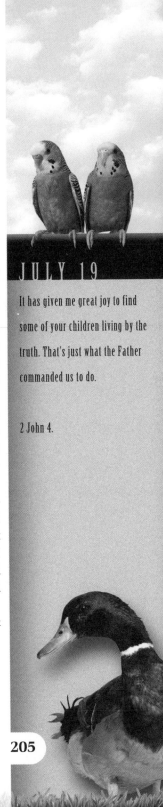

JULY 19

It has given me great joy to find some of your children living by the truth. That's just what the Father commanded us to do.

2 John 4.

Recently Cinnamon and Henrym, my cockatiels, had babies. When they were about 3 weeks old, we took them out of the punchbowl where they had been born to hand-feed them so that they would be tame. As I was feeding them, I noticed that they were walking backward. I thought it was a little odd, but when I showed them to my dad, he said his puppies had done the same thing when they were learning to walk.

While I don't know why they walk backward, I do know that it can be dangerous. If they walk only backward, they can't see where they are going and could fall off the table. Or if they were in the wild, they could wind up in a predator's lair.

It seems kind of silly to walk backward, but sometimes we as Christians do something like that. We'll get into something that maybe we shouldn't and that will hurt us, such as drugs or alcohol. But just as I make sure that my cockatiels don't fall down, God will help us to know what we're getting into. And hopefully we will make the right choice.

Dear God, please help me not to walk backward in my life, but guide me to see where I am going. Amen.

APOLLO 11 DISEASE

Then Jesus said, "I am the bread of life. No one who comes to me will ever go hungry. And no one who believes in me will ever be thirsty."

John 6:35.

Mom remembers when the first men walked on the moon in 1969, because the people in Accra, Ghana, where she was living at the time, were extremely afraid that the lunar module would bring back a new disease from the moon.

Around the time the module touched down, an epidemic of conjunctivitis (we call it pink-eye) started going around Accra. People panicked. They called it *Apollo 11* disease.

Mom went to a small church school for the missionary kids. Each person had their own towel next to the sink, where they could wash their hands and faces after recesses and trips to the restroom. But all the towels hung so close together that the infection spread rapidly through the whole class. It took weeks to clear up.

Until Mom was in nursing school, she always insisted that she had caught *Apollo 11* disease. Now (as a nurse) she knows that conjunctivitis is not uncommon and not a big deal. It's been around a lot longer than the space program and is easily treated.

Sin is not uncommon either. It can be easily treated now, because Jesus died to give us the antidote. Although sin brings pain, suffering, and death, we don't have to be afraid of it. Nor do we have to just live with it and accept the pain as part of life. Instead, we can go to Jesus, and He will heal our lives through the time spent with Him. We just have to ask for help. He has promised to give it to us!

Thank You, God, for healing my sin disease and making a way to keep me from getting reinfected. Amen.

HOW TO AVOID SPIRITUAL ROAD RASH

JULY 21

Put on all of God's armor. Then you can stand firm against the devil's evil plans.

Ephesians 6:11-17.

My favorite sport right now is skateboarding. My mom considers it very dangerous, and it can be. When you fall, it hurts, and you do fall if you ever try anything new. But you have to get back up and try again. I like to skateboard at a big skate park in Harrisonburg. They have big ramps and curbs for the serious skateboarder. Because a beginner playing in a skate park can get some serious road rash, it's important to use pads and protective equipment. I always wear a helmet and elbow and knee pads. Sometimes I think some leather gloves would be a good idea too.

Last week when I was skating, I fell three feet from the ramp I was on, but I skidded six more. Without my protective equipment I would have been really chewed up.

When God sends us to do something we don't think we are ready for, He also gives us the Holy Spirit as our protective gear. Without the Holy Spirit's help we would wipe out and would not only become a failure but also get hurt. But with Him as our protection, we can go anywhere and do anything that God suggests.

God, it's scary how many ways Satan can find to hurt me, but it's really awesome that You've got even more ways to protect me. Thanks so very much. Amen.

THE PIED PIPER

God loved the world so much that he gave his one and only son. Anyone who believes in him will not die but will have eternal life.

John 3:16.

Today is Rat Catchers Day. It celebrates the anniversary of the pied piper of Hamelin, Germany. Apparently Hamelin had a problem with rats. Rats lurked everywhere. No matter what the people did, they couldn't get rid of them.

In 1376 the pied piper came to Hamelin. He offered to remove the rats for a price. Desperate, the people were willing to agree to anything. According to the story, the pied piper played his flute and hypnotized the rats. They all followed him to the river, jumped in, and drowned.

The people were overjoyed but didn't want to pay the exorbitant price they had already agreed to. When the pied piper asked for his payment, they just laughed at him and told him to get lost! Becoming angry, he went out into the street and began playing his flute again. The children of the town started pouring out of the houses and into the street. He walked up and down each street in the town until every child in the entire town was following him. Without a glance back toward the parents, he led them to Koppelberg Hill, where all but one trooped into a cave that miraculously opened up.

No matter how much or how little of the story is based on fact, the principle is the same: Eventually everyone has to pay for their choices. We will too, unless we let Jesus pick up the tab. *He* will pay the piper. If we don't, we must pay with our lives, just as the children of Hamelin.

What a wonderful God!

I can't thank You, God, often enough for what You've done for me. I'm grateful today. Amen.

WHEN MISS AMERICA WASN'T SO COOL

O n this date back in 1984 the first Miss America ever to resign lost her crown. She left her job amid a huge scandal when the media uncovered the fact that she was a single mother and had had a baby out of wedlock. You would think that she might have become discouraged and faded into oblivion after that, yet she didn't. Even though she was publicly punished for a private mistake, Vanessa Williams went on to pursue her career as an actress, singer, and dancer. She performs today on videos and CDs, and few people even remember the scandal attached to her name all those years ago.

I got into trouble one time, and the police came and picked me up on the lawn in front of the whole campus. Everyone in town either saw what happened or heard about it from someone else who had witnessed it. They all knew that I had been really stupid and was in trouble.

Have you been publicly punished? Do you feel humiliated and mortified and unable to go on? There is life after scandal. Ten years from now nobody will probably remember it. Have the courage to admit your mistakes, then ask God's forgiveness. He has promised to give it to you (and me too!). Now go on to a wonderful life.

Thank You, God, for Your promise to forgive and remain with me. Amen.

JULY 23

But God is faithful and fair. If we admit that we have sinned, he will forgive us our sins. He will forgive every wrong thing that we have done. He will make us pure.

1 John 1:9.

209

FRIENDLY FIRE

He will not break a bent twig. He will not put out a dimly burning flame. He will be faithful and make everything right.

Isaiah 42:3.

On this date the U.S. military commissioned the first guided missile ship. Ships launched missiles before that, but navies had a lot of what they termed "friendly fire." "Friendly fire" happens when people get injured from bullets and missiles shot by their own side.

Unfortunately Christians are not immune to "friendly fire." One research project revealed that most people who left the Adventist Church had no problem with its doctrines or beliefs. The majority departed because someone else had hurt their feelings or said something that made them uncomfortable going to their churches again. They were wounded by friendly fire.

We need help from the Holy Spirit with the things that we say. So often people's words act like unguided missiles. We need the Holy Spirit to enable us to speak guided missiles that will hurt only Satan. It's important for us to remember who the real enemy is, and with the Holy Spirit's help, shoot only guided missiles and thus stamp out friendly fire in the church.

Please God, help me to recognize which of my friends may be feeling wounded, and remind me not to do things that might hurt them even more. Amen.

WHY ME, LORD?

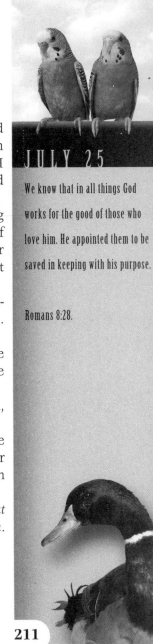

Sometimes nothing in my life goes right, and I find myself asking God, "Do You even care? Why did You let this happen to me?" I was feeling this way recently when I heard a story that I have to share.

A man who had been shipwrecked was living alone on a desert island. He had finally built himself a little refuge out of palm branches that would shelter him from the sun and the rain. That night his hut caught fire and burned to the ground.

"What are You doing, God?" he cried. "I have so little left in life, and yet You let my house burn down. How could You let this happen to me?"

A few hours later a British ship picked him up. "We saw your fire signal," the crew said. "We didn't realize these were inhabited islands. We'll take you home."

The man closed his eyes in embarrassment. "Uh, thank You, God," he said finally.

Sometimes I wonder that if I could really see everything that God does, would I be embarrassed for the questions that I ask too? Maybe I would then close my eyes and say, "Thank You, God."

Thank You, God. And please help me remember that even when things look bad, You're still in control. Amen.

JULY 25

We know that in all things God works for the good of those who love him. He appointed them to be saved in keeping with his purpose.

Romans 8:28.

So he said to me, "A message came to Zerubbabel from the Lord. He said, 'Your strength will not get my temple rebuilt. Your power will not do it either. Only the power of my spirit will do it,' says the Lord who rules over all."

Zechariah 4:6.

YOU GOTTA HAVE THE RIGHT EQUIPMENT

Not all skateboards are created equal. The old-fashioned ones are flat and have no kick tail on them. Making a comeback right now, they are good for flat skateboarding, but you can't do new tricks on them, because they weren't designed for that. Without the right board, you just can't learn anything new.

Reading the Bible without the Holy Spirit is like trying to ollie (that's the name of a type of jump, for you nonskaters) on a skateboard without a kick tail. It's not good enough to just have a skateboard. Nor is it good enough just to have a Bible. You need a kick tail. And you need the Holy Spirit. The Bible was not designed for learning new things without the Holy Spirit's help. People who do study the Bible without the Holy Spirit's assistance end up confused and tangled over many issues. Yet, with His guidance we can learn more of God's love for us, and His plan for our lives becomes clearer and clearer. Use the right equipment. You'll accomplish much more.

Thanks, Holy Spirit, for being the kick tail in my spiritual life. Amen.

UNLOCK THE DOOR

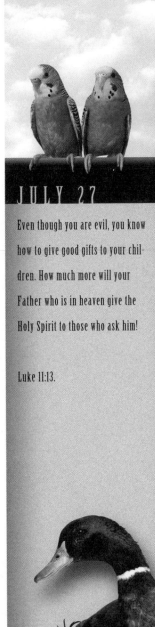

On this date in 1921 Fred Banting discovered injectable insulin. I'm especially glad he did. My aunt Yostie is a diabetic. A diabetic can eat or digest enough nutrition for their cells, and it can be floating around in their bloodstream, but the food can't get from the bloodstream to inside the cell. It needs a key to unlock the cell.

In my body I produce insulin, which unlocks the cell doors and lets the nutrition in. Aunt Yostie has never been able to produce insulin. Since she was a baby she has had to be injected with insulin. When her blood sugar gets high, Aunt Yostie gives herself a shot of insulin. It opens the cell doors, and the sugars in her blood enter the cells and nourish them, then her blood sugar comes back down. It drops too low when it is time to eat again. This makes her hungry, and she eats. Aunt Yostie has to pay careful attention to all that. I don't. My body just knows what to do.

God created our bodies in the beginning to know how to do everything. Spiritually He fashioned our minds to know how to live like Him too. But sin has damaged our minds. We need a dose of the Holy Spirit to act as a key to let the good things all around us in. Without the help of the Holy Spirit all kinds of wonderful things can be around us, but we won't be able to absorb them. I'm thankful that Fred Banting discovered insulin in 1921, but I'm even more thankful for the Holy Spirit.

Please come into my mind today, Holy Spirit, and unlock the door to my understanding. Amen.

Even though you are evil, you know how to give good gifts to your children. How much more will your Father who is in heaven give the Holy Spirit to those who ask him!

Luke 11:13.

IT'S EASIER WITH THE RIGHT TEACHER

JULY 28

But the Father will send the Friend in my name to help you. The Friend is the Holy Spirit. He will teach you all things. He will remind you of everything I have said to you.

John 14:26.

Carl was the first person in my group of friends to become a skateboarder. He became interested in skateboarding before books, magazines, and videos on the topic floated around our class and before other people were interested in it. He just took his skateboard out every day and practiced. It was nine months before he could ollie up a curb. Now there are three of us together who skateboard all the time. Working together, we can teach someone to ollie (jump with the skateboard) in a week.

Carl is frustrated because it took him so long to learn, and the new guys are picking it up so quickly. What's the difference? Carl didn't have a teacher. He had to learn by himself.

Thankfully, Jesus came to be our example, and He gave us the Holy Spirit to be our teacher. We don't have to learn the Christian life the way Carl did skateboarding. It doesn't have to be that hard. The Holy Spirit is willing to show us how to do it and to help us with every step along the way.

Jesus, thank You for showing us the way to live. Now please help me follow Your example. Amen.

214

THE RAINS CAME DOWN, AND THE FLOODS CAME UP . . .

JULY 29

I have put my rainbow in the clouds. It will be the sign of the covenant between me and the earth.

Genesis 9:13.

Today, as I write this, is a rainy day. Rain is a good thing. It helps my three grapefruit trees grow. I have been growing them from seeds I found in a grapefruit my aunt brought me from Florida, and they are an inch and a half tall now.

I'm not the only one who appreciates rain. I live in a farming community, and all the farmers are glad that the rain has come. Their corn is very dry.

After Noah's time, people feared the rain. Remembering the terrible Flood, they built the Tower of Babel as a place to escape to in case God ever sent another deluge. Because God promised He would never again destroy the entire world with a flood, His people didn't have to be afraid or worry about that.

Because I believe God, I don't worry about it either. Rain is good. It's OK to get a little wet. Not the end of the world, it will make the crops grow.

Thanks for taking the scariness out of my life, God. It's secure knowing that You're always with me. Amen.

215

I'M NOT WEIRD!
I'M A COCKATIEL!

JULY 30

But I will keep 7,000 people in Israel for myself. They have not bowed down to Baal. And they have not kissed him.

1 Kings 19:18.

For two and a half years, my cockatiel, Miss Cinnamon, has lived in my bedroom and the parakeet room. For a while she wasn't sure whether she was a human or a bird. But in time she came to decide she was a parakeet.

I always felt a little sorry for her. She probably thought she was just an extra-large and not-very-attractive parakeet.

When Mom's friend Tommy was finally able to go to Southwestern Adventist University, in Texas, he bequeathed Mom his two birds. Henry and Pretty Boy moved in.

When Mom opened the cage door, Henry flew out and perched next to Miss Cinnamon.

As the two cockatiels became inseparable, Miss Cinnamon started acting differently. It was as if she suddenly realized she wasn't a parakeet after all. She became very noisy. It was as if she was letting the whole world know, "I'm not weird! I'm a cockatiel!"

Sometimes when we think we're the only Christian in the world, we feel as if we're a little odd too. People do treat us differently, and we don't always fit in. That's why it's important for us to hang around with other Christians. Then we have someone to share our lives with, someone who goes through many of the same things as we do. Suddenly we can shout just like Miss Cinnamon, "I'm not weird! I'm a Christian!" It helps a lot when we Christians stick together.

Thanks, God, for giving me friends who feel the same way I do about You. Amen.

STEREOTYPES

Not all skateboarders have been courteous in their skating habits. And because of that, many skaters have a bad reputation. In fact, signs in many places say "No Skateboarding." That is because some skaters have left blue streaks on park benches from their skateboards. They can chip sidewalks from grinding on them. Such behavior destroys public property. As a result, many people view all skaters as a menace to society. It happens in my town. When they see someone with a skateboard, they automatically think he or she's a bad person, and they look around for the things the skateboarder might destroy.

But it comforts me to know that when God looks at me, He sees who I really am and not just what other people have damaged or what I might break if He looks the other way. He sees a kid that He likes. To be like Him we need to look past outward appearances and to appreciate people for who they really are too, and not judge them just by our prejudices against certain stereotypes.

Thanks for seeing who I am inside, God, and for loving me. I love You too! Amen.

JULY 31

But the Lord said to Samuel, "Do not consider how handsome or tall he is. I have not chosen him. I do not look at the things people look at. Man looks at how someone appears on the outside. But I look at what is in the heart."

1 Samuel 16:7.

BE CAREFUL WHAT YOU TRY TO TAKE TO MOROCCO

When my brother and I went on our band trip to Spain and Morocco, one of the new experiences that stuck in my mind was going through customs. Today is the anniversary of the beginning of United States Customs Service. Every country has some sort of customs service you must clear before entering. Each one has rules about what you can and cannot bring into the country. And the guards will go through your baggage, checking everything to make sure you have nothing illegal.

God even has a customs point for heaven. He will examine all of our baggage too. As we are getting ready for our trip and doing our packing, we need to get rid of anything that might not be acceptable to Him and might not make it through the pearly gates. Be careful what you pack. Do everything you can to be acceptable to God, but don't be afraid, because unlike customs in Morocco, God's customs service has grace.

Thanks for being gracious and understanding us poor sinful humans. We really do want to please You; it's just that we're unable to do it on our own. We need Your help. Lots of help! Amen.

218

TODAY IS THE REAL INDEPENDENCE DAY

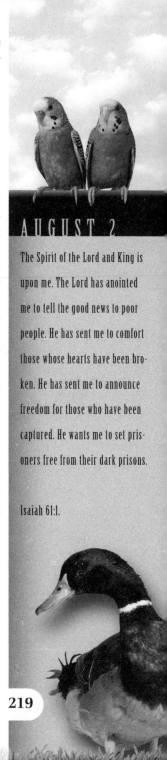

All Americans have learned about the Declaration of Independence proclaimed on July 4, 1776, but not many know that it didn't make a real legal difference until this date, August 2, 1776. On this day the patriots each made a personal commitment. They signed the Declaration of Independence.

It was fine for a rebel group to declare their independence, but to actually put their names on the line meant that should royalist soldiers catch them, they could be hanged for treason. It took courage to sign their names on the document, yet the document meant nothing without their personal commitment.

Jesus declared our independence 2,000 years ago when He stretched out His arms and died in exchange for our lives. But it's not real to you until you sign the bottom line. It is not your declaration of independence until you actually make a personal commitment to it. The fact that Jesus died for you is not good enough. You have to accept it. Sign the dotted line today.

Here I am, God. I want to sign up and declare my independence from sin and my dependence on You. Amen.

AUGUST 2

The Spirit of the Lord and King is upon me. The Lord has anointed me to tell the good news to poor people. He has sent me to comfort those whose hearts have been broken. He has sent me to announce freedom for those who have been captured. He wants me to set prisoners free from their dark prisons.

Isaiah 61:1.

YOU CAN'T SKATE IF ONE OF THE PIECES IS MISSING

AUGUST 3

The body is not made up of just one part. It has many parts.

1 Corinthians 12:14.

I guess all of us at one time have felt like we were unimportant and that life would be just the same even if we weren't here. And while those feelings are common, they aren't accurate.

When I look at my skateboard, I know that every single part of it is vital. Without wheels it wouldn't go. Without bearings the wheels wouldn't turn. Without the trucks there would be no place to mount the wheels on the board. And without the deck there would be no point in having it. I wouldn't have anywhere to stand. All of those are important parts, but even they're no good without a little bag of $3 nuts and bolts. They hold everything together.

Being part of the body of Christ is kind of like that. And even if you feel that God has made you only a tiny little nut, He still needs you to hold something important together. He needs you. Christ needs His whole body, and you're important to Him.

God, I'm glad that I'm important to You, even when I don't feel that important to myself. And I'm even more glad that You've got some important jobs for me to do. Amen.

220

OBSTACLES

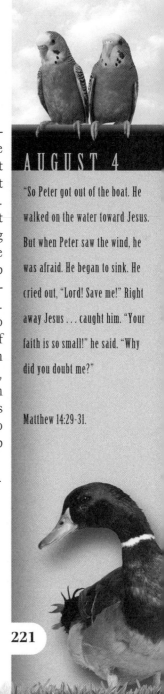

As my buddies and I practiced our skateboarding, we came to the place where we could ollie a foot and a half into the air at top speed, land, and keep going without falling over. It was time to add obstacles.

We found that even though we could jump a foot and a half when there was nothing in the way, adding a little obstacle like a three-inch piece of plastic pipe would make us fall. What was wrong? We could jump much higher than that. But the presence of the obstacle seemed to make it much harder than it really was.

I learned that to get over the obstacle I had to keep my eyes focused straight ahead and jump as if nothing were there. As long as I focus my gaze in front of me, I do fine. But when I look at the obstacle, I trip on it. Perhaps this is how we should deal with our obstacles in life too. As long as we keep our eyes on Jesus, we're going to be OK. It's when we forget to look at Him and dwell on the obstacle that we trip and fall.

Lord Jesus, help me keep my eyes always on You. Amen.

AUGUST 4

"So Peter got out of the boat. He walked on the water toward Jesus. But when Peter saw the wind, he was afraid. He began to sink. He cried out, "Lord! Save me!" Right away Jesus ... caught him. "Your faith is so small!" he said. "Why did you doubt me?"

Matthew 14:29-31.

YOU'VE GOT TO MASTER THE BASICS

Like babies that were just born, you should long for the pure milk of God's word. It will help you grow up as believers.

1 Peter 2:2.

My friend Matt likes to skateboard with Carl and me. But he gets hurt more often than Carl or I do. And there's a reason for it. Carl is very cautious, and I suppose I am moderately so. We practice the basics in his driveway for hours before we try the fancy stuff.

Matt is into extreme sports. The basics bore him. He started right away trying to ride his skateboard off a four-step porch. Naturally he crashed and burned.

Having high goals is good. Being willing to take on challenges is a good thing too. But it is important to master the basics and learn them well before you try to do it. God sent Moses to the wilderness for 40 years to master the basics before He let him lead the children of Israel. And He has sent me to school to learn the basics before He uses me in whatever way He decides to in this world.

Yes, I have high goals too. But I have learned from watching Matt that mastering the basics is vital.

God, please help me be patient while I'm learning the basics of life in You. Amen.

CHEAP CHURCH?

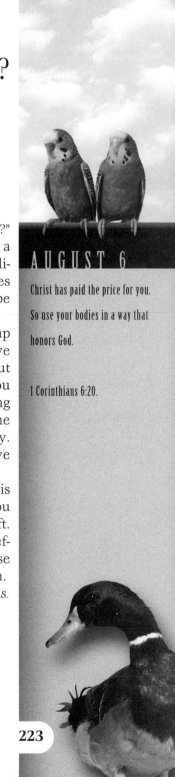

Why don't you pick an easier religion?" a friend once asked me. "Being a Seventh-day Adventist is so complicated. There are a lot of churches you could belong to that would be easier than that. Grace is cheaper at my church."

I smiled and looked at my skateboard. Cheap skateboards can be found these days. You don't have to spend very much for one if you don't want to, but cheap skateboards often don't roll straight. When you try to do tricks with them, you find the deck isn't long enough because it isn't the standard size. Often the bearings are sticky and haven't been oiled properly. Matt had one like that. Carl and I worked on it, but we couldn't fix it. You just need the real thing.

There is no true easy religion, either. And grace is not cheap, no matter how you look at it, when you consider what it cost God to offer it to me as a free gift. No, I'm not interested in an easy religion. With the effort and value that Jesus placed on me, my response needs to be the real thing, not some cheap imitation.

I'm glad You thought I was worth the effort, Jesus. Thank You! Amen.

AUGUST 6

Christ has paid the price for you. So use your bodies in a way that honors God.

1 Corinthians 6:20.

223

REVOLVING DOORS

Jesus answered, "What I'm about to tell you is true. No one can enter God's kingdom without being born through water and the Holy Spirit. People give birth to people. But the Spirit gives birth to spirit."

John 3:5, 6.

When I was a real little guy, revolving doors terrified me. I would bury my face in Mom's neck until we got through. When I got too big for her to carry me anymore, it put me in a terrible quandary. I was terrified of being in one of those compartments by myself and even though they were fairly small, I would try to jump in with Mom at the last minute. She would reach out to grab me and try to stop the door. We both fell down and generally made a spectacle of ourselves, amusing all the people around (except Dad).

Mom tried and tried to explain to me how the door worked and tried practicing with me going through it together again and again until I wasn't scared anymore. Then she would have me practice doing it on my own. But the next time we came to one, I would panic and jump in with her, and the whole thing would happen all over again. It was something I just had to learn to do by myself.

Getting into heaven is kind of like that. God allows people into heaven one at a time. Each person enters only because of his or her relationship with Jesus. I can't jump in at the last minute and get in because of Mom's relationship with Him. I have to have one of my own.

God, I want to know You myself, not just know about You from somebody else. Let's be friends today. Amen.

THE $500 PICKUP TRUCK

AUGUST 8

But here is how God has shown his love for us. While we were still sinners, Christ died for us.

Romans 5:8.

One of the things I've learned about life is that you get what you pay for most of the time. But there are exceptions. The exceptions seem to come with people who love you a lot. My brother was able to buy a fantastic little red pickup truck for $500. It even had a cap.

What was the catch? There wasn't any. It was a great truck that he bought from Grandpa. He got a lot more than he paid for, not because of Donnie's financial genius but because Grandpa loved him.

When you add love to the equation, none of the numbers make sense anymore. Think about it. It cost my parents more than $700 for me to be born and then to bring me home. But I wasn't able to do things around the house to help and wasn't much of a conversationalist. In fact, I couldn't do anything, yet they were willing to pay a whole lot of money for someone who could do nothing—because they loved me.

When God looks at me, He doesn't see some kid who is still in school and can earn only minimum wage and isn't worth much. He has placed such a high value on me that it was worth trading the life of His only Son in exchange for mine. The numbers don't make sense. But the value He puts on me tells me how much He loves me. It makes me love Him and want to be worth it.

I love You too, Jesus. Amen.

225

BUCKLE UP!

Jesus was in the back, sleeping on a cushion. The disciples woke him up. They said, "Teacher! Don't you care if we drown?" He got up and ordered the wind to stop. He said to the waves, "Quiet! Be still!" Then the wind died down. And it was completely calm.

Mark 4:38, 39.

On this day the first roller coaster built in the United States made its debut. Before inviting Jesus to be King of my life, life seemed like a real roller coaster, and it was scary. I love roller coasters, but the reason they don't scare me is because of the safety harnesses. Even when I ride on roller coasters that turn me upside down at high speeds, I know that the padded safety harness that comes down across my chest will keep me from flying out of the car and that I will end up safely at the end of the ride.

Life is a roller coaster, but Jesus is our safety harness. As long as we hold Him close to us, He will hold us firmly next to Him. While life may have lots of ups and downs and even turn us upside down once in a while, we can always lean on Him and He will get us safely to the end of the ride.

Don't forget our safety harness. Ask for it every morning.

Please strap me in today, God. Thanks! Amen.

226

WHAT IS IN YOUR HAND?

Recently I attended a concert with a bunch of my friends at the Nissan Center in Washington, D.C. It was a festival featuring many different bands playing many different types of contemporary Christian music. The adults in our group enjoyed some of the music. Other parts were a little heavy for them. My friends and I loved it all.

While some people might object to some of the music there, I don't think I do. I believe that music is a tool. God gives everyone tools. He expects us to use whatever He has given us to bring more honor to Him. If music is the tool that some people have received, then they need to use it to praise Him. When nursing is a tool, as my mom has, then they need to use that to bring honor to God.

Whether it be gardening and landscaping, or computer know-how, or whatever God gave you, remember God's question to Moses in the wilderness: "What do you have in your hand?" Take a look. What do you have? Use that to bring honor to God.

Please show me how to honor You today, God. Amen.

AUGUST 10

Moses answered, "What if the elders of Israel won't believe me? What if they won't listen to me? Suppose they say, 'The Lord didn't appear to you.' Then what should I do?" The Lord said to him, "What do you have in your hand?" "A wooden staff," he said. The Lord said, "Throw it on the ground." So Moses threw it on the ground. It turned into a snake."

Exodus 4:1-3.

227

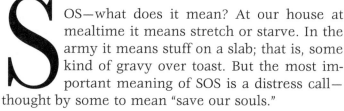

So he said to me, "A message came to Zerubbabel from the Lord. He said, 'Your strength will not get my temple rebuilt. Your power will not do it either. Only the power of my Spirit will do it,' says the Lord who rules over all."

Zechariah 4:6.

SOS—what does it mean? At our house at mealtime it means stretch or starve. In the army it means stuff on a slab; that is, some kind of gravy over toast. But the most important meaning of SOS is a distress call—thought by some to mean "save our souls."

Today is the anniversary of the first SOS call put out by an American ship. The ship was in trouble. Its crew had tried everything they knew to fix the problem, and now knew that without outside help, they were going down. They recognized it was something they could not handle on their own and that they had to turn to outside help.

We need to send out an SOS more often than we do. Often we try to handle by ourselves problems that are bigger than we are. We need to recognize that it's not something we can handle, and then turn to God and send out an SOS message: "Save our souls." It's what He specializes in—and He will. But we have to invite Him first. He does not force anything on us—even our salvation.

Take a hard look at your life. Can you really handle it by yourself? Then get on your knees and send out your SOS message. I'll see you in port.

Please save my soul, God. I can't do it myself. Amen.

228

KNOW YOUR ENEMY

I have a friend who doesn't believe the devil exists. He says that gives him great freedom and a feeling of safety because he doesn't have to worry about the devil all the time, as some Christians do. But I think it's a dangerous position.

Back in the early 1800s doctors did not believe in the germ theory. When Joseph Lister came along, wanting to use disinfectant in surgery, they made fun of him. They treated his germ theory as personal paranoia and thought he probably needed therapy. But Joseph Lister persisted and is the father of the antiseptics we use today.

The problem with those doctors was that because they didn't believe in germs, they did nothing to stop them, and the germs really had free reign to hurt their patients. Surgical mortality was extremely high during those days, as was the death rate of mothers delivering babies. Both dropped significantly once doctors started using Joseph Lister's disinfectant.

If you don't believe in Satan at all, then you do nothing to protect yourself, and he has free reign to mess with your life in whatever way he wants to.

Fortunately God gave us all the information we need. We don't have to wait until someone comes along and discovers it, as Joseph Lister had to. The Bible tells us everything we need to know to protect ourselves. While we don't have to fear Satan, we do need to believe he's there and to defend ourselves against him.

God, thanks for warning us about Satan. And thanks for protecting us from him too. Amen.

Control yourselves. Be on your guard. Your enemy the devil is like a roaring lion. He prowls around looking for someone to chew up and swallow.

1 Peter 5:8.

229

"STEE-RIKE THREE! YOU'RE OUT!"

AUGUST 13

Trust in the Lord with all your heart. Do not depend on your own understanding. In all your ways remember him. Then he will make your paths smooth and straight.

Proverbs 3:5, 6.

This day has been designated as Umpire Appreciation Day. Often the sports world does not appreciate umpires very much. They have a lot of hard calls to make and often don't see things the same way as the player involved in the problem. Players can blame all their problems on the umpire's poor eyesight. While sometimes umpires or people in authority do make mistakes and some bad calls, we have to accept it. If you aren't willing to submit to the umpire's authority, you can't play on the team. It also works the same way when you get a job.

I work part-time in a box recycling factory at my academy. The same rules apply there. If you aren't willing to submit to the authority of the manager, you can't work there. It even works that way with God. God is our umpire. He doesn't always see things as we do. In fact, sometimes His eyesight looks terrible to us from where we are, but we have to trust Him. And God, unlike my manager at work, is infallible. He doesn't make mistakes. But if I'm not willing to submit to my Umpire's authority, then I can't play on His team.

Come, be part of God's team. He's the most reasonable Umpire you'll ever have.

God, thanks for being completely fair. And thanks also for seeing the end from the beginning so clearly. Amen.

230

THIS ISN'T WHAT I PLANNED!

AUGUST 14

The Lord looks with favor on those who are godly. His ears are open to their cry.

Psalm 34:15.

Today is the birthday of the whiffle ball. The man who invented it assumed that the holes drilled in it would allow the air to pass through it, and therefore there would be less resistance, so it would weigh less but you could hit it just as far.

My mom bought two whiffle balls last week because of the holes in them. She was not interested in the lesser air resistance, but because she thought that Skippy and Wamml, our two parrots, would find it easier to hold onto the ball with their beaks.

Mom was delighted with the whiffle balls. She brought them home and gave one to Skippy and the other to Wamml. They were pleased with them too. But their ideas were different. They shook the ball a few times and realized there was a jingle bell in the middle, so they promptly sat down and ate the whiffle balls so they could get the bell.

Mom bought the whiffle balls because she wanted Skippy and Wamml to have fun—and they did. So she enjoyed it, even though it didn't turn out the way that she planned.

Life can be like the whiffle ball sometimes. Our plans make lots of sense to us, but when we put them into practice, sometimes they turn out totally different than we expected. We need to develop the ability to sit back and look at a situation, remember what our primary purpose is for life, and then laugh. Life is too short for us to take it so seriously that we're upset and angry all the time.

God, please help me to see all of my little annoyances from Your perspective. Amen.

231

WHAT WILL HEAVEN SOUND LIKE?

AUGUST 15

It is written, "No eye has seen, no ear has heard, no mind has known what God has prepared for those who love him."

I Corinthians 2:9.

My friends were having an argument the other day. "Do you think there will be contemporary Christian music in heaven?" someone asked.

"Yes," said one friend.

"No," replied another.

"Do you believe there will be Christian heavy metal in heaven?"

"Yes," one friend argued.

"No," protested another.

Soon a heated argument was going on. Everyone's opinion reflected the things they liked and how they saw God. I don't know what kind of music will be in heaven, but I truly believe that God accepts all sincere worship from any of us that we direct toward Him. Besides, heaven's technology will be awesome. Who wants to settle for just this kind of music?

God, I love You and want to find a creative way to praise You. And I can't wait to hear the music the heavenly choir makes! Amen.

232

BY THE BOOK

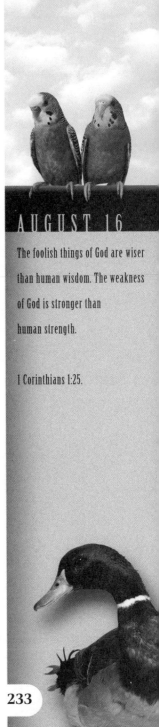

AUGUST 16

The foolish things of God are wiser than human wisdom. The weakness of God is stronger than human strength.

1 Corinthians 1:25.

Every once in a while it's not such a bad thing to be ignorant. I'll explain. My vet assured me that parakeets usually don't breed well in captivity. My parakeets, however, are extremely ignorant little birds, and having read no veterinary magazines or books, they breed like a herd of bunnies. I've had to give away more than 30 parakeets to friends, acquaintances, and anyone else who wanted one.

I have finches, too. My bird book says that finches are highly strung emotionally and that if you have a swing in your finch's cage, you should tie both sides down, or it will become frightened. Apparently my finches can't read, either. They love to play on their swings. Fred and Wilma, the Flintstones, play on theirs all the time, but Barney and Betty Rubble especially enjoy theirs, squabbling over it all day until it gets too dark, whereupon they both sit on top of it until it's light enough to play again.

According to the laws of physics, bumblebees shouldn't be able to fly either, but they do.

When God calls us to do something or gives us the opportunity to serve Him, it's important to just go ahead and do it. Don't worry about what the books say.

God, thank You for providing the power and ability to do everything that You ask me to do. And help me remember that when someone or something tells me that I can't. Amen.

233

WAMML'S WISDOM

Moses answered the people. He said, "Don't be afraid. Stand firm. You will see how the Lord will save you today. Do you see those Egyptians? You will never see them again. The Lord will fight for you. Just be still."

Exodus 14:13, 14.

One day while Wamml was still sitting on his perch on his cage (Wamml is not a morning bird and generally doesn't venture out to his climbing tree until the afternoon), Puff, in his travels, began exploring Mom's bedroom. He climbed up the bedspread and approached Wamml's cage. Puff has a little problem respecting property, and he climbed right up onto the cage as if he didn't know that it was Wamml's special territory. Wamml pulled himself up to the top one of his cage and perched there, glaring down at Puff and yelling for Mom.

Wamml could have handled the situation himself, although in a fight between a 42-inch iguana and an African gray parrot with a big hooked beak, I'm not sure whom I would vote for. But Wamml knew he would get into trouble, so he sat there shouting for Mom. As soon as Mom came in, she realized the problem and moved Puff back to his territory. Wamml's cage was his own again.

Sometimes people in our church family can be annoying too. But it is important for us not to take matters into our own hands. Just like Wamml, we need to wait for God to resolve it. If we do it ourselves, we may get hurt, as well as the person we're trying to straighten out, and we'll both get in lots of trouble. When in that situation, use Wamml's wisdom. Stay out of reach and call for help. Let God fix it. He will.

God, please help me to wait for You to solve the problems with the people that bother me. Amen.

234

A BALL OF BABY POSSUMS

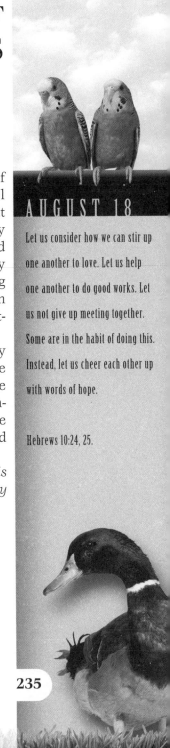

O ur baby possums easily learned lots of lessons. Even under their little flannel blanket that Mom put over them at night, they were still chilly. But they quickly discovered that if they could find their brothers and sisters and snuggle up, they had a much better chance of survival. Every morning we would pull back their little blanket and find them all curled up sleeping in a big ball of possum's with little noses and tails everywhere.

Possums aren't the only ones who do better by sticking together. Christians can too. Often we are much better off by staying together, even though we sometimes annoy each other, than by trying to venture off on our own. God intended for Christians to be together as a family and support each other, and surely we're at least as smart as baby possums.

God, please help me to remember how important it is to stick together with my spiritual family, even when they may annoy me. Amen.

Let us consider how we can stir up one another to love. Let us help one another to do good works. Let us not give up meeting together. Some are in the habit of doing this. Instead, let us cheer each other up with words of hope.

Hebrews 10:24, 25.

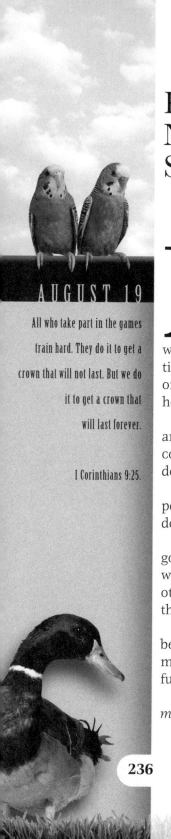

All who take part in the games train hard. They do it to get a crown that will not last. But we do it to get a crown that will last forever.

1 Corinthians 9:25.

KEEPING THE NEIGHBORHOOD SAFE FROM MOM

My brother and I love bike riding. We used to ride with Mom a lot until her car accident. Mom was riding her bike, and no, the car didn't hit her—she hit it. What added insult to injury was that it was parked at the time. Even more upsetting was that it wrecked her bike. She left scratches on the car. But the worst thing of all was that it was her car.

Mom's doctor told her she couldn't ride that bike anymore. Now she has one on a little stand in the corner of her bedroom that she pedals away on, but doesn't go anywhere.

Mom's bike was a good one, but no matter how expensive your bicycle is and how fancy it is, it doesn't do you any good without balance.

The Christian life is like that. It won't do you any good without balance either. In living the Christian way, it is just too easy to go off on one side or the other. It is vital to keep our eyes on Jesus and to ask the Holy Spirit for balance.

A speaker I heard at a writer's conference said it best. "The main thing is to keep the main thing the main thing," he stated. Here is the secret to successful Christianity.

God, please help keep me aimed at You and do not let me veer off one way or the other. Amen.

236

WATCH OUT FOR PARKED CARS

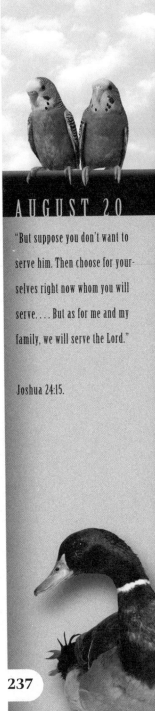

AUGUST 20

"But suppose you don't want to serve him. Then choose for yourselves right now whom you will serve.... But as for me and my family, we will serve the Lord."

Joshua 24:15.

Yesterday a car hit me—well, it seemed that way. Actually I was just trying to jump my skateboard. The jump went fine, it was the landing that did not work out well, and I careened into a car. Thankfully it was parked at the time. But it still hurt. Fortunately I was wearing my helmet, my knee pads, and my elbow pads, so even though I crashed into it pretty hard, I was protected from a concussion, cracked kneecaps, and broken elbows. However, even though I had protection, it did not keep me from having to face the consequences of my jump. Since I had hit someone's car, I had to talk to the person. I had to deal with the possible damage I had caused.

When we ask the Holy Spirit for His protection, He does protect us, just like my safety gear I wear when I skateboard. However, just because we've asked the Holy Spirit to safeguard us does not make us immune to any consequences of our choices after that. The Holy Spirit will often keep us from getting badly hurt, but if we make poor choices, we will still have to deal with the consequences. I wasn't hurt, but I had hit someone's car. That is why it is important to ask not only for the Holy Spirit's protection, but also for His guidance and wisdom as we make the many choices we face every day.

God, thanks for giving me Your protection. And thanks for offering guidance along the way so I don't need Your protection quite so much. Amen.

237

A HOME FOR THE BATTERED, BRUISED, AND NEGLECTED

AUGUST 21

Come to me, all of you who are tired and are carrying heavy loads. I will give you rest. Become my servants and learn from me. I am gentle and free of pride. You will find rest for your souls. Serving me is easy, and my load is light.

Matthew 11:28-30.

Our house feels like a retirement home for nonfurry critters. It's a haven of rest for animals with mental and physical difficulties. Wamml, our African gray parrot, arrived here after a life of neglect and feather plucking. Puff, our iguana, came to us from on top of Grandpa's woodpile, cold and starving and with dog bites. We acquired the Flintstones and the Rubbles, my two finch couples, because the first-grade teacher had asthma and was allergic to their feathers, so they became homeless. Mr. Kiwi had a broken wing and had been labeled a "problem bird." We have two of our three cockatiels because their owner went away to college.

Each one of these characters Mom has accepted, gently cared for, and brought back to health, and now they are all a part of the family and adore her.

I think heaven will be a lot like that. As you walk around it, everyone in heaven will have a story to tell, and like our critters and Mom, they will all focus on Jesus and how He saved them from all of their troubles. And I plan to be as happy in heaven as Mom's critters are here in our house.

Jesus, thank You for making a place for us to spend eternity away from the pain and problems we have here. Please come soon and take us there. Amen.

WHEN BIRDS GRIEVE

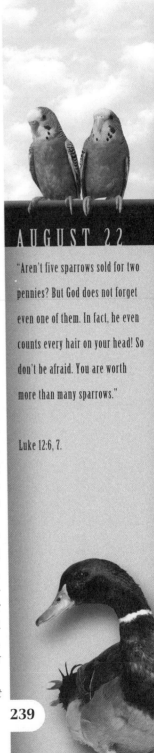

I have always wondered about Jesus' answer to the Pharisees when they asked Him about the widow in heaven (Matt. 22:23-33). It wasn't a very satisfying answer. What would happen to the widow? Then I got to thinking. The Pharisees were asking this question on purpose to trip Jesus up. His answer might have been different if it had been a concerned widowed person asking instead of someone seeking to catch Him in a mistake. I believe He would have been much more reassuring.

I have had some widowed parakeets come to my flock. Mr. Beckett was given to me after his mate escaped and he became so depressed that he wouldn't eat or play with the other birds. Miss Itchy lost her first mate before they were old enough to have a family, but she grieved for several months. I do my best to keep all of my parakeets contented, and I provide them with appropriate mates until they find someone they can be happy with.

If I care so much about my budgies, not only enough to make sure they have food and water and toys but an appropriate mate to share their lives with, then I can trust Jesus to be concerned about my happiness too. He made us and understands our need for a mate. So if He really has no plan for marriage in heaven, then He has something even better in mind. Because if I care that much about my budgies, I know He cares even more about me.

God, help me to trust Your choices for me, not just with a mate but in everything. Amen.

AUGUST 22

"Aren't five sparrows sold for two pennies? But God does not forget even one of them. In fact, he even counts every hair on your head! So don't be afraid. You are worth more than many sparrows."

Luke 12:6, 7.

"THAT'S NOT FUNNY!"

We have a high priest who can feel it when we are weak and hurting. We have a high priest who has been tempted in every way, just as we are. But he did not sin.

Hebrews 4:15.

Sometimes I watch *America's Funniest Home Videos* on TV, and a lot of them are very funny. But my mom occasionally gets all bent out of shape viewing them. Even though she is retired now, she still thinks like a nurse. She'll sit there and say, "That's not funny. He could get a serious head injury from that."

Last week one of the "humorous" episodes showed a sulphur-crested cockatoo, like my Skippy, except that he was naked but for the feathers in the middle of his back and the top of his head. He was a feather plucker.

I knew right away it meant that he was unhappy. Instead of biting the people around him who were making him unhappy, he pulled out his own feathers. The video clip showed him running back and forth on the back of a couch next to a man reading a newspaper. The bird danced and screamed, then fell off.

The people in the studio were convulsed with laughter as the bird danced even more and more frantically. It wasn't funny—it was pitiful. That poor bird obviously had serious emotional problems that had developed into physical ones. Most feather pluckers who get to that point eventually die of it. It made me wonder if some of the things that we laugh at appear as heartbreaking to God as the little cockatoo did to me.

God, I'm glad that You don't laugh at us when we hurt. Please teach me the same compassion for the people around me. Amen.

LIFE'S LITTLE VOLCANOES

O n this date in A.D. 79 Mount Vesuvius erupted in Italy, completely destroying the city of Pompeii. Mom has been to the ruins of the city of Pompeii and has shown me pictures of it. I became fascinated with volcanoes.

For my first-grade science project Mom and I built a volcano. I used wire and papier-mâché for the mountain and then fit a small cup in the top of the volcano for the volcanic bowl. Putting an acid and an alkaline together made a great volcanic eruption that would sputter and spatter and pour suds everywhere. I used baking soda and Coca-Cola, with a drop of red food coloring to make it look like red-hot lava.

I learned a lot from my volcano and was even invited to demonstrate it in children's church. It reminded me of my temper. Keeping your temper is hard, I said, but once it has blown (and I would set off my volcano), you cannot get all the lava back, and it hurts everyone around you. I did my project on a large plastic tablecloth so that it wouldn't stain the carpet on the floor in Sabbath school, but it was very obvious to everyone that you could not get all the foam and dribbles back into the volcano.

Life is like that too. Not only do you save yourself a lot of hurt and trouble by keeping your temper, but you prevent a lot of hurt to the people around you. It is much easier to hang on to your temper than to have to apologize to so many people afterward. Don't be a volcano. Ask for God's help, and hang on to it.

God, please help me to control my temper. Amen.

My dear brothers and sisters, pay attention to what I say. Everyone should be quick to listen. But they should be slow to speak. They should be slow to get angry. A man's anger doesn't produce the kind of life God wants.

James 1:19, 20.

241

I LOVE MY PASTOR BECAUSE HE'S MY FRIEND

No one has greater love than the one who gives his life for his friends.

John 15:13.

Many kids my age would say "I love my pastor because he is so great and he tells good children's stories." Pastor Rick Greve is an OK preacher, and his children's stories are good. But I don't love him because he is my pastor. He's my friend.

Near the end of my eighth-grade year, it began to look like I might be kicked out of school before the class trip. My mother was my only buffer, diffusing my frustration and thereby keeping me in school. Then she went into the hospital, and I was on my own. Things became worse at school. One day Mrs. Greve came to see my mom in the hospital. Mom told her that she was really worried about me. Instead of saying "Yes, we will pray for him," Mrs. Greve promised her that Pastor Rick would help me stay in school.

He did exactly that. He even took me golfing and out for ice cream while Mom was still in the hospital.

The school had invited Pastor Rick to come along on our class trip. He hadn't planned on it, because the day we were leaving was his wedding anniversary. But he came anyway—especially for me. Halfway through the class trip they could have sent me home if it hadn't been for him. He is really good at diffusing awkward situations and helping me not to feel so angry. Now we play basketball and lift weights together. On Sabbath he may be Pastor Greve, but on the other six days he's my friend Rick.

God, thanks for sending me a friend when I needed it the most. Amen.

242

FROM A LUMP OF COAL TO A DIAMOND

My brother and I have enjoyed putting all different kinds of rocks in our rock tumbler. But we learned something about types of rocks. One day we put in several different rocks and turned it on. When we checked it again, both the piece of slate and the piece of sandstone had completely disappeared. "Where did they go?" we asked. "How could they get out of here?" The thing had been shut tightly the whole time.

Mom laughed. She explained to us that slate and sandstone consisted of compressed sand, and as they tumbled against the harder rocks, they just crumbled apart.

My brother and I learned a lot as we played with our rock tumbler. As we looked things up in our nature books, we discovered other things about rocks. We knew that slate couldn't take tumbling in a rock tumbler. But in the ground, if slate was put under enough pressure, it turned into diamond. It reminded me of a bumper sticker I saw once that said that "the diamond is just a lump of coal that could take the pressure."

Sometimes when I feel like there is way too much pressure in my life, I think about slate and coal and diamonds. It may be hard now, but someday I'm going to be a diamond too.

God, sometimes I look at myself and see a lump of coal. But I'm glad You see a diamond. Now, please help me to remember that the problems I go through are just one of the ways You're using to make that big change. Amen.

AUGUST 26

You are tempted in the same way all other human beings are. God is faithful. He will not let you be tempted any more than you can take. But when you are tempted, God will give you a way out so that you can stand up under it.

1 Corinthians 10:13.

243

PROJECT GENESIS

I saw a new heaven and a new earth. The first heaven and the first earth were completely gone. There was no longer any sea.... He who was sitting on the throne said, "I am making everything new!" Then he said, "Write this down. You can trust these words. They are true."

Revelation 21:1-5.

In the *Star Trek* movies *Wrath of Khan* and *Search for Spock* the crew of the *Enterprise* worked on something called the Genesis Project. As they ejected the Genesis module and fired it toward the barren planet, it gave me goose bumps and also made my hair stand on end as I watched the planet transform from a barren nothing to sprouting trees and plants, animals, and becoming a habitable world. Is that anything what it was like watching God create the world? I don't know, but it must have been exciting.

According to the calculations of a professor at Cambridge University in England named John Lightfoot, Creation began at 9:00 a.m. on this date in the year 4004 B.C. That would make it exactly 6003 years ago, providing Professor Lightfoot was correct. Can you imagine sitting there with the beings from other planets watching as suddenly this shapeless ball of water developed dry land, an atmosphere, and started sprouting plants, animals, and finally people? Awesome!

What really excites me is knowing that I will someday find out just what it was like. For after this world is destroyed, God has promised He is going to create a new earth, and we will all be there to watch! It won't be a mystery anymore, and I bet it will be a whole lot better than the makers of *Star Trek* ever dreamed.

Jesus, I can't wait to see You make everything all over again. I know that it's going to be great living there with everything "very good." Amen.

"I'M THE SKIPPY. GOTTA LOVE ME!"

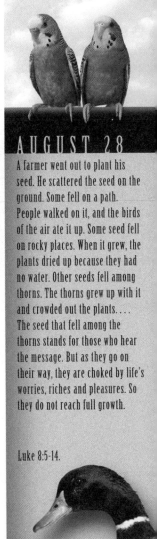

AUGUST 28

A farmer went out to plant his seed. He scattered the seed on the ground. Some fell on a path. People walked on it, and the birds of the air ate it up. Some seed fell on rocky places. When it grew, the plants dried up because they had no water. Other seeds fell among thorns. The thorns grew up with it and crowded out the plants.... The seed that fell among the thorns stands for those who hear the message. But as they go on their way, they are choked by life's worries, riches and pleasures. So they do not reach full growth.

Luke 8:5-14.

Skippy is our friendliest parrot. He will go to almost anyone, bob up and down, and beg for attention. The problem comes when they lose interest in him and want to continue their conversation or leave. Then Skippy screams and yells for attention.

Skippy needs a lot of work on his manners and maturity. He may learn better behavior with time, but a lot of Christians still act the same way toward God. As long as God is making them feel good, they love Him. But whenever they think He's not paying enough attention, they demand, "Are You answering my prayers, God? Where did You go? Don't You love me anymore?" Skippy reacts this way when we leave to get him food or a drink. God may be preparing something a person needs, but if God appears silent or inattentive, the individual becomes angry.

When Skippy does that, it's very annoying, yet I try to reassure him firmly that I do love him.

God is even more patient than I am with Skippy. And He tries gently to explain to us that many times when we think He is leaving us and not paying attention to us, He is actually in the process of bringing us even greater blessings.

We as Christians don't have to act like Skippy. We can grow up and just trust God, knowing that He loves us, instead of screeching and screaming and biting like a spoiled cockatoo.

God, I can be impatient and demanding at times. Please help me to remember that You're always paying attention, even if it doesn't seem like it to me. Amen.

245

HOW TO GET OUT OF YELLOWSTONE PARK

AUGUST 29

You can't be saved by believing in anyone else. God has given us no other name under heaven that will save us.

Acts 4:12.

When I was a little guy, my mom used to tell me stories about her trip to Yellowstone National Park as a child. She described bears begging for cinnamon rolls from passing cars, elk grazing along the side of the road, bad-tempered moose bounding through the shallows on the edge of the river and sending birds flapping in all directions, feeding little pieces of peanut-butter sandwiches to the friendly little marmots who lived under the cabins in the park camp areas, and deer grazing on the edge of picnic areas and watching the campers with a curious eye.

One of the funniest things Mom told me about was of their efforts to leave the park. The roads through the national park are fairly well marked, and many signs indicate the park entrances. But none point to the exits. After driving around for several hours, they figured out that since roads go both ways, you could exit the way you came in.

Unfortunately, life isn't that simple. It is a lot more like a city parking garage. You can't get out the way you came in. Jesus is the only exit. He is the only way out for humans to go without hurting themselves and others. Like a city parking garage, life may be huge and may have many entrances, but there is only one way out.

Jesus, I know that You are the Way and that You've left us a road map. Now please help me follow You more closely. I really want to get out of this world. Soon. Amen.

246

"YES, VIRGINIA, THERE *ARE* STUPID QUESTIONS!"

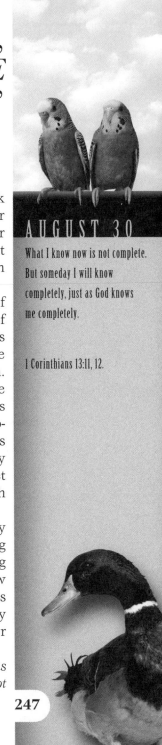

At Yellowstone National Park the park rangers keep a list of some of the sillier questions people have asked them. For example, "Does Old Faithful erupt at night?" "How do you turn it on?" "When does the guy who turns it on get to sleep?"

To the guides who care for the area and take care of the human traffic, the idea that humans have control of a natural phenomenon like the Old Faithful geyser is just laughable. The concept of a person in an office pushing a button to turn it on makes no sense to them. Yet many of us who have lived in cities can't imagine anything in nature as outside of human control. And as much as we might laugh about the questions some people ask, perhaps to God some of our own questions might seem even sillier. Questions that seem perfectly serious to us, such as "What if Jesus comes before I get a chance to get married?" "What if there is no such thing as marriage in heaven?"

Our minds are limited because we can think only in human terms. It would be like a 3-year-old trying to imagine what Disney World is like, never having been there. Yet God is patient with us. No matter how stupid our questions may appear, He never makes fun of us. He gently guides us and gives us as many answers as we can handle right now. God will never treat you as if you're stupid.

God, please help me to start to think in Your terms and to see things the way You do. And thanks for not making fun of my "stupid" questions. Amen.

AUGUST 30

What I know now is not complete. But someday I will know completely, just as God knows me completely.

1 Corinthians 13:11, 12.

247

AN AWESOME OLLIE

AUGUST 31

Suppose you can be trusted with very little. Then you can be trusted with a lot. But suppose you are not honest with very little. Then you will not be honest with a lot.

Luke 16:10.

A few days ago I was out skateboarding with my buddies. Carl, Matt, and I are pretty good on our boards. Brian was with us and trying to ollie. He was getting frustrated because he couldn't make his board leap very high. He struggled and struggled.

My buddies and I tried to help him. When we asked him to show us how high he could jump without being on his skateboard, he gave a little hop that looked about the same height as he could ollie.

"There is your problem," I said. "If you can't jump very high without a skateboard, then you won't be able to ollie high either. An ollie is more complicated. You have to start by practicing the smaller skills."

I've found that life is a lot like skateboarding. If you are having trouble with big things, chances are there are smaller parts of it that you need to master first. Once you get the hang of the smaller things, then the bigger ones will work out too. Too many people want to do big things for the Lord without being willing to do all the small stuff first. But the small stuff is often what the Lord uses to train His people for the big things.

I'd like to do awesome things for God—be a missionary pilot, save lives, something big. Doing my English homework wasn't exactly what I had in mind. Yet this is what God expects me to be faithful with right now, and the bigger stuff will come later.

God, thanks for having big plans for me. Now, please **248** *help me be patient and make all the necessary preparation. Amen.*

BOISE, OHIO?

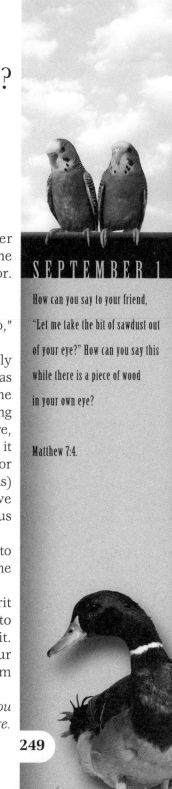

SEPTEMBER 1

How can you say to your friend, "Let me take the bit of sawdust out of your eye?" How can you say this while there is a piece of wood in your own eye?

Matthew 7:4.

S am Goldwyn, of Metro-Goldwyn-Mayer Studios (MGM), was an opinionated guy. One day he was talking with a newly signed actor. "Where do you hail from?" he asked. "Idaho," replied the actor.

"Out here, young man, we pronounce it Ohio," Goldwyn declared.

When we try to correct other people and we only think we know what we are doing, we look as silly as Sam Goldwyn did. Unfortunately, it happens a lot. One time my grandpa's Sabbath school class was arguing about God and Jesus and the Holy Spirit. As I sat there, I started to wonder if God was listening to this and if it was making Him laugh. We know so little about what or who He really is. How can we (as ignorant humans) make sweeping statements about Him? After all, we know for sure only what His Spirit and His Son Jesus have told us in the Bible.

Does the Father really get offended if we pray to Jesus instead of to Him? What about "Hear, O Israel, the Lord our God is *one*" (Deut. 6:4)?

The same thing also applies to playing Holy Spirit Junior and trying to tell others how God reacts to their behavior, when it is really how *we* feel about it. Jesus said, "Make sure you get the beam out of your own eye before you try to remove the speck from your brother's." Still sounds like good advice to me.

God, Jesus, and Holy Spirit, I really need all of You to help me and guide me as I try to live for You here. Amen.

249

ARE YOU SURE THIS IS THE MILLENNIUM?

No one knows about that day or hour. Not even the angels in heaven know. The Son does not know. Only the Father knows.

Mark 13:32.

O n this day in 1752 Britain became one of the last nations in Western Europe to adopt the Gregorian calendar. The Gregorian calendar is the one we currently use.

In 1582 the pope abolished the Julian calendar, the one Christians had used up until that time. He discarded it because every 128 years it became another day off. Pope Gregory XIII changed it to the calendar he humbly named the Gregorian calendar. However, Protestant nations refused to accept that calendar for quite some time. The Russians kept the Julian calendar until the year 1918.

This way of labeling the year is not how everyone has always looked at it or necessarily still does. On September 14 this year the year 7508 begins according to the Byzantine calendar. The Jewish calendar would call it year 5760 after September 10. In the Chinese calendar it is the year 4698. The Islamic calendar would label this the year 1421. But on the Julian calendar it would be the year 6713.

Some people are concerned that the world will end next year. It's important to remember that this is a millennial year only on the Gregorian calendar and not even necessarily 2,000 years from when Jesus was born.

As Christians, we should focus on our day-to-day walk with Jesus rather than on trying to figure out when the world will end. As long as we're walking with Him, it will be just fine.

Jesus, I want to be ready when You come back,
250 *whether that's next week or next year. Amen.*

WATCH OUT WHERE YOU STAND WHEN MOM GOES BOWLING

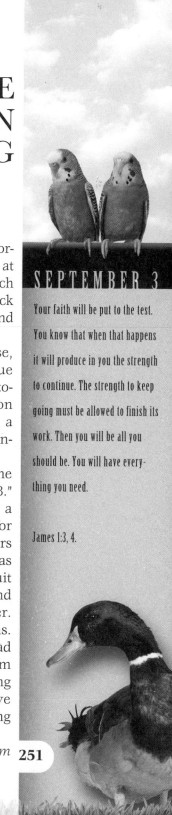

My mom always loved bowling. Unfortunately, she just wasn't very good at it. The first time a guy tried to teach her to bowl, she swung the ball back and it slipped right off her fingers and landed on his foot!

We have several bowling trophies in our house, because Mom persevered and found a bowling league to join in which other young moms like her got together to bowl. It even provided a nursery for Don and me to play in. The bowling league gave Mom a place to practice and play with other people who enjoyed bowling too.

My favorite bowling trophy is the largest one she won. It is 18 inches tall and says: "Lowest Average: 98." A relic of Mom's first year in the league, it holds a place of pride among her others, including a plaque for the highest score in the league (won several years later) and several 200 + pins and patches. Mom was able to win the other trophies because she didn't quit when her average was only 98. Without patience and perseverance she would have still been a lousy bowler.

Some of us don't feel very good at being Christians. Every time we try, we end up in trouble. Just as a bad bowling average will improve with practice and from meeting with the bowling league each week for a long time, so our Christian behavior will improve if we practice walking with Jesus and continue meeting each week with others who also love Him.

Jesus, help me to persevere when it doesn't seem worth the effort to follow You. Amen.

SEPTEMBER 3

Your faith will be put to the test. You know that when that happens it will produce in you the strength to continue. The strength to keep going must be allowed to finish its work. Then you will be all you should be. You will have everything you need.

James 1:3, 4.

"WHERE'S THE ELEVATOR?"

Those who trust in the Lord are like Mount Zion. They will always be secure. They will last forever.

Like the mountains around Jerusalem, the Lord is all around his people both now and forever.

Psalm 125:1, 2.

This has been designated as National Wilderness Week, a week for all couch potatoes (and tater tots) to get out and enjoy nature. It is surprising how ignorant some people are of God's wonderful creation! *The 365 Stupidest Things Said* has a list of real questions people have asked the Grand Canyon National Park rangers. I've included some of them below:

"Was this man-made?"

"Do you light it up at night?"

"I bought tickets for the elevator to the bottom. Where is it?"

"Is the mule train air-conditioned?"

"So where are the faces of the presidents?"

Seventh-day Adventists have an advantage when it comes to nature. We have one whole day set aside every week when we remember to honor our Creator and all the neat stuff He made for us. On it we can go out hiking and enjoying the things He fashioned and use the Sabbath hours to learn more about nature as we study it, play with it, and get our Pathfinder nature honors.

If I were God and had made everything out there, I would be hurt and offended if people didn't even notice it and knew nothing about it. To please God and honor Him as your Creator, get yourself outside this week. Appreciate nature. And remember while you are admiring the creation to thank the Creator!

God, thanks so much for all the effort You put in to making our world beautiful for me. Please help me to show my appreciation by taking good care of it. Amen.

NOT MUCH CRIME HERE EXCEPT FOR ALL THE MURDERS

SEPTEMBER 5

Everything that belongs to the Father is mine. That is why I said the Holy Spirit will receive something from me and show it to you.

John 16:15.

A recent mayor of Washington, D.C., had a few problems with his administration. We can say in his defense that Washington, D.C., had a lot of problems that were there before he took over, but when even the mayor is accused of breaking the laws, it is hard to enforce them on everyone else. The mayor once said, "Outside of the killings, [Washington] has one of the lowest crime rates in the country." Possibly so, but it makes no sense at all to consider crime while ignoring murder rates.

It would be like saying "Except for my little stealing problem, I'm a really good person." We can evaluate goodness only by including *all* the rules, whether it involves a city or personal behavior. What would you think if someone tried to buy an item that cost $1 and said, "I have the money I need for this—except for a dime." Very few stores would accept that as adequate payment!

Some people believe in the Ten Commandments and assume they keep God's laws—well, all but that Sabbath one. Yet Jesus asked us to show that we love Him by obeying *all* His commandments. That would include not killing, not stealing, and keeping the Sabbath.

If you choose to follow God and be His friend, go all the way. Don't be like the person who said, "I followed You and did everything You said—except for . . ."

God, I want to follow You all the way. Please show me what to do to please You today. Amen.

253

CHEER UP, YE PILGRIMS

Hearing good news from a land far away is like drinking cold water when you are tired.

Proverbs 25:25.

In the year 1620, 102 brave and frustrated people set sail from Plymouth, England. The Pilgrims were looking for a new world. They were so frustrated with life as they knew it that they were willing to brave incredible dangers to find a better place.

To see the replica of the *Mayflower* is a sobering experience. It's not very big. The upper deck has no protection from the weather, and down below, it is small, dark, and cramped. It is almost impossible to envision more than 100 people sharing that space for any amount of time. It gives us a new appreciation for what they were willing to go through to find another life.

One of my ancestors was one of those who survived the trip and started a family in the new world. When I look at the *Mayflower,* it makes me stand a little taller. In my veins flows the blood of people who weren't willing just to sit and complain about their circumstances, but who did what it took to make a better life.

Life can be frustrating for all of us. I know. It certainly gets frustrating for me at times. Yet what makes us who we are are not the difficult things that happen to us, but how we deal with them. How about you? Are you going to sit and complain, or are you going to do what it takes to make changes? Perhaps you might have to endure danger, but most of all you need to do something to make your life and your world a better place.

God, please show me what I can do today to make the world a little more like Your kingdom. Amen.

254

POW

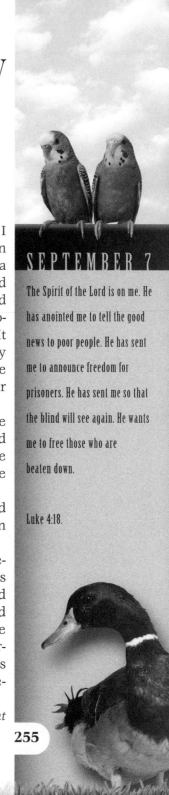

When I was 4 years old my mom and I went to the Vietnam Memorial in Washington, D.C. I was drawn to a man wearing camouflage fatigues and sitting at a card table. He said hi and offered me a pin for my jacket. It had the silhouette profile of someone looking down and said POW-MIA. (It stood for prisoner of war—missing in action.) I proudly told him that I knew what all those letters stood for. He had a bamboo cage next to his table. Four feet tall, four feet wide, and four feet long, it fascinated me.

I listened to him as he explained to Mom that the Vietcong had captured his buddy during the war and kept him in a cage like that one for three years. The man was unable to stand up or lie down in it. The Vietcong treated him cruelly.

I was horrified that anyone could ever be treated so meanly (though I wished I could have his cage in my bedroom for me to play in).

Satan has taken a lot of prisoners in the war between good and evil. He treats people as cruelly as possible. Yet, just as the man's buddy was rescued and brought to a place of safety where others could feed and care for him, so Satan's prisoners will be freed. Jesus sets some free now. Others He will liberate when He returns in the clouds and defeats Satan's plan to take over the world. Jesus came to bring freedom to the captives. What a wonderful Person!

Jesus, please come soon and make everything right again. Amen.

SEPTEMBER 7

The Spirit of the Lord is on me. He has anointed me to tell the good news to poor people. He has sent me to announce freedom for prisoners. He has sent me so that the blind will see again. He wants me to free those who are beaten down.

Luke 4:18.

255

"LET'S JUST SHOOT THE WOUNDED. THAT'LL CURE 'EM."

He stands up for those who are beaten down. He gives food to hungry people. The Lord sets prisoners free.

Psalm 146:7.

Edwin Meese, a Cabinet official in the Reagan administration, wanted to issue a tax on unemployment benefits at Thanksgiving time in 1982. When the press asked Mr. Meese about his rather hard-hearted stand, he said, "[We want to] make it less attractive to be unemployed."

Even though I can't remember Edwin Meese, I *do* remember what it is like to have my dad unemployed. While I kind of liked having him around for the first few days, it became one of the hardest times in our lives—his, mine, Mom's, and my brother's. It affected the whole family, and no one could have done anything to make being unemployed *less* attractive.

When God gave His laws to the children of Israel, He tried to impress on them again and again: "Don't kick people when they are already down." While He didn't use those exact words, He did forbid them from charging interest to poor neighbors who borrowed desperately needed money from them. He told them that if a poor person had to leave his or her cloak as collateral for a loan, they could not keep it overnight, but must give it back to the person so he or she had something warm to sleep in.

God cares about the unemployed, the single moms, and the kids without dads. If I want to be like Him, I need to treat such people with compassion and *not* go out of my way to make their circumstances "less attractive."

God, please teach me to see people and their situations the same way as You do. Amen.

THE ENERGIZER BUNNY

In September of 490 B.C. the Battle of Marathon, between the Greeks and Persians, took place. The smaller Greek force won, but other Persians were on their way to attack the city of Athens. The Greeks at Marathon realized that the people of Athens were not soldiers and could be overwhelmed by the Persians. They also knew that if they could get the message of their victory to them, the Athenians would probably hang in there and resist until reinforcements arrived.

According to legend, a Greek soldier ran from Marathon to Athens. Twenty-six miles at maximum speed without pacing yourself can be fatal. It was to the soldier. He did arrive in Athens, and as he collapsed in the town square, he is supposed to have gasped, "Rejoice, we are victorious!"

Living the Christian life is like a marathon. It isn't a onetime event—a short sprint. We have to keep going and going and going like the Energizer bunny. Sometimes it just seems too far, and yet, by our example, we can bring hope and victory to others too. This may be what Paul meant when he wrote our text for today. He was old and in poor health as he waited in jail for his execution. Yet he wrote: "There is laid up for me a crown of righteousness which the Lord, the righteous judge, shall give me at that day: and not to me only but unto all them also that love his appearing" (KJV). That means me. That means you. Just keep going. The end is almost in sight.

God, please come soon and fix this mess. And please give me the strength to hold on until You do. Amen.

I have fought the good fight. I have finished the race.... Now there is a crown waiting for me. It is given to those who are right with God. The Lord, who judges fairly, will give it to me on the day he returns. He will not give it only to me. He will also give it to all those who are longing for him to return.

2 Timothy 4:7, 8.

257

No one's ears have ever heard of a God like you. No one's eyes have ever seen a God who is greater than you. No God but you acts for the good of those who trust in him.

Isaiah 64:4.

THE BIGGEST, THE BEST, THE FASTEST, THE TALLEST, THE FARTHEST

Did you know that the largest leaves of any plant belong to the raffia palm? The leaf blades measure up to 65 feet in length. Did you know that the tallest grass is the bamboo and it can grow to 12½ feet tall? Did you know the largest butterfly is the Queen Alexandra birdwing, from Papua New Guinea, which can have a wingspan of up to 11 inches?

I didn't either until I started reading the *Guinness Book of Records* with my cousin Eric. Eric and I had a great time citing incredible records to each other. How about the longest species of earthworm, 22 feet long, collected in South Africa? I'd like to see a bird try to eat that one.

The oldest living person, according to the 1995 edition, was Jeanne Louise Calment, born in France on February 21, 1875. She lived to be 122, dying in 1997. But the Bible tells us of someone who lived much longer. Methuselah lived to be 969 years old. The *1995 Guinness Book of Records* gives the oldest reported age for a woman to become a mother as 63. But Sarah had Isaac in her 90s.

The *Guinness Book of Records* is fascinating, but it covers only the period of time since its editors have been around to validate and measure the various records.

I can't wait till I get to heaven and am able to find some of the real records. I think Eric and I will have a ball discovering who was the fastest, the oldest, the biggest, could run the farthest, jump the highest, and throw the farthest.

I can't wait to have fun with You in heaven, Jesus. Please come get us soon! Amen.

HAVE A DIRTY, NO-GOOD, LOUSY, ROTTEN, BAD DAY

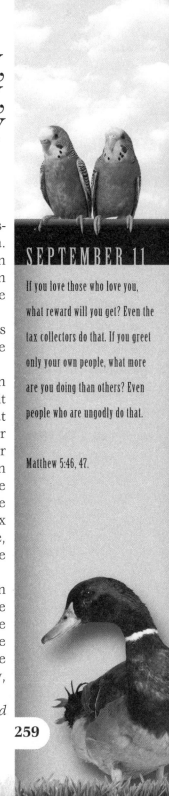

I found a funny quote by Hugh Durham, a basketball coach from the University of Georgia. He said, "It's not how good you can play when you play good. It's how good you play when you play bad, and we can play as bad as anyone in the country."

Perhaps it doesn't matter how we act as Christians on good days. Perhaps what really makes a difference is how we act when we are having a bad day.

Jesus said something similar, though He stated it in a way that made more sense. "You have heard that it was said, 'Love your neighbor. Hate your enemy.' But here is what I tell you. Love your enemies. Pray for those who hurt you. Then you will be sons of your Father who is in heaven. He causes his sun to shine on evil people and good people. He sends rain on those who do right and those who don't. If you love those who love you, what reward will you get? Even the tax collectors do that. If you greet only your own people, what more are you doing than others? Even people who are ungodly do that" (Matthew 5:43-47).

Anyone can be nice to someone they like or when they are having a good day. What really counts is if we can be nice to people when we are having a terrible day, and if we can be nice even to people whom we don't like. The way people will really be able to tell we are friends of Jesus is by how we act on those dirty, no-good, lousy, rotten bad days!

God, please help me to be like You all the time, and not just when it's easy. Amen.

SEPTEMBER 11

If you love those who love you, what reward will you get? Even the tax collectors do that. If you greet only your own people, what more are you doing than others? Even people who are ungodly do that.

Matthew 5:46, 47.

259

WHEN KETCHUP WAS A VEGETABLE

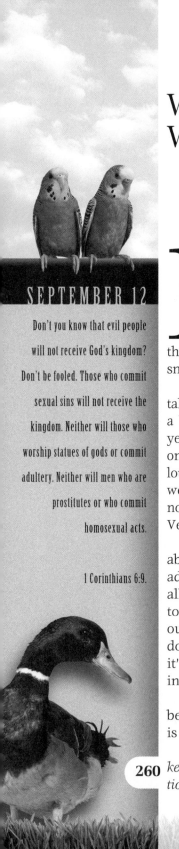

Don't you know that evil people will not receive God's kingdom? Don't be fooled. Those who commit sexual sins will not receive the kingdom. Neither will those who worship statues of gods or commit adultery. Neither will men who are prostitutes or who commit homosexual acts.

1 Corinthians 6:9.

During the Ronald Reagan presidency, nutritionists could consider the school lunch program as balanced only if they counted ketchup as a vegetable. George Bush didn't even try to pretend, announcing that he hated broccoli and that his favorite on-the-road snack was fried pork rinds and Tabasco sauce.

Hopefully, as young Seventh-day Adventists, we will take our nutritional advice from better sources! We have a big advantage when it comes to diet. More than 100 years ago Mrs. White gave our church a lot of information on healthy nutrition. We have had it long enough that a lot of us take it for granted and don't even follow it very well. It comes as a big surprise to us that other people are now teaching the stuff we knew about so long ago. Vegetarianism is becoming very popular in the world.

God has given us all that we needed to know about salvation in the Bible. Some of His nutritional advice is in there too. He didn't keep it a secret! It is all right there for us, if we just look. God expects us to be smart enough to do our homework and to find out who knows how to give food advice and who doesn't. If we end up thinking ketchup is a vegetable, it's not His fault! How good of Him to make all that information available for anyone who wants to know.

Since my body is His temple, it seems that the best advice would come from the architect, and that is the advice I plan to follow.

Thank You, God, for all the best information. Please keep reminding me where to go when I've got other questions about life. Amen.

PUNCTUATION COUNTS

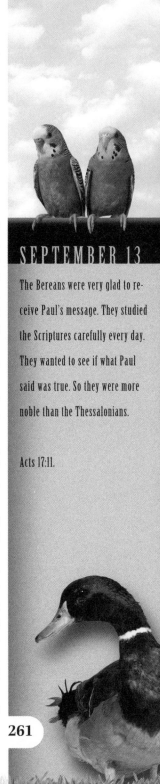

A friend of mine was trying to convince me that what Jesus said to the thief on the cross was proof that people go straight to heaven when they die. Since there was very little punctuation used in Aramaic or Greek (the first and second languages that New Testament people spoke), Jesus' statement could have been taken to mean "I say to you today, You will be with me in Paradise" instead of "I say to you, Today you will be with me in Paradise."

See what I mean? It reminds me of a couple newspaper headlines I saw that could have meant something else if they had been punctuated differently:

"Fire at Mount Pleasant Causes Small Damage Starts in Wastepaper Basket Occupied by Two College Students" (Wyandotte *News*, Michigan). (What were those students doing in a wastepaper basket?

"Government to Concentrate on Exterminating School, Sex, Organized Violence Next Year" (Korea *Times*). (Exterminating school? Let's get out of here!)

Punctuation *does* count, and without it we sometimes have to see what the rest of the Bible has to say in order to understand the exact meaning of a text. It *never* hurts to compare everything the Bible teaches on a subject. Smart Bible students will do their homework before accepting anything another person says. The new Christians in Berea were like that, and God was pleased. They searched the Scriptures carefully.

Dear God, please help me to do my homework before just accepting what other people think You said. Amen.

SEPTEMBER 13

The Bereans were very glad to receive Paul's message. They studied the Scriptures carefully every day. They wanted to see if what Paul said was true. So they were more noble than the Thessalonians.

Acts 17:11.

Trust in the Lord with all your heart. Do not depend on your own understanding. In all your ways remember him. Then he will make your paths smooth and straight.

Proverbs 3:5, 6.

GOING NOWHERE BUT MAKING GOOD TIME

My brother is going through the agony-and-ecstasy experience of being a senior. He is one of the hotshots on the campus, but also is having to figure out what he wants to do next year—where he wants to go to school and what he wants to major in. That means figuring out what he might want to do for a living. Tough stuff! He isn't the only one who is having a little trouble finding some direction in life.

Woody Harrelson said, "My main hope for myself is to be where I am." Now, there is an achievable goal!

Claudia Schiffer walked into an occupied elevator, hit a button that didn't light up, and continued to hold down the button. A man asked her, "Where do you want to go?"

"I don't know," she replied. "I've never been there."

Still others realize that they haven't a clue but are trying to get there as fast as they can. Phil Rizzuto, in a car with Yogi Berra (both oldtime baseball players), driving to a banquet, said, "Yogi, we're lost."

"Yeah," Yogi replied, "but we're making good time."

When it comes down to the final analysis, who cares if we are making good time if we are lost? Fortunately, God promised us help with our big decisions in life. Since my brother is one of His friends, I know he'll make a wise choice.

Dear God, thank You for being willing to direct our paths. Amen.

TURNING POINTS

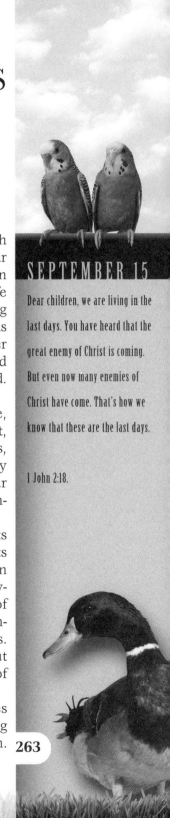

On this day in 1940 was what the British consider the turning point in World War II. The Germans planned an air invasion of Britain. Wave after wave of Luftwaffe flew across the British Isles, dropping tons of bombs. But the British don't commemorate this day for the destruction that took place. They remember the bravery of their Royal Air Force pilots who destroyed 185 German aircraft that day. Britain was not invaded. Eventually the Allies defeated the Axis powers.

The important thing to remember about this date, in my opinion, is that although it was a turning point, still the war didn't actually end for five more years, and the Nazis continued to hold the territories they had conquered for quite some time. Prisoners of war continued to be prisoners, and many died in concentration camps. Soldiers continued to fight.

In the war between good and evil, Calvary was its turning point. Until that time, humanity had given its allegiance and obedience to Satan. Jesus' death on Calvary was our declaration of independence for anyone who chose to accept it. But it was not the end of the war. Satan still has prisoners. Many people continue to be mistreated in his concentration camps. Brave soldiers continue to fight the battle and die. But Calvary was still the turning point. Jesus, the king of the universe, is going to win the war.

Feel like a prisoner of war behind enemy lines sometimes? Take courage. We're past the turning point. The end is in sight, and our side is going to win.

Dear God, You are my hero! Come quickly. Amen.

Dear children, we are living in the last days. You have heard that the great enemy of Christ is coming. But even now many enemies of Christ have come. That's how we know that these are the last days.

1 John 2:18.

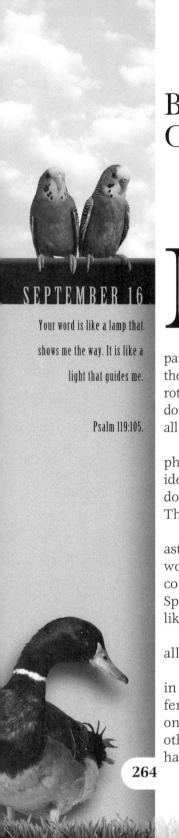

SEPTEMBER 16

Your word is like a lamp that shows me the way. It is like a light that guides me.

Psalm 119:105.

BUNGLED FLIGHT OF THE NAVIGATOR

My family and I were on a trip to Virginia Beach. I had read in my bird magazine that there would be a parrot convention near there, but forgot the magazine that listed the meeting.

We searched and called everywhere, trying to find the parrot meeting. The first time dad talked to the person at the local chamber of commerce and asked where the parrot convention was being held, she said rather stiffly, "We don't call them that here. You will find their celebration all along the beachfront," and hung up on him.

When he called her back, she was even more emphatic. "The chamber of commerce supports our residents and visitors of Latin American descent, and we do not appreciate those who call them parrotheads." The third time she wouldn't talk to him.

Finally we gave up trying to find the bird enthusiasts and went to the beachfront. There we found a wonderful party to honor several Latin American countries that had gained their independence from Spain in 1821. Also I discovered that people who didn't like Hispanics called them "parrotheads."

I had a good time seeing the sights and tasting all the awesome food they were serving.

In life those who lose their directions can end up in big parties too but the consequences are much different. I missed just the parrot convention (the *real* one). Others are missing eternal life. I will have another chance to attend a parrot fest, but they will not have another opportunity after the final judgment.

264

Thank You for being my navigator, God!

DON'T FORGET YOUR SIGNATURE

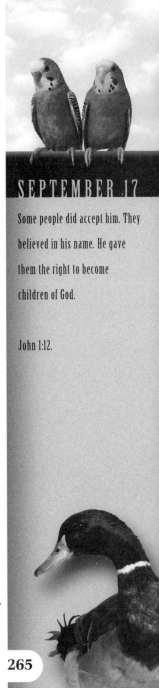

Some people did accept him. They believed in his name. He gave them the right to become children of God.

John 1:12.

On this day in 1787 the delegates to the Constitutional Convention in Philadelphia completed the American Constitution, and a majority of them signed it. When I was a little guy, my mom took me to see it.

Even though we celebrate the Fourth of July as the day our country's independence was made available to all those who chose to be Americans, the people didn't really have their freedom and live under the Constitution that we have today until the delegates to the convention were willing to put their names on it. Representatives from nine states had to sign the Constitution in order for all to be a part of it.

God wrote our constitution in the New Testament. It spells out our rights and responsibilities. It makes it possible that we, who are Gentiles, can be adopted and have the same rights and the same treatment as God's children by birth. Our constitution in the New Testament guarantees those rights to all of us who choose to be His citizens. It happened 2,000 years ago. What didn't happen then was the signing. Until you put your name on the bottom line and choose to be a part of God's family, the constitution does not apply to you. You have a choice. It counts only if you sign on the dotted line.

Thank You for inviting me to sign up to be part of Your family. Amen.

CONSTRUCTING WITH CORNERSTONES

You are a building that is built on the apostles and the prophets. They are the foundation. Christ Jesus himself is the most important stone in the building.

Ephesians 2:20.

O n this day in 1793 President George Washington laid a cornerstone for the Capitol building, in Washington, D.C. As with all the other important historical stuff in Washington, my mom took me down there to see it. It is huge. It wasn't until later that I learned a little more about its construction.

Where weight-bearing walls meet, they have to cope with extra pressure. It is important to use strong materials. The farther down the building you go, the more pressure is on the materials. So the strongest piece of material in the whole building needs to be the cornerstone at the bottom. Builders have known this for thousands of years.

The Bible talks about Jesus being our cornerstone. Unfortunately, not everyone has chosen Jesus as their cornerstone on which to support the rest of the structure of their lives. Even Jesus referred to Himself as the cornerstone the builders rejected. Each of us is building our own life today. And many are still rejecting Jesus, the strongest cornerstone ever known to humanity. We've seen people build their lives on money, fun, and many other things. And we've seen many lives crumble around people's ears. The materials in them weren't strong enough.

Jesus is still available to be your cornerstone. Don't let Him be the cornerstone you rejected. Build your life on the only thing strong enough to hold it up.

Dear God, please let Jesus be my cornerstone. Amen.

BACON OR BLESSING

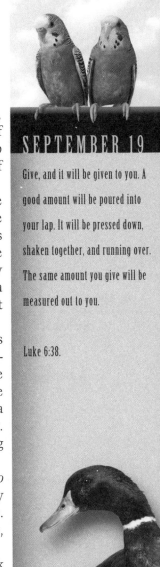

SEPTEMBER 19

Give, and it will be given to you. A good amount will be poured into your lap. It will be pressed down, shaken together, and running over. The same amount you give will be measured out to you.

Luke 6:38.

This is Farm Animals Awareness Week, sponsored by the Farm Animal section of the Humane Society. Its goal is to help people appreciate the unique qualities of farm animals.

My brother and I started out as city people. We were born in the Chicago suburbs, so our lives were pretty civilized. Then Donnie started preschool. His first field trip was to a dairy farm. Afterward he came home very cynical. As I lay on the floor drinking my bottle, he raised an eyebrow as he stared at me for a moment, then shook his head and said, "You wouldn't drink that if you knowed where it came from!"

When I was in second grade, my parents moved us from the suburbs of Washington, D.C., out to the middle of nowhere: Timberville, Virginia. We live in a wide spot in the road between two cow pastures. Timberville is getting pretty civilized, though, now that we have a post office, a gas station, and even our own traffic light. Out here, farm animal awareness means watching where you step when walking across the field!

When we had to read the first chapter of *Steps to Christ* in school, I did notice one thing that really stands out about farm animals. They all help others. No farm animal lives just to be selfish—and if it does, it ends up being bacon!

Perhaps during Farm Animals Awareness Week we should take a look at our lives. Do we live to help others? Or are we being pigs? The choice is up to us.

Dear God, please make me a blessing to those around me. Amen.

267

UNQUOTABLE QUOTES

SEPTEMBER 20

Jesus replied, "You are mistaken, because you do not know the Scriptures. And you do not know the power of God."

Matthew 22:29.

Bill Clinton, while criticizing antigovernment protesters during his campaign, said, "The last time I checked, the Constitution said, 'of the people, by the people, and for the people.' That's what the Declaration of Independence says." My history class taught me the phrase actually came from Lincoln's Gettysburg Address.

I have learned that it is not just presidents that can be misinformed sometimes. It is always good to do your homework before you believe the things you hear. As an Adventist kid, I have heard many quotations from the famous, but nonexistant, book *Ellen White Says* . . . . The trouble is, many times she didn't ever say a certain thing, but has been quoted so many times that people think she did! Some famous "Ellen White says" statements that she didn't make include:

We will have Sabbath lunch on a planet on the way to heaven.

Ellen White will be one of the 144,000.

Christ will come at midnight.

Who the president of the United States will be just before the Second Coming.

I have learned that it is very useful to have a set of the Ellen White indexes. You can use them like a Bible concordance to check out EGW quotes. It is important to do your homework. Check things out. Use your Bible. And don't forget to ask the Holy Spirit for help.

Dear God, thanks for giving us resources to find out what is really true. Amen.

268

ONLY THE LONELY

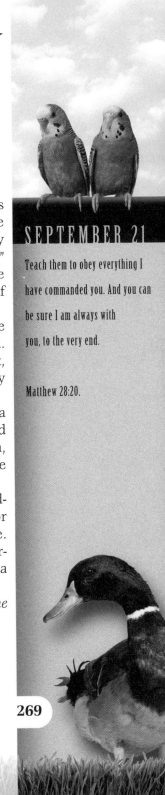

George Steinbrenner, New York Yankees owner, once describing his favorite pitcher, said, "David Cone is in a class by himself with three or four other players." Though that was a silly thing to say (if he had thought about it), often God's people have felt as if they were the only ones still loyal to Him.

Elijah was the only representative of God before 450 prophets of Baal and 400 prophets of Asherah. When he later complained to God how alone he felt, God told him there were 7,000 people in the country who had not bowed their knees to Baal.

I learned on the Internet that if you are one in a million, then there are 260 other people in the United States just like you. And if you are one in a billion, then you will have nearly seven other people in the world just like you!

Senator Orin Hatch once quoted what he considered a stupid courtroom question: "Were you alone or by yourself?" Believe it or not, there *is* a difference. As friends of Jesus, we may sometimes feel by ourselves but we will never be alone. Perhaps it wasn't a stupid question after all.

Dear God, thank You for promising never to leave me alone. Amen.

SEPTEMBER 21

Teach them to obey everything I have commanded you. And you can be sure I am always with you, to the very end.

Matthew 28:20.

ONE LIFE TO GIVE

But suppose you don't want to serve him. Then choose for yourselves right now whom you will serve. You can choose the gods your people served east of the Euphrates River. Or you can choose the gods the Amorites served. After all, you are living in their land. But as for me and my family, we will serve the Lord.

Joshua 24:15.

O n this day in 1776 Nathan Hale, an American patriot or a treasonist rebel, depending on your point of view, was hanged. The Loyalist forces of King George III executed him for treason. Americans consider him a great hero. He is best known for his famous last words. As they fastened the rope about his neck, he said, "I only regret that I have but one life to lose for my country."

Considering the barbaric suffering that hanging often caused, they were pretty noble words. But that's all they were. We remember Nathan Hale and his words, but his death didn't change anything.

Jesus had only one life to give too. But unlike Nathan Hale's, His life was enough to make a difference. When Jesus died, Satan lost the war. Everything bad that happens from now until the end is just his being a poor loser and hurting God's kids as much as he can before it's all over.

Why isn't it finished yet? Because not everyone has chosen the government they want. People are still making a choice. Are they going to be loyal to the King of the universe, or are they going to be rebels? Are they going to do things their own way and end up being dominated by the prince of darkness? The war continues only until everyone has made their choice. But whatever happens, Jesus' life was enough to make the difference. His death guaranteed your freedom. Do you want it? Just reach out and accept it. He died for you. It's all yours.

Thank You, Jesus. Amen.

MACHO COMMACHO'S MATH BOTCHO

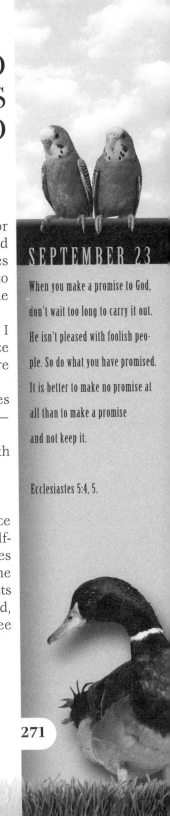

I read a quote from a fighter named Hector Macho Commacho that made me think he had hit his head once too often—or else he does math like my brother. Speaking of his return to the ring, he said, "I can happily say I've made a 100-degree turn in my life."

Since math isn't my problem area at school, I know that it takes 180 degrees to make an about-face turn. A 100-degree turn would be just a little more than half an about-face turn.

Unfortunately, a lot of conversions and promises to God are 100-degree turns. You know the type—often made under duress:

"God, if You will just get me through this math test, I'll do anything You want me to . . ."

"God, if You will just make her like me, I'll . . ."

"God, if You will just . . ."

Often God does exactly what we asked, but once the crisis is over, we forget, or we make only a half-hearted attempt at what we promised. But God takes us seriously. Be glad—sometimes He is the only one who does! When we promise something, He expects us to follow through on it. If you are turning to God, don't be like Macho Commacho. Make a 180-degree turn! Go all the way!

God, help me to be Yours—all the way! Amen.

SEPTEMBER 23

When you make a promise to God, don't wait too long to carry it out. He isn't pleased with foolish people. So do what you have promised. It is better to make no promise at all than to make a promise and not keep it.

Ecclesiastes 5:4, 5.

EXCUSES, EXCUSES

SEPTEMBER 24

The man said, "It was the woman you put here with me. She gave me some fruit from the tree. And I ate it." Then the Lord God said to the woman, "What have you done?" The woman said, "The serpent tricked me. That's why I ate the fruit."

Genesis 3:12, 13.

People have been making excuses for behavior since the Garden of Eden. Some recent creative ones:

"It wasn't a shark attack, but a shark accident. More than likely he ran into [the swimmer's] leg, and it got caught in his mouth" (an explanation by town spokesman Joe Rubio to try to explain away rumors that a shark had attacked a woman while she was swimming off South Padre Island, Texas).

Someone saw Representative Martin Hoke on the House of Representatives floor with his eyes closed during the debate on the Republican Contract With America. When it was reported, his aide replied, "It's not true [the Congressman was sleeping during the debate]. He was just taking a few moments for deep reflection." Yeah, right. My mom calls it "just resting her eyes."

God is looking for people who will tell the truth—or even if it hurts the tourist industry or makes them look bad. It takes a stronger man or woman to tell the truth than to make up a quick excuse. Stand up and admit the truth—even if it is unpopular. God will be pleased with you—and let's face it, who else's opinion is really more important than His?

Dear God, please give me the courage to always be truthful—even if it hurts. Amen.

272

SPEAK BEFORE YOU THINK . . . WAIT . . . NO . . .

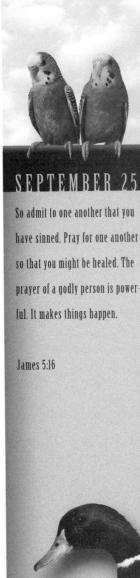

SEPTEMBER 25

So admit to one another that you have sinned. Pray for one another so that you might be healed. The prayer of a godly person is powerful. It makes things happen.

James 5:16

A headline from the Little Rock, Arkansas, *Gazette* read: "Minister Suggests Ladies Take Off Miniskirts in Church." Of course, I can just imagine the hullabaloo that would occur in my church if a bunch of girls and women took off their miniskirts. Most of the women in my church wear really long skirts, but if they did take his suggestion, let's just say that it wouldn't go over well here!

I am sure that the well-meaning minister never intended his suggestion to come out the way it sounded. (That's why the newspaper staff took such delight in publishing it!) Often when we try to change people's behavior by telling them what they should do instead of praying for them and asking the Holy Spirit to help them make a decision, we find ourselves misunderstood too. Often it results in tears and anger and hurt feelings. Sometimes it even leads to people not coming to church anymore.

I thoroughly believe that if we spent as much (or more) time talking to God about the offending person as we do talking *about* them and *to* them about their problem, we'd have more changed behavior in our churches than we do now. The Holy Spirit is much better at handling people's feelings than we are. Not only that, it is *His* job, not ours.

Should I care? Yes, it is my church too. But I should be telling God about my concerns, and not other people's.

Dear God, help me to talk about things to You first. Amen.

273

NONEXISTENT PROMISES

SEPTEMBER 26

He has also given us his very great and valuable promises. He did it so you could share in his nature. He also did it so you could escape from the evil in the world. That evil is caused by sinful longings.

2 Peter 1:4.

I am an incurable bookworm. I get it from my mom's side of the family. So it is no surprise to anyone who knows me that my favorite store is Paper Treasures, a used-book store in New Market, Virginia, near where I live. Because I have had so much fun at Paper Treasures, I tend to notice used bookstores everywhere now.

One bookstore sign in Jacksonville, Florida, really caught my attention. It read: "Rare, Out-of-Print, and Nonexistent Books." Now, I am familiar with rare books and out-of-print books—but nonexistent books? Never heard of those. They don't exist, as far as I am concerned.

I have learned that a lot of people will promise things they can't deliver. Sometimes it is because something comes up and they just can't; other times they were just lying in the first place. Either way, it makes life disappointing. One thing I have discovered though: Even though people you really love can disappoint you sometimes, God will never let you down. He will never promise something He can't come through with, nor will He ever be surprised by circumstances that prevent Him from keeping His promise. God never gets sick at the last minute or has a financial problem crop up (such as car repairs) so that He can't afford what He promised you. The Lord never forgets, and He doesn't change His mind. If He promises you something, you can count on it—as definitely as if it were already in your hand!

Thank You, God, I really count on You. Amen.

SCOOTER JOCKEYS AND OTHER FRIENDS OF GOD

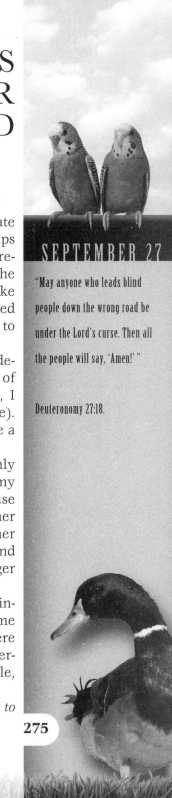

SEPTEMBER 27

"May anyone who leads blind people down the wrong road be under the Lord's curse. Then all the people will say, 'Amen!'"

Deuteronomy 27:18.

I get pretty offended by people who discriminate against those with physical disabilities. Perhaps that is because I've seen my mom on the receiving end of a little of that. Usually she laughs or makes a joke about it, but I don't like it at all. It is different if Mom or her other disabled friends make the cracks. Mom sometimes refers to them as a group of scooter jockeys.

Actor Peter Falk (the legendary Colombo of detective movie fame) had Harry Cohn (head of Columbia Pictures) tell him, "For the same price, I can get an actor with two eyes" (Falk has a glass eye). As it turned out, that actor with only one eye made a lot of money for the studio that hired him!

My friend Jason has only one eye (at least only one that doesn't come out at night) but none of my friends make fun of him for it. Perhaps it is because they know that God values him just as much, whether he has one eye or two, just as He valued my brother when he was deaf (though he hears fine now). And just as He values my mom when she can no longer walk and run and lift heavy patients.

In Bible times people often viewed a disabled individual as someone whom God was punishing. Some still do. But Jesus always treated people who were physically disabled with gentle respect and no differently than other individuals. Since He is my example, I try to do that too.

Dear God, help me always to act like Jesus would to others. Amen.

275

JUSTINE JUSTIFIED

First of all, here is what you must understand. In the last days people will make fun of the truth. They will laugh at it. They will follow their own evil longings.

2 Peter 3:3.

I enjoy humor and satire. Also I enjoy reading famous quotes. When I can read both at once, I really have fun. One book I really liked this year was *The 365 Stupidest Things Ever Said.* However, one quote in the book didn't seem that stupid to me. It was a statement made by Justine Bateman (Mallery on *Family Ties*) on *Total TV.* She said: "[God is,] like, so cool. Think of the coolest person in your life. He made that person. And He's cooler than that."

Why did they think that was stupid? Actually, I feel the same way she does. God *is* cool. Cooler than the coolest person in my life. Cool enough that He defies my vocabulary for words awesome enough to describe Him.

The psalmist David had instructions for us regarding this:

"Shout to God with joy, everyone on earth!
Sing about the glory of his name!
Say to God, 'What wonderful things you do!
Your power is so great that your enemies bow
down to you in fear'" (Psalm 66:1-3).

It seems to me as though Justine Bateman was understating things. Perhaps we should list Ross and Marilyn Petras in *The 365 Stupidest Things Ever Said* for including Justine's statement in their book at all.

God, You are just awesome! Amen.

GETTING INTO HEAVEN IS EASIER THAN VOTING IN ARKANSAS

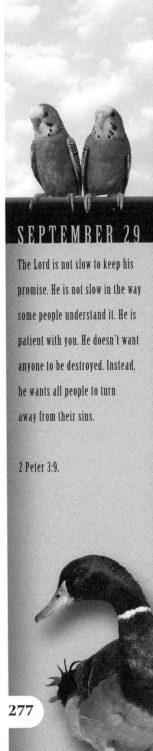

SEPTEMBER 29

The Lord is not slow to keep his promise. He is not slow in the way some people understand it. He is patient with you. He doesn't want anyone to be destroyed. Instead, he wants all people to turn away from their sins.

2 Peter 3:9.

I am not usually into law. Just reading it makes me sleepy, but this one is special. I had to read it twice before I started laughing.

"And no person shall be permitted, under any pretext whatever, to come nearer than fifty feet of any door or window of any polling room, from the opening of the polls until the completion of the count and the certification of the returns" (Arkansas Law, section 4761) *(Pope's Digest)*.

Any pretext whatever? What about *voting?*

Some people feel that God has a similar attitude about letting people into heaven. It seems so hard when you read their books. Yet the Bible tells us that God isn't willing that *anyone* should perish (die), but He wants so much for all of us to be saved. He is not into making rules that will keep us out, but designing a whole plan to let us in. We call it the plan of salvation.

However, God isn't going to force anyone to go to heaven. He is the ultimate gentleman, and though He went out of His way to provide a way for us to get in, even to giving up His Son's life in exchange for ours, He still allows us to choose whether we will accept it or not. Our freedom of choice was tremendously important to Him. Important enough for Him to die for. And important enough that we can choose to die for it too. But we don't have to. He opened the door, made the plan, paid the bill. We just have to say yes. Don't give up your rights by abstaining—when He died so you could vote!

Thank You, God. I choose You! Amen.

277

ESCHEW OBFUSCATION (DON'T MAKE THINGS SO COMPLICATED)

SEPTEMBER 30

God loved the world so much that he gave his one and only son. Anyone who believes in him will not die but will have eternal life.

John 3:16.

Disposable diapers. You wouldn't think there was much to say about them. Yet, read this: "In muted hues of pink, blue, and green, done not quite in Empire style and without either a court train or redingote, but flared about the bottom in an Alençon lace effect and sprinkled throughout with tiny pink dots not unlike stephanotis adorning the Plaza Hotel's Grand Ballroom."

What the press release was trying to say was that the diapers had colored polka dots and lace printed on them. It must be human nature to try to complicate everything. Perhaps it was just too embarrassing to admit that they were just pink-spotted diapers. Yet we Christians do that too. John 3:16 pretty clearly states the plan of salvation. God made it even simpler in a picture lesson for the Israelites in their tabernacle structure and services.

Today, many consider the sanctuary complicated and hard for adults to understand, let alone children! Why? Why was the concept of living with Jesus as my example and accepting His perfect life in exchange for mine and then living as if I love Him so hard to accept? Why do humans feel the need to add hundreds of extra rules and qualifiers on it? God's plan was perfect the way it was—perfect the way it is.

God so loved Mike Dillon that He gave His only Son, that if Mike believed in Him he could have everlasting life. Period.

Thank You, God! Amen.

278

SAVING SEALS (AND GOD'S KIDS)

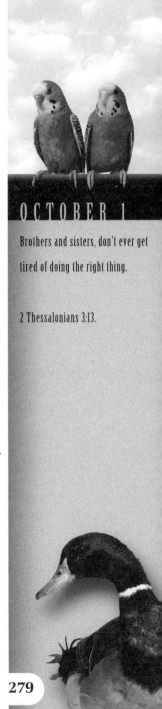

OCTOBER 1

Brothers and sisters, don't ever get tired of doing the right thing.

2 Thessalonians 3:13.

The oil spill in Alaska from the *Exxon Valdez* was one of the greatest environmental disasters that has happened in my lifetime.

I read on the Internet that the average cost of rehabilitating a seal coated by the oil was $80,000. The Internet also told a story of two seals who had been a couple of the most expensively saved creatures after the spill. The people working with them held a special ceremony as they released the creatures back into the wild. The onlookers had tears and applause as the two seals swam out into the ocean. Then the horrified crowd watched as a killer whale ate both of them.

My mom likes teenagers. We have had several troubled teens living in our home as they tried to get their lives back together again. Every time we have a teen live with us, it costs our family. It takes money, time, some patience and some space, and a lot of Mom's emotional energy and prayers.

Most of the people who have lived with us have done very well and gone on to get their lives straightened out—but not everyone. Sometimes we feel like the crowd who stood there watching the killer whale eat the two seals.

God asked us to help each other. He wants us to love people and to help those who are hurt and needing some rehabilitation. But He never promised that things would always turn out all right. We still live in enemy territory, and terrible things happen in this world.

Dear God, I can't wait till You come and make everything right. Amen.

UNLICENSED ANGEL

The Lord will command his angels

to take good care of you.

Psalm 91:11.

One day mom and I went to the grocery store. I pulled her scooter out of the van and hooked up its two heavy batteries. Then Mom realized she had forgotten her purse—*again!* (When Mom is going through a bad spot, she gets very forgetful.) It meant no scooter key and no checkbook to shop with anyway.

My brother Don was planning to meet us there in an hour to help put the scooter back in after we were done shopping. Taking the scooter apart, I tried to lift it back into the van. I could handle the batteries and smaller parts OK, but the rest of it was too big.

Suddenly I saw a man approaching us from a van parked across from ours. A small wiry man about the size of my grandpa, he was Black. That fact really stood out because New Market has only one Black family, and Timberville none. I said hi to him.

Nodding but not speaking, he just picked up Mom's heavy scooter and put it in the van. When Mom started babbling profuse thanks, he just smiled, put his hand on her shoulder, and then walked back to his van. As he drove away I looked to see if his license plate was from out of state. His van didn't even have one!

Our friend Mitzi suggested he might have been a migrant worker here to help with the apple orchards. Many of them don't speak English, and he might not have talked to us because he didn't know English either. Or he might have been an angel. I guess I don't care which.

God, thank You for sending angels and other friends of Yours when I need help. Amen.

GOD'S KIDS ARE EVERYWHERE

I don't speak in tongues, although sometimes when I try to type, it looks like that. However, I have been in places where people were speaking in tongues. Last week my brother and I heard a preacher making fun of people who do. He was babbling like a person speaking in tongues and then making little nonsense rhymes that went along with it.

And he said, "Now, folks, if you are going to pray to the Lord, you better tell Him what you really want, because as long as you're just babbling, you don't even know what you really want."

Now, even though I don't speak in tongues, his comments made me very uncomfortable and feel very defensive. For a start, I believe that God understands what I want and need no matter how poorly I express myself. And secondly, if God really feels like a parent to us, then He probably doesn't like it when we make fun of His other kids. Here at home, if I start teasing or ridiculing my brother and really putting him down, Mom gets mad at me. Don't you think God might feel the same way?

I believe we should be very careful about treating other Christians with respect, even though they may believe differently than we do. After all, I'd really like them to treat me with respect too, and I know my heavenly Father wants me treated well.

Lord, please help me recognize that people who go to other churches are Your people too. Amen.

OCTOBER 3

I have other sheep that do not belong to this sheep pen. I must bring them in too. They also will listen to my voice. Then there will be one flock and one shepherd.

John 10:16.

281

IS ANYBODY OUT THERE LISTENING?

Again, here is what the kingdom of heaven will be like. A man was going on a journey. He sent for his servants and put them in charge of his property.... The man gave each servant the amount of money he knew the servant could take care of. Then he went on his journey.... His master replied, "You have done well, good and faithful servant! You have been faithful with a few things. I will put you in charge of many things. Come and share your master's happiness!"

Matthew 25:14-21.

I heard a preacher (not my pastor) talking about behavior. He said, "You can't please God, no matter how hard you try. You're just not going to be able to please Him with anything you do. God said, 'Be ye therefore perfect, even as your Father which is in heaven is perfect' (Matthew 5:48, KJV). Are you perfect? Well, then, you don't please God." He went on for quite a while until everyone was feeling pretty guilty, and then he explained to us that we all needed to throw ourselves on His mercy, and that the blood of Jesus would cover us.

I don't believe this. Certainly Jesus did tell the disciples to try to be just like their Father in heaven, who was perfect, but I believe that we can please Him. I believe that even though I'm not able to do everything the way that my Father can, it's still possible to please Him. When you talk to your parents and spend time with them, it pleases them. Or when you do nice things for them, it pleases them. And I think my dad gets a special charge out of seeing me trying to be like him, doing the things that he does, even if I don't do them as well as he does.

I believe the Bible shows us that God is a parent who delights in watching us grow more like Him. But I don't believe that He gets mad at us when we do make mistakes. That was why He provided a plan to take care of them. I believe that by doing what He asked and spending time with Him, I do please Him, even though I'm not perfect yet.

God, thanks for loving me, even though I'm not perfect yet. Amen.

282

BLOOD BROTHERS

But suppose we walk in the light, just as he is in the light. Then we share life with one another. And the blood of Jesus, his Son, makes us pure from all sin.

1 John 1:7.

W hen I was a little dude, my best friend and I had a lot of secrets. If we had a really super secret that we both were swearing to protect, we would often seal it in blood. Each one of us would prick our finger and put a little drop of blood on the paper. To us it signified the absolute, highest importance of the secret or agreement we were signing.

It made me feel good to find out that God worked that way too. When God set up the plan of salvation, He sealed it in blood. Adam and Eve sacrificed a lamb. That was their side of the agreement. And when Jesus came to earth and hung on the cross, He sealed the agreement in His blood. It was absolutely the most important agreement, and it required blood to confirm it.

My great-great-grandfather, who helped forge the peace between the Chippewa Indians and the Scandinavian settlers in northern Minnesota, established a blood treaty with Chief Mickinock. They both cut their hands and mingled their blood. That was before people worried about AIDS and infected body fluids. But it made them blood brothers.

I like to think that when I offer my body to God as a living sacrifice (aren't you glad He gave us that option?), I am offering Him my blood too. Jesus gave me His, and I'm giving Him mine. Not only is He my king, but that makes us blood brothers, and it's an agreement of highest importance.

Jesus, now that we're blood brothers, we can share lots of stuff. How about we spend today together and have some fun? Amen.

GET OUT THE BUGGY WHIPS

Those who aren't Jews do not have the law. Sometimes they just naturally do what the law requires. ... They show that what the law requires is written on their hearts. The way their minds judge them gives witness to that fact. Sometimes their thoughts find them guilty. At other times their thoughts find them not guilty. People will be judged on the day God appoints Jesus Christ to judge their secret thoughts.

Romans 2:14-16

Ellen White once said that every girl should learn to harness a horse. But in the Adventist Church today, only people with a lot of money or a ranch have horses available to learn to harness. In some cases, sticking to the literal rule makes no sense.

The rule was based on a good principle. Women need to know how to get where they want to go if there isn't a man around. Today, she might say that all girls should learn to drive a car and change a tire.

As Christians, and especially as Seventh-day Adventists, we need to examine more closely our principles and not be so rigid with our rules, just because we've always done it that way. The principles will never change, and if we focus on those and live by our principles, we'll never look silly later.

God, thanks for giving us good principles to live by. Please help me today to apply them to the situations I'll have to deal with. Amen.

PROMISES, PROMISES

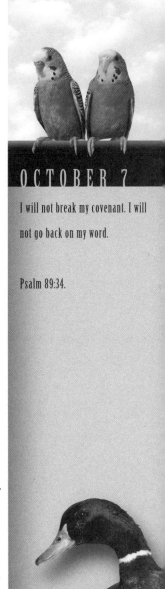

I will not break my covenant. I will not go back on my word.

Psalm 89:34.

In 1963 the U.S.S.R., Britain, and the United States signed a nuclear test-ban treaty. Just the title makes us laugh, because those of us born in the eighties know that nobody's nuclear testing ceased in 1963. The Russians didn't stop; neither did the United States; and I'm not sure about the British. It's like the peace accords that get signed all the time right before one country continues to bomb another one. All the treaties in the world don't seem to prevent violent people from doing violent things. And the politicians who sign them have trouble living up to the terms that they agreed to.

It can leave you cynical about treaties and contractual agreements. But one thing I know for sure: God always keeps His part of a bargain. If you make a treaty or a covenant with God, He holds up His end of the deal. He never changes His mind. His covenant with Abraham lasted for thousands of years, and it wasn't God who backed out on the terms of the agreement.

Now we have a new covenant between God and Christians. You can trust Him. Keeping up His end of the deal, He'll never back out, He'll never sneak around the edges, or just plain lie. God always fulfills His part of a treaty. What makes or breaks a treaty with Him is what you do with your part.

God, thanks for being so faithful and keeping all Your promises. Amen.

"CHOOSE WISELY, MY SON"

But suppose you don't want to serve Him. Then choose for yourselves right now whom you will serve. You can choose the gods your people served east of the Euphrates river. Or you can choose the gods the Amorites serve. After all, you are living in their land. But as for me and my family, we will serve the Lord.

Joshua 24:15.

Mrs. O'Leary probably didn't think her cow was very important. She and her cow both lived in 1871 in Chicago, yet when legend says her cow kicked over the lantern and started the great Chicago fire, they suddenly became very famous. The act of kicking over the lantern was not such a big deal. It was a small event—if looked at by itself.

Sometimes I make choices that I think are insignificant and maybe even funny at the time, but they end up coming back to bite me and affecting my life much longer and more seriously than I ever imagined.

I'm not the only one this happens to. Remember Abraham? Having a child with Hagar at his wife's urging really didn't seem like anybody else's business to him at the time, yet we see the results in the Middle East even today as the descendants of the two brothers fight each other.

Some choices don't seem like a big deal, yet the consequences are so massive that we would have chosen differently if we had any idea they would turn out that way.

God has offered us protection against such dangers. He has given us guidelines so that any choice we make can be smart. If we are always careful to choose the road God would want us to, we'll have much less trouble in our lives. Abraham would have, I would have, and Mrs. O'Leary probably would have put her lantern out of reach of her cow.

God, please help me to make good choices today. Amen.

WHO DISCOVERED AMERICA?

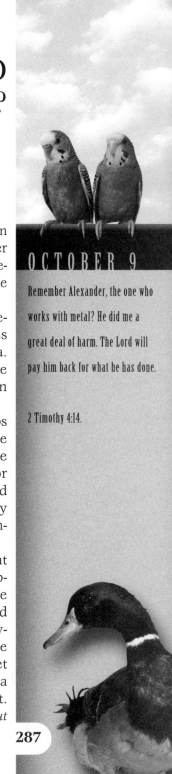

Today Norwegians celebrate Leif Ericsson Day. Leif Ericsson was a Norwegian explorer who landed in North America 492 years before Columbus. Yet Columbus receives the credit for discovering the New World.

This has always bothered me. Perhaps it is because I get so angry when someone at school takes credit for something that was my work or my idea. Perhaps it is because I have Scandinavian blood in me and feel that the Norwegians should have gotten credit for their exploring.

Perhaps there's even more to it than that. Perhaps Leif Ericsson never claimed to have discovered the New World because people were already there: the Native Americans who lived there and had done so for hundreds of years. Can you really discover a new land in which people already dwell? Hadn't they already found it? Whatever the reasons, today people remember Leif Ericsson for getting here before Columbus.

I'm not very old, but I've already learned that many things in this life are just not fair. This is probably only one of the small things. I am glad that we serve a God who does know exactly who did what and who didn't. Someday He's going to straighten everything out. Setting everything right, He will make everything fair. And Christopher Columbus will get credit only for things he actually did. It may not be a great day for him, but I'm really looking forward to it.

God, I'm glad that You'll straighten everything out when You come. Please make it soon. Amen.

Remember Alexander, the one who works with metal? He did me a great deal of harm. The Lord will pay him back for what he has done.

2 Timothy 4:14.

287

AVOID THE SMOKING SECTION

OCTOBER 10

Christ has paid the price for you. So use your bodies in a way that honors God.

1 Corinthians 6:20.

When my mom worked at the hospital, she had a sign in her office that said, "If you are smoking in here, you had better be on fire, and will be treated accordingly." It always used to make me laugh. Also it reminded me of the story Mom told me about Sir Walter Raleigh, who had come to what is now Virginia and established a colony. One of the things he has been known for was bringing tobacco back to Europe.

The story is told of how one day, when Sir Walter Raleigh was smoking in the Tower of London, a servant came rushing in with a bucket of water and threw it on him. Sir Walter sputtered in anger, wondering why the servant would do such a thing. The poor servant replied that he thought that the respected English knight had been on fire!

Many people feel that smoking should be a personal choice, even though we know now that it causes terrible health problems, destroys people's bodies, and costs our country millions of dollars in health care that wouldn't have been necessary if people hadn't used tobacco. Regardless of how people choose here on earth, I'll bet that when they decide for eternity, they'd rather not be in the smoking section.

God, please help me make and keep my body fit and strong for You to use when You need it. Amen.

SOME KIDS ARE JUST DIFFERENT

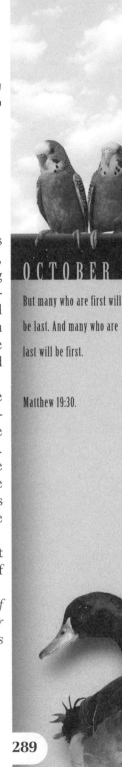

OCTOBER 11

But many who are first will be last. And many who are last will be first.

Matthew 19:30.

October is Learning Disabilities Awareness Month. Not long ago, and even still today, society labeled many kids with learning disabilities as just dumb, or slow, or having behavior problems. It wasn't until they became adults and accomplished something with their lives that others recognized them as worthwhile people. Yet many people who have done good things did have learning disabilities and trouble reading.

When my brother went to a writing conference with my mom, he met Bodie Thoene, who has written many Christian best-sellers. The hot book on the market at the time was her *Twilight of Courage*. Donnie learned that Bodie Thoene has a hard time reading. Yet Bodie and her husband, Brock, wrote scripts for John Wayne movies back when he was alive and have written countless best-sellers in the Christian market.

Kids who have trouble learning to read aren't dumb—they're just different, and someday some of them may be more famous than you.

God, thanks for making all of us special. And even if we have problems in one way or another, thanks for making a special plan for each of us that will make us successful in Your eyes. Amen.

289

CHRISTOPHER COLUMBUS

OCTOBER 12

The scroll of the prophet Isaiah was handed to him. He unrolled it and found the right place. There it is written, "The Spirit of the Lord is on me. He has anointed me to tell the good news to poor people.

He has sent me to announce freedom for prisoners. He has sent me so that the blind will see again.

He wants me to free those who are beaten down."

Luke 4:17, 18.

Today many people in the United States celebrate Columbus Day. As I mentioned earlier, most people accept the fact that he was not the first one to reach the New World. People already lived here, and other explorers had arrived before he had. Unfortunately, something he did help establish in this part of the world was slavery. When he returned from one of his earlier trips to the Americas, he took back a group of Caribbean Indians to the royal family in Spain.

Fortunately, Queen Isabella had a more sensitive conscience than Columbus and wrote a letter to a religious leader named Fonseca, asking whether selling Indians was legal. The bishop and his friends could not decide, and Queen Isabella ordered the Caribbean Indians returned to their home. However, that did not dampen Columbus' enthusiasm for selling the people he found in the New World, and four years later another shipment of them arrived in Spain.

On Columbus Day not everyone is inclined to honor Columbus. Instead, I would like to spend today honoring Jesus, who also left His comfortable home to go to a faraway and uncomfortable place, but He went to set people free and to end slavery forever. In my book He's a lot more deserving of our respect and appreciation.

Jesus, thanks for coming here to win us back. Now please hurry and return to get us so we can all be together. Amen.

290

MOM'S AVOCADO TREES

OCTOBER 13

When Mom was a little girl, she lived in Nigeria. Mom planted mango and avocado trees all around her yard in Nigeria during the five years they lived there.

Trees take a while to grow, and the avocado trees started bearing the year she and her parents left. We have had people who have been there tell us that the mangoes and avocados produced by the trees in that yard are just wonderful and that everyone on the campus enjoys them because they bear so many. It makes Mom growl in frustration, having never gotten to enjoy even one piece of fruit from the trees she worked so hard to grow as a little girl.

Moses experienced those same feelings. He spent 40 years leading the ornery Israelites through the wilderness, got right up to the edge of the Promised Land, and then never had a chance to live in it.

Christians experience this too. Often they start projects that other people benefit from. Many times we never see the results of work we have done or the witnessing we have been involved in. Yet someday God is going to reward all of us for everything we have done. And someday He is going to show us the results of our hard work, and we will understand and be able to see our rewards. Yet all of it will seem pretty puny compared to what Jesus has done for us.

God, I'm looking forward to seeing the results of what I've done when I get to heaven. Can we all go there soon? Amen.

Look! I am coming soon! I bring my rewards with me. I will reward each person for what he has done.

Revelation 22:12.

291

GO FOR IT!

Don't let anyone look down on you because you are young. Set an example for the believers in what you say and in how you live. Also set an example in how you love and in what you believe. Show the believers how to be pure.

1 Timothy 4:12.

The *Literary Digest* in 1899 contained this prediction: We see "a dim future for the horseless carriage or the automobile." It will never "come into as common use as the bicycle." What if the makers of cars had let the opinion of those at the *Literary Digest* discourage them, and they had quit making cars?

There are always people who think they know it all and are willing to discourage others. In 1910 W. J. Jackman and Thomas Russel wrote a book about the construction and operation of flying machines. It contained this quote: "In the opinion of competent experts it is idle to look for a commercial future for the flying machine. There is and always will be a limit to its carrying capacity. . . . Some will argue that because a machine will carry two people, another may be constructed that will carry a dozen. But those who make this contention do not understand the theory." How foolish Mr. Jackman and Mr. Russel would feel if they were to take a ride on a 747 today.

If you have a passion for something, go for it. Don't listen to people who try to discourage you. Anyone who has ever tried something different has always had to face people like that.

But God put your creativity in you, your talents, and your passion to do things. Make Him your partner, and He'll help you get things done, whether or not other people think you can.

God, You've given all of us talents. Now please help us develop them so we can use them to help You. Amen.

THORKEL THE SKULL-SPLITTER AND ROBERT DE BRUCE

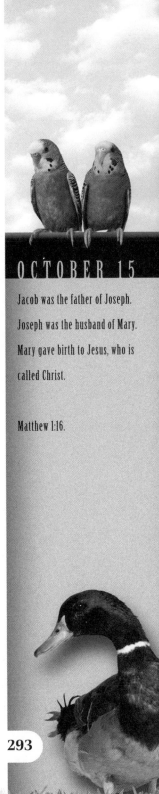

OCTOBER 15

Jacob was the father of Joseph. Joseph was the husband of Mary. Mary gave birth to Jesus, who is called Christ.

Matthew 1:16.

Mom likes the story of Scottish leader William Wallace because his grandmother was a Dillon. My mother likes digging in genealogies. It wasn't until last weekend that she discovered that Robert de Bruce—who was sort of the bad guy in the movie *Braveheart* but who was so moved by William Wallace's death that he took up the Scottish cause, fought the English, and became king of Scotland—was one of her ancestors. She learned that on her great-grandmother's side the family had been descendants of Robert de Bruce. This means I am too. Also on my mom's grandfather's family tree was George Soule, who came over on the *Mayflower* to the New World.

Finding out your genealogy is fun. It makes history seem more alive when you know that someone from your family with the genes and blood that runs in your own veins was there, right in the thick of the action. And though tracing my family's genealogies uncovers people both good and bad (like Thorkel the Skull-splitter, another ancestor), it's comforting to know that Jesus' genealogy in Matthew reveals the same thing—good people as well as people with serious moral problems.

Jesus had a family tree just like mine. He had the genes of good people and bad people passed on to Him. And yet He took what He was given and lived His life to bring honor to God, and that's what I intend to do too.

God, You know that we're all a mixture of good and bad. Please help us use the good and get rid of the bad. Amen.

293

HURRICANE SEASON

A thousand may fall dead at your side. Ten thousand may fall near your right hand. But no harm will come to you.

Psalm 91:7.

About this time of year the hurricane season comes to an end. It's a big relief to people who live in areas that suffer from tropical storms. This year I was glad to see it end too. One of my friends, who went to school last year here in Virginia with me, was back in his home in Puerto Rico, unable to return to school. We heard on the news that a hurricane had completely destroyed his village. Hundreds across the island were dead and many more were missing. We weren't able to phone and find out how he was because there was no village left to call. We could only wait.

Yesterday I found out that he and his family were OK—that is, they're alive. The storm smashed their home and wiped out their village, and they escaped with only their bodies intact. They will have to start life over again.

In the Virgin Islands the people have a day set aside as their Thanksgiving Day, in which they thank God that the hurricane season is over. I'm thankful too this year. Sometimes, because we might live in an area where we don't have storms like that, we don't realize what we have been protected from and how good our lives are. But this year, having the hurricanes hit people I cared about, I'm especially grateful that hurricane season is over and that my friends and their families are still alive. In spite of the hard things that happen, God is good.

God, thanks for taking care of us and helping us through the bad times. Please come soon so there won't be any more bad times to go through. Amen.

294

THE BENEFIT
OF MY WISDOM

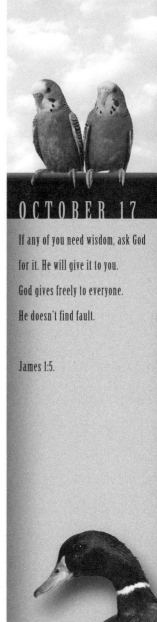

If any of you need wisdom, ask God for it. He will give it to you. God gives freely to everyone. He doesn't find fault.

James 1:5.

I have been offended a couple times when a person at church has thought I had a problem and tried to straighten my life out. So I was very amused to read this story on the Internet.

A woman came home and saw her husband in the kitchen. He seemed to be shaking frantically and looked like he was connected to the electric griddle with a wire. Sure that he was being electrocuted, she searched about for some way to help him. Grabbing a big piece of wood that was laying outside the back door, she rushed into the kitchen and whacked him with it to separate him from the electric current. The blow broke his arm in two places. As it turned out, he had been listening to music on his Walkman.

He probably felt a lot like I did at church at times. As we grow in Jesus we often see people who are making mistakes and want to help them. It is important, whenever we feel that way, to ask the Holy Spirit for wisdom first so that we don't end up just hurting them and then feeling bad about what we've done, especially when we find out that perhaps what they were doing was not a problem anyway. The book of James promises that any of us who lack wisdom can ask God and He will give it to us. I'm glad He's willing to do that, and so will the people who do not end up getting hurt by receiving my "help."

Holy Spirit, please give me the right words to say when I think someone needs the benefit of my wisdom. And also please teach me when to keep my big mouth shut. Amen.

295

WHAT A DEAL!

OCTOBER 18

God loved the world so much that he gave his one and only Son. Anyone who believes in him will not die but will have eternal life.

John 3:16.

In 1867 the United States bought Alaska from the Russians for $7.2 million. Popular opinion held that the whole deal was just ridiculous and that the United States government was once again wasting taxpayers' dollars. Almost everyone considered Alaska worthless, and the few pennies an acre that the government did spend to purchase it seemed a bigger waste than dropping it down an outhouse.

People commonly referred to Alaska as Seward's Folly, after Secretary of State Seward, who helped negotiate the deal. Today, we view Alaska much differently. Not only is it our largest state, but it is one of the richest in natural resources. Its vast oil fields provide petroleum and energy for our country. Alaska has turned out to be a worthwhile investment, and no one any longer considers it a folly.

Jesus left His home in heaven and came to earth to give up His life for a planet full of selfish, not-too-bright humans. Perhaps some would consider that His folly. But in the long run, what divides a folly from a wise investment is how things turn out.

It's up to you and to me. Are we going to be a worthwhile investment of Jesus' blood, or will people look at His sacrifice, shake their heads, and think, "What a pity!" You and I are the ones who get to decide. I choose to be a worthwhile investment. I want to be something that Jesus can be proud of to present to the entire universe and say, "Look what I bought!"

296

Jesus, thanks for buying me back from Satan, even if my value isn't really apparent at first glance. Amen.

AT LEAST WE KNOW

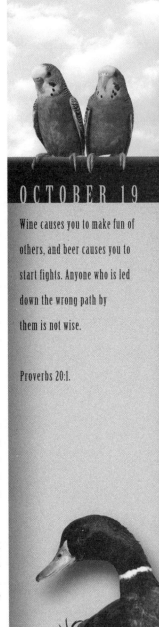

Wine causes you to make fun of others, and beer causes you to start fights. Anyone who is led down the wrong path by them is not wise.

Proverbs 20:1.

This week is National Collegiate Alcohol Awareness Week. More than 3,000 college campuses in the United States are offering their students alcohol-awareness classes and encouraging them not to drink, especially the binge drinking that students often indulge in.

As I am writing this devotional, so far this year 500 college students have died as a result of binge drinking on college campuses. In one of the interviews I saw on TV a student whose best friend had just died seemed bewildered, as if she had never understood before that drinking could hurt someone so badly.

As Adventist kids, we have a great advantage. We should have grown up knowing this. Many of us have been taught this from the time we were little. Sometimes the rules that we've lived with may have seemed kind of confining and arbitrary. But as I was watching the interviews on TV, it struck me that we were lucky. Whether or not we choose to follow the principles we've been taught, at least we know the dangers involved in drinking and other things.

God has been good in sharing information with us, letting us know what is dangerous and what is not. At least as His kids we can make informed choices and not be surprised by the terrible things that can happen.

Thanks, God, for letting us know so much. Now please make us smart enough to follow Your plan. Amen.

297

Let the whole earth have respect for the Lord. Let all of the people in the world honor him. He spoke, and the world came into being. He commanded, and it stood firm.

Psalm 33:8, 9.

TELL ME WHAT YOU KNOW

At the writer's conference I attended, I learned that one of the best pieces of advice for would-be authors is to write about what you know. Ian Fleming did this. After studying languages in Switzerland and Germany, he worked as a reporter in Moscow. Later he also worked in the banking and stock market worlds, and he was a naval intelligence officer in World War II. Since these were things he knew about, that is what he wrote about. It resulted in the stories of James Bond, secret agent 007.

Ian turned out 12 novels and seven short stories with the character James Bond, and they sold millions of copies, though most of us know him best for his movies. One reason his works were so successful was that Ian Fleming really knew about the world he created for James Bond to live in.

In order for us to communicate well about Jesus, whether we are writing, preaching, or just witnessing to our friends, we need to know what we are talking about too.

If we don't know Jesus, all the theology in the world will mean nothing. And our witnessing won't be successful. Just as it is important to write only what you know, it's also vital to only witness about whom you know.

Jesus, I want to know You so I can tell other people what You're like. Amen.

WHAT SHIPS?

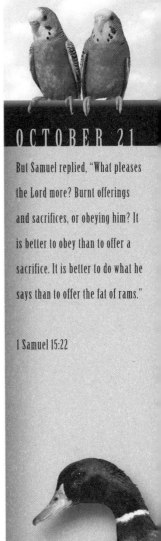

On this date in 1805 the British Navy, led by Horatio Nelson, defeated the combined Spanish and French naval fleets at the Battle of Trafalgar. This ended Napoleon's power on the seas. Historians, especially British ones, think the battle was extremely significant.

Several years earlier Nelson had attacked Danish forces at Copenhagen. His superiors had seen the huge fleet coming against them and sent a message to Lord Nelson commanding him to retreat. One of his crewmen pointed it out to him. Nelson had only one eye, having lost the other in a previous battle. When the crewmen told him they were receiving a message from the other British ships, Nelson put his spyglass up to his patched eye and said, "Ships? I see no ships," and led the British to a resounding victory.

Sometimes we act like Lord Nelson. When the Holy Spirit sends us a message, "No, don't do that," we turn a blind eye or a deaf ear and pretend that we don't know what He's talking about. The Bible warns us not to grieve, or resist, the Holy Spirit.

Saul also turned a deaf ear to the Holy Spirit, and eventually it cost him his life. No matter what type of reward we think we might be able to pull off, it's just not worth it. God doesn't want sacrifices and apologies later. He would prefer obedience. If Saul had obeyed, he might have lived a lot longer and enjoyed his life. Obedience is better than sacrifice.

God, help me to remember how important obedience is to You and to trust You to take care of everything. Amen.

But Samuel replied, "What pleases the Lord more? Burnt offerings and sacrifices, or obeying him? It is better to obey than to offer a sacrifice. It is better to do what he says than to offer the fat of rams."

1 Samuel 15:22

"I WON'T DO IT AGAIN, GRANDMA"

OCTOBER 22

Stand up in order to show your respect for old people. Also have respect for me. I am the Lord your God.

Leviticus 19:32

I believe that showing respect for old people goes further than just saying "Please" and "Thank you" and not making fun of them. Sometimes it can mean saving them from embarrassment too.

Grandma Tadman is in a nursing home. I go with Mom to visit her. Because she's old and sick, Grandma Tadman now wears diapers. One day when we were visiting her, something fell out on the floor. She was terribly embarrassed as she looked around and realized everybody saw it. Turning to my aunt Esther, she said, "Esther, did you drop that?" Maybe blaming Aunt Esther would make her feel less embarrassed. Then she faced my mom. "Sally, was that you?"

"No way," Mom replied.

Grandma was getting redder and redder and looked as if she were about to cry. She glanced over toward me. "Was that you, Michael?" she asked.

Knowing full well it was she, I grinned at her. "I'm sorry, Grandma, I won't do it again."

Suddenly the tension broke. Grandma broke into a really big smile and reached toward me. "I love you, Michael," she said. And then Grandma relaxed and wasn't embarrassed anymore. It didn't take much to help her.

I believe that respecting her includes things like that. And I love her too.

Jesus, thanks for taking the blame for me. I love You too. Amen.

THE SKATEBOARD I GOT FROM THE SEWER

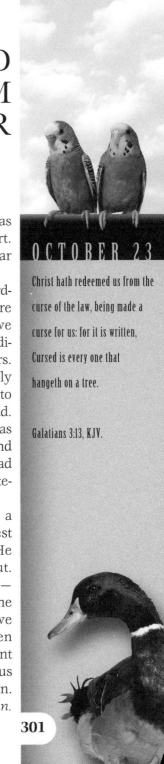

OCTOBER 23

Christ hath redeemed us from the curse of the law, being made a curse for us: for it is written, Cursed is every one that hangeth on a tree.

Galatians 3:13, KJV.

My skateboard is new. My first one was a cheap one that eventually fell apart. This time I saved up for almost a year to get a really high-quality one.

Friday afternoon I was skateboarding with my friends Carl, Matt, and Willie. We were boarding down Willie's street, which is on a hill, so we can get going really fast. He lives in a very quiet subdivision of New Market, so we weren't expecting any cars. On our last run we were cruising right along. Suddenly we spotted a car turning onto Willie's road. It seemed to be racing toward us, and I was in the middle of the road. Carl swerved and dived into the grass. All I could do was jump off and hit the ground running, but I tripped and slid on the pavement. Although I got some nasty road rash, that wasn't what upset me. My brand-new skateboard rolled neatly into the brand-new storm drain.

We walked back up to Willie's house and got a pickax, a rope, and a flashlight. Prying up the nearest manhole cover, we let Willie down with the rope. He found my skateboard and then we lifted him back out.

My skateboard was mine—because I paid for it—but it still had to be rescued when it went down the storm drain, or it would be lost. In a similar way, we belonged to Jesus. He made us—we were His. When humanity chose to disobey, we pretty much went down the drain too. Rather than let us go, Jesus climbed down into it too. Now we belong to Him again.

Jesus, thanks for rescuing me from the sewer of sin. Amen.

301

THE NEW CINDERELLA

He suffered the things we should have suffered. He took on himself the pain that should have been ours. But we thought God was punishing him. We thought God was wounding him and making him suffer.

Isaiah 53:4.

In the most recent movie version of Cinderella, titled *Ever After,* one scene really caught my attention. A group of bandits had captured the prince, and the Cinderella character had just impressed them with her swordplay. The bandits offered her anything she could carry away on her back. However, they refused to release the prince. Instead of taking clothing, jewels, or other valuables, she walked over to the prince, hoisted him up onto her back, and set out for home.

Later I found out that it wasn't just some filmmaker's romantic idea. In 1140 King Conrad III, founder of the Hohenstaufen dynasty of holy Roman emperors, captured the Welf fortress in Weinsberg. His soldiers lined the men up against the wall, telling the women they could leave the castle with anything they could carry on their backs.

The women of Weinsberg fortress had no trouble choosing what they would carry out. Each woman left the fortress with someone on her back.

People are more important than things. Jesus left His lofty position in heaven and came to earth to be a child in a poor family in a country under Roman occupation, giving up His life to prove to us this very point. With the King of the universe placing such tremendous value on us, how could we ever feel bad about ourselves?

Jesus, You carried us away from Satan on Your back. I'll never be able to thank You enough. But since You've given me eternity, I'll give it a good try. Amen.

302

"FORWARD THE LIGHT BRIGADE"

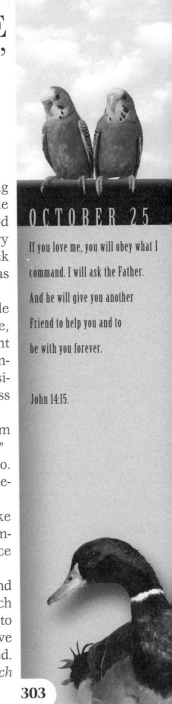

I have never minded being obedient or doing what my parents asked me to when it made sense to me. Mom has always been pretty good about giving me a reason why. However, every once in a while, it makes the hair on the back of my neck stand on end when I get such reasons as "because I'm your father, and I said so."

On this date in 1854 the charge of the light brigade took place. If you have played the Authors card game, you know that Alfred, Lord Tennyson made the light brigade immortal with his poem about them. Six hundred of them received orders to attack in an impossible situation during the Crimean War, in Europe. Less than a third of the men survived.

Lord Tennyson's most famous quote from the poem is: "Theirs not to reason why, theirs but to do and die."

As followers of Jesus, the words could apply to us, too. God doesn't always give us reasons He tells us to do something, and things at first don't always make sense to us.

Seventh-day Adventists were told not to smoke during a period of history when doctors recommended it to soothe people's nerves. Later science showed us why smoking was dangerous.

Many things may make sense to us later on, and some things we may never understand until we reach heaven, but He has promised us that once we are able to see the end from the beginning, we won't wish to have done things any other way than what He recommended.

God, I need constant reminding that You're much smarter than I am. Amen.

OCTOBER 25

If you love me, you will obey what I command. I will ask the Father. And he will give you another Friend to help you and to be with you forever.

John 14:15.

303

MULE DAY

OCTOBER 26

Have you traveled to the springs at the bottom of the ocean? Have you walked in its deepest parts? Have the gates of death been shown to you? Have you seen the gates of darkness? Do you understand how big the earth is? Tell me, if you know all of those things.

Job 38:16-18.

Today is Mule Day. On this day in 1785 the first mules arrived in Boston, Massachusetts, as a gift from King Charles III of Spain. While sending a gift sounds like a friendly thing to do, I'm not sure how friendly a gift of mules really is.

My grandpa grew up on a farm. He says that mules are some of the most stubborn, bad-tempered farm animals he has ever encountered. The term "stubborn as a mule" is common everywhere today, even among people who have never seen the animal.

I learned that a mule is actually a cross between a female horse and a jack. I'm not sure why anyone would want to do this, especially the horse and the jack. God created all of His creatures perfect. They were strong and able to do everything He intended them to, including have babies. But I learned that mules are sterile. The only way to get more mules is to mix more jacks and horses.

Humans can't create any new animals, and the best they can do is to mix up animals God has already created, sometimes producing stubborn, bad-tempered, ornery ones. How wise God is, and how silly humans can sometimes be! Perhaps we would all be better off just to sit back and let God be God and use our energy appreciating how wonderfully He has done things instead of trying to compete with Him, looking foolish and having questionable results in the process.

OK, God, I'll try letting You be God today. Please run my life for me. Amen.

304

MY CAMP BLUE RIDGE BOXERS

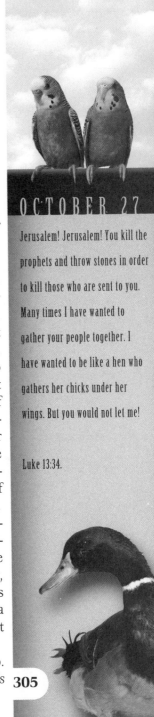

Boxer shorts appeared on this date in the year 1901. However, I didn't discover them until 89 years later, in the year 1990. I thought they were cool. I bought my first pair of boxer shorts at Camp Blue Ridge, and yes, they had "Camp Blue Ridge" printed all over them.

Unfortunately, I didn't realize that since they were underwear, I was supposed to wear them under regular shorts. Instead, I proudly wore them everywhere. Fortunately I had underwear underneath them, or it could have been more embarrassing than it already was.

I proudly wore them on the bus back home to Mom. Mom was highly amused, but didn't laugh out loud. After I had gotten settled at home and shown off my Camp Blue Ridge souvenirs, Mom gently explained to me how to tell regular shorts from boxer shorts. And she also explained that boxer shorts are underwear. I felt mortified. However, Mom was gentle and supportive, keeping her chuckles to herself and soon restoring my dignity. But I still like boxers.

As we grow in Jesus we make a lot of new discoveries. But sometimes we haven't learned everything we need to, and occasionally our ignorance makes us look pretty silly to other people. However, God gently gathers us close to Him and never laughs out loud at us. Like Mom, He leads us one step at a time and teaches us what we need to know without wounding our fragile dignity.

The least we can do is treat other people that way too.

God, please help me to be gentle with other people's feelings. Amen.

OCTOBER 27

Jerusalem! Jerusalem! You kill the prophets and throw stones in order to kill those who are sent to you. Many times I have wanted to gather your people together. I have wanted to be like a hen who gathers her chicks under her wings. But you would not let me!

Luke 13:34.

305

THE STATUES
OF LIBERTY

God has breathed life into all of Scripture. It is useful for teaching us what is true. It is useful for correcting our mistakes. It is useful for making our lives whole again. It is useful for training us to do what is right. By using Scripture, a man of God can be completely prepared to do every good thing.

2 Timothy 3:16, 17.

Last year on a trip to New York I had the opportunity to visit the Statue of Liberty. At the time I learned that the French gave it to the American people in 1886, but I've discovered more about it since then.

I found out that our Statue of Liberty is actually not unique. It is one of two. The other one is in France, and it faces our own statue. They were to be symbols of friendship—two statues facing each other, two parts of one whole. Yet one has almost been completely forgotten. While Americans revere their statue, they look at it as an American symbol and not as a symbol of the bond of friendship between two countries.

Something similar has happened with the Bible. The New Testament and the Old are two halves of a whole. They are a pair facing each other, each one filling in the blanks that the other one has left, making sense of the prophecies in the Old Testament by the stories in the New. Yet just like the statue on the French coast, many people have ignored the Old Testament. And by paying no attention to the Old Testament, we lose much meaning out of the New.

Ever since I learned this, whenever I see the Statue of Liberty, I also think of the French half and how the two of them together are a symbol of friendship between two peoples. Just like that, the Old and New Testament fit together and symbolize the friendship between God and the human race.

God, thanks for both halves of the Bible. Together they help me understand You better. Amen.

"DOCTOR LIVINGSTONE, I PRESUME?"

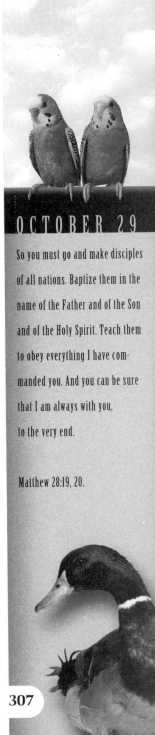

OCTOBER 29

So you must go and make disciples of all nations. Baptize them in the name of the Father and of the Son and of the Holy Spirit. Teach them to obey everything I have commanded you. And you can be sure that I am always with you, to the very end.

Matthew 28:19, 20.

David Livingstone was a Scottish doctor. But what he was most famous for was his mission work and exploration in Africa. When people had not heard from him in years, a New York journalist named Henry Stanley went to Africa to rescue Dr. Livingstone or bring his body back if he was not alive.

He found Dr. Livingstone busily doing his thing. Stanley's famous opening remark was "Dr. Livingstone, I presume." Mr. Stanley soon found out that Dr. Livingstone needed no rescuing and didn't want to go back. He sadly returned without him.

David Livingstone loved Africa and the people who lived there. He stayed there until he died. Dr. Livingstone's friends sent his body back to England for burial in Westminster Abbey, but before they sealed the casket, they removed his heart from his chest and buried it in Africa.

Dr. Livingstone's body may have gone home, but his heart stayed where it had always been. Jesus went back to heaven in honor and glory. But His heart has stayed here with us, though not a literal heart buried somewhere in Palestine. His love and His attention, and even His Holy Spirit, have remained here with us to comfort us and help us and show us His love in a much more real and personal way than Dr. Livingstone's heart ever could.

Thanks, Jesus, for loving us so much that You came and are still here in the form of the Holy Spirit. Amen.

THE TIME OF TROUBLE

So don't worry. Don't say, "What will we eat?" Or, "What will we drink?" Or, "What will we wear?" People who are ungodly run after all of those things. Your Father who is in heaven knows that you need them.

Matthew 6:31, 32.

Ted Daniels, who publishes *Millennium News,* says, "There are hints that more people are getting ready to move into compounds and withdraw from the world at large. They're taking the attitude of 'we're sitting out until the end.'"

One of my friends at school belongs to a family who feels that way. Distrusting the government, they are stockpiling food and other things they feel will be valuable during the difficult time they believe is coming soon in the future.

I can still remember watching TV with my mom and seeing the Branch Davidian compound, in Waco, Texas, going up in smoke in 1993. The people there felt that way too. Not only had they withdrawn into a compound, but they had stashed lots of weapons to defend themselves. Ultimately it wasn't enough.

I too believe hard times await us, but I don't think we need to hide and spend our money and our energy stocking up on things that we assume will get us through the time of trouble. I believe God wants us to use our money to help people here and now and to rely on Him to aid us in the future. He has promised us that our bread and water will be sure. And we can trust Him to do just what He said. No matter what comes up, God will be able to handle it. What a relief to be able to trust Him to take care of things and not have to worry about it!

Jesus, I know that before You come back there's going to be lots of hard times. But thank You for promising to take care of us, no matter what. Amen.

308

LUTHER'S 95 GRIPES

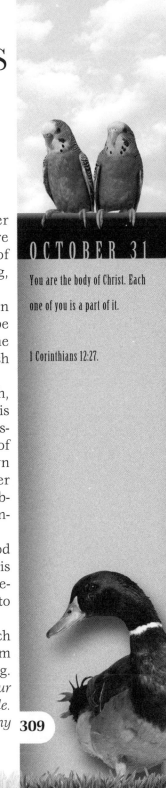

You are the body of Christ. Each one of you is a part of it.

1 Corinthians 12:27.

On this day in 1517 Martin Luther nailed his list of 95 things that were wrong with his church on the door of the castle church in Wittenberg, Germany. What a guy!

Occasionally, I get frustrated at my church. Martin Luther's idea was cool. Sometimes I think it would be fun to write down all the things that are bugging me and nail it to our church door. However, our church has glass doors, and it wouldn't be the same.

One thing I did learn from Martin Luther, though, still is the same. He never intended to leave his church. Loving it and loving God, he was just frustrated when he saw things that weren't right, kind of like me. But he didn't just go off and begin his own denomination, as you might think. Martin Luther worked very hard to try to straighten out the problems in his church from the inside. Luther never intended to start a new religion.

I believe that Martin Luther was doing what God expects us to do. Rather than be critical of what is wrong in our churches and going off in a huff, I believe God wants us to work from the inside to try to make them better.

If Luther is my example, I will stay in my church and do everything I know how to make it better from the inside, because that has been God's plan all along.

God, I know that there are things wrong with Your church. That's because it's filled with imperfect people. Please help me be one of the things that's right with my church. Amen.

309

SAFER THAN UNCLE SAM

Do not put away riches for yourselves on earth. Moths and rust can destroy them. Thieves can break in and steal them. Instead, put away riches for yourselves in heaven. There, moths and rust do not destroy them. There, thieves do not break in and steal them.

Matthew 6:19, 20.

Mom is pretty cynical about our post office. The people there have had a few problems delivering the mail. Of course, they've lost only a couple rejection letters and no incoming checks that we know of, so she shouldn't mind much. However, they've had some problems with outgoing mail, too.

One time Mom had paid our monthly bills and mailed them on time, yet she received phone calls from several of our creditors asking for the money. Mom explained she had sent the checks and on what date, but they weren't very impressed. She ended up sending them more money. Almost a month later the bills arrived, and credits for double payments showed up on all the accounts. Uncle Sam had just been a little slow.

When I told Mom I had found that the U.S. Post Office Department had introduced the money order system in 1864 so they could provide people with a means to make payments safely through the mail, she just laughed. Sending money through the mail then apparently was as frustrating as trying to do it now.

However, there is a safe way to get your money where you want it to go. You let God take care of it. If you put your money in His hands, He keeps it safe and makes sure it reaches the person who needs it. You can always trust Him. He's faster than the pony express and a lot more reliable than the U.S. Postal Service. It's good to know we can always count on Someone.

Dear God, I am glad I can always count on You. Amen.

310

COMPLAINTS AND BIRDBRAINS

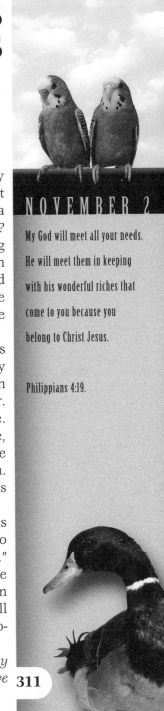

My God will meet all your needs. He will meet them in keeping with his wonderful riches that come to you because you belong to Christ Jesus.

Philippians 4:19.

My little finches aren't as smart as my parrots. Of course, I don't expect them to be. With a brain the size of a pea, how much can go on in there? Mom takes good care of them, giving them clean water and stalks of millet to chew on, with plenty of seeds in their dish and little tidbits of fruit and fresh veggies. Yet sometimes even the finches have complaints. Their most common protest is that they're out of water. It sounds something like "Tweet, tweet!"

It's not that Mom doesn't give them water. She fills up their little water dishes with more water than any bird could drink in one day, but they like to rush down and jump in immediately when they get clean water. They squawk and chirp and throw it all over the place. The water splashes on each other, the rest of the cage, and on the piano. By the time they are finished, the water gets pretty shallow, and then they complain. They are probably saying, "Why doesn't Mom give us enough water? She knows we need water."

Perhaps they're not that different from humans after all. Sometimes we complain, "God promised to provide all our needs, and yet we're always broke." But perhaps some of it has to do with the way we use what God already gave us. Watching my finches in their water has made me ponder a lot. Perhaps I'll think twice before complaining about God not providing what I need.

Dear God, thank You for providing so well for my needs. Help me to be more sensible with what You give me and not complain like my little finches. Amen.

311

SIN AND SEIZURES

He will wipe away every tear from their eyes. There will be no more death or sadness. There will be no more crying or pain. Things are no longer the way they used to be.

Revelation 21:4.

November is National Epilepsy Awareness Month. People have often misunderstood the disease. Perhaps that is because grand mal seizures can look so frightening. In the olden days many people thought seizures indicated demon possession. If you have ever seen one, you can understand why they might have concluded that. It can be scary. But epilepsy is a disease. Doctors can treat it with medicine, and people with epilepsy can live normal lives. As I have gotten older I have found out that several people I know have seizure disorders. I wouldn't have known if someone hadn't told me. They seem pretty normal to me.

Epilepsy and demon possession are two separate things, but they can be both devastating and fatal if not treated. I am glad that the God we worship has the power to cure both. We can trust Him with whatever problems crop up in our lives, medical or spiritual, because He is all-wise and all-powerful. No matter what the problem is, He can take care of it.

I'm looking forward to the day when He will come and make everything perfect again. There will be no more epilepsy, and Satan will hurt no more people either, because all of those terrible things will be completely gone. Until then, I'm trusting Him to handle things for me.

Even so, come, Lord Jesus. Amen.

MOM, MOSES, AND KING TUT

On this day in 1922 Howard Carter, an archaeologist poking around in the Valley of the Kings, discovered King Tut's tomb. King Tut was a boy king who died young. Yet his people buried many incredible treasures in his tomb with him.

King Tut has made me think about Moses. If Moses had made different choices, perhaps archaeologists would be finding his tomb in the Valley of the Kings too, surrounded by gold and treasures—if someone hadn't already stolen them.

Moses faced a difficult choice. He had to decide whether he wanted to be pharaoh of Egypt or to follow God's plan, which included 40 years off in the wilderness with a bunch of sheep and 40 years with an even more frustrating group of stubborn people, trying to lead them to the Promised Land. At the time, being pharaoh may have looked more attractive.

Today Moses is in heaven hanging out with God and probably happier than he ever was on earth. Had he chosen to be pharaoh, he would be in a tomb, perhaps still surrounded with his treasures, but a smelly mummified corpse just the same. If you look at the big picture, it's a no-brainer.

You and I encounter choices too. As you decide what you're going to do with your life, take the long-term view. It's a no-brainer and confusing only if you look just at the present and don't consider the future.

Dear God, thank You for giving me a choice. I want to live forever with You. Amen.

NOVEMBER 4

Moses had faith. So he refused to be called the son of Pharaoh's daughter. That happened after he had grown up. He chose to be treated badly together with the people of God. He chose that instead of enjoying sin's pleasures for a short time. He suffered shame because of Christ.... He considered it better than the riches of Egypt.

Hebrews 11:24-26.

313

FAILURE AND FIREWORKS

Look! I am coming soon! I bring my rewards with me. I will reward each person for what he has done.

Revelation 22:12.

When my mom was my age, she lived in England. Over there, for obvious reasons they don't celebrate the Fourth of July, but they do have their day for fireworks. It is November 5, and they call it Guy Fawkes Day. Guy Fawkes tried to blow up the House of Lords in the British Parliament building. In 1605 he and other conspirators filled the basement under the House of Lords with gunpowder, and the plot might have worked if the authorities hadn't caught him. Instead, he was hanged, drawn, and quartered (what they did with those who committed treason in those days). And ever since, the British have celebrated November 5 as a failed rebellion.

Kids make scarecrow dummies and push them around in strollers asking, "Penny for the guy?" Adults will toss pennies in the guys' cups, and the kids use the money to buy fireworks. November 5 is bonfire night, and people shoot off fireworks as impressive as the House of Lords might look exploding into the sky.

I'm looking forward to an even bigger celebration someday, a celebration of another failed rebellion in heaven in which we will remember the defeat of sin and the victory of Jesus. I'm sure that the fireworks in heaven will be "totally out of this world!" And we'll be able to celebrate the close of a rebellion that will never ever happen again.

What a celebration that will be, God! I'm glad I am on Your side. Amen.

314

MAKING A
JOYFUL NOISE

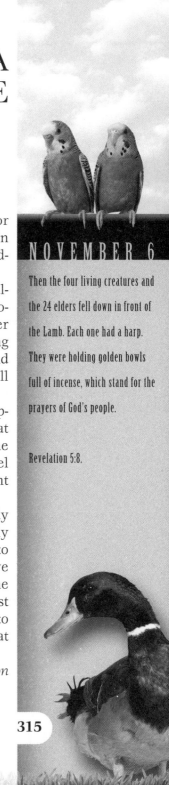

Today is Saxophone Day, named in honor of Adolphe Sax. Mr. Sax was born in 1814. He invented the first brass woodwind, the saxophone.

Being a trombone player myself, I always tell my brother that people who play saxophones are pretty wimpy. However, my brother thinks that Mr. Sax's invention was the coolest thing ever. He can play alto, tenor, and baritone sax, and he performs in the academy band and in a small Dixieland jazz band at school.

Musical instruments are a lot of fun, and I suppose I'm glad that Mr. Sax did his inventing so that my brother could have so much fun with it, since he isn't cool enough to play the trombone. But I feel sorry for people who don't have a musical instrument or don't know how to play one.

I'm looking forward to heaven, where anybody who wants to will be able to play in the heavenly band and make the most fabulous music and praise to Jesus without having to worry about how expensive instruments are and without having to go through the "tortured cat" phase of learning to play. It almost drove my mom nuts. Someday anybody who wants to will be able to make beautiful music together. What fun we will have living with Jesus!

Dear God, I am looking forward to praising You on more than just my trombone! Amen.

Then the four living creatures and the 24 elders fell down in front of the Lamb. Each one had a harp. They were holding golden bowls full of incense, which stand for the prayers of God's people.

Revelation 5:8.

GRANDMA SWANSON

The King will reply, "What I'm about to tell you is true. Anything you did for one of the least important of these brothers of mine, you did for me."

Matthew 25:40.

My cousins, Eric and Andrew, share Grandma Betty with me, but they have another grandmother whom I am not related to. Her name is Grandma Swanson. Grandma Swanson lives in a nursing home because she has Alzheimer's disease. Her husband kept her at home as long as he could, but Grandma Swanson would wander outdoors, and one day she climbed over the fence into the street, where she got hurt. Now she lives in a nursing home, where somebody can watch over her all the time.

Grandpa Swanson visits her every day, and Eric and Andrew stop by often. Although Grandma Swanson no longer remembers their names, she loves their visits. As she shuffles restlessly up and down the hall, my cousins walk along with her. She stops every few seconds to hug them, especially Andrew. While she doesn't know who my aunt Janice is, she senses it's someone she really likes, and she's always happy to see her.

November is National Alzheimer's Disease Month. While your grandma may not have this condition, you will know of people who do. Sometimes being around them can be a little uncomfortable, but remember, people with Alzheimer's need love too. This month, make it a point to be nice to one of them. They still appreciate visits and kindness and attention. And they still like people to talk to them.

Dear God, help me to love You by loving other people. 316 *Amen.*

COME FLY WITH ME

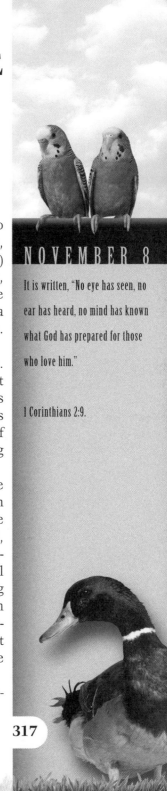

You've probably heard the saying "Two wrongs don't make a right." (Actually, two Wrights made an airplane.) November is Aviation History Month, but this date does not commemorate the accomplishments of Wilbur and Orville. It honors a pair of brothers who came along before the Wrights. They were the Montgolfiers.

The Montgolfiers developed hot-air balloons. Without the accomplishments and knowledge that people gained from hot-air balloons, the Wrights might never have invented the airplane. Humans have always wanted to fly. History is full of stories of people trying to invent flying machines and jumping off buildings, often injuring themselves terribly.

Close to my home is an airport where, if you have enough money, you can purchase flying lessons both for powered planes and also gliders. Such lessons are probably not something that I can realistically afford, at least not until I graduate from college. But someday I will fly. When we go to heaven, we will have all of our greatest hopes and dreams fulfilled, including being able to fly. I plan to spend very little time on the ground. The discoveries of those in aviation history may or may not help me to fly before then, but by being friends with Jesus, I will fly someday. Come fly with me.

Dear God, I can't imagine all the fun we will have together someday. Amen.

NOVEMBER 8

It is written, "No eye has seen, no ear has heard, no mind has known what God has prepared for those who love him."

1 Corinthians 2:9.

FEEDING GOD'S TEMPLE

Don't you know that your bodies are temples of the Holy Spirit? The Spirit is in you. You have received him from God. You do not belong to yourselves.

1 Corinthians 6:19.

November has also been designated as Good Nutrition Month. It is a good opportunity to review the four basic food groups. Contrary to what my brother might think, the four basic food groups are not pizza, veggie burgers, Veja-Links, and chocolate.

I believe that my body is the temple of the Holy Spirit. I've invited Him to live here, and I want to take the best care of it I can. In addition to getting lots of exercise, fresh air, plenty of water to drink, and enough rest, I am learning to pay attention to what I eat.

Fruits and vegetables are awesome. Ever since I was a little boy, Mom has kept a big bowl of fruit in the kitchen, and she allows my brother and me unlimited snacking from it.

Carbohydrates are cool and are one of my favorite forms of food. I love rice, potatoes, and pasta. Bread and cereals are OK too.

Protein is the third group. It's also good stuff for my body.

The fourth category is fats and oils. I probably need to go easy on them, so that I don't end up looking like a fat Buddha.

If I eat things from each of these four food groups, my body will become strong and healthy. And I hope it's a comfortable home for the Holy Spirit to live in. I want Him to stay with me a long time.

Dear God, I want my body to be a place where You will be comfortable living. Amen.

NO MORE GO-BETWEENS

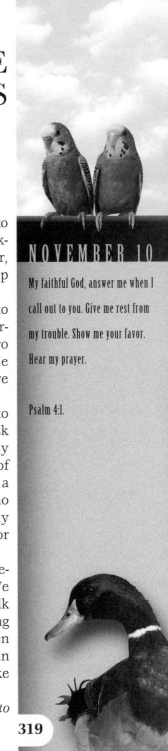

NOVEMBER 10

My faithful God, answer me when I call out to you. Give me rest from my trouble. Show me your favor. Hear my prayer.

Psalm 4:1.

Long-distance phone calls are pretty easy to make. According to my mom, I've been making them a long time. When I was a toddler, she used to have to put all the telephones up high where I couldn't reach them.

But people in the United States have been able to make long-distance calls without the help of an operator only since 1951. Before that they had to dial zero and ask the long-distance operator for help. While that sounds like a real pain to us now, people were used to doing it.

Having to go through a third person to talk to someone reminds me of the way people had to ask for forgiveness before Jesus came. Back then they had to take a lamb and sacrifice it. From the time of Moses until Jesus arrived, everything went through a third person, the high priest. He was the one who took the blood from the lamb into the Most Holy Place once a year so people could have atonement for their sins.

Jesus' death on the cross eliminated the go-between. He made it possible for us to dial God direct. We don't even have to sacrifice a lamb. Instead, we can talk to Him anytime and receive forgiveness for anything anywhere without anyone else's help. That is even cooler than being able to call long distance. What an awesome connection we've been given! But just like your telephone, it works only if you actually use it.

Dear God, thank You for giving me direct access to You. Amen.

319

Then I heard a voice from heaven. "Write this," it said. "Blessed are the dead who die as believers in the Lord from now on." "Yes," says the Holy Spirit. "They will rest from their labor. What they have done will not be forgotten."

Revelation 14:13.

HONORING THE UNKNOWN SOLDIERS

Today is Veterans Day in the United States and Remembrance Day in Canada. When my family lived in Maryland, Mom took me to a lot of the famous sites in the area.

One I especially remember (because I got lost during the ceremony) was visiting the Tomb of the Unknown Soldier at Arlington Cemetery. It was fascinating to watch the changing of the guard as the soldiers in their flashy uniforms marched with their guns and medals. Mom explained to me that no one knows who the soldier inside the tomb is, but they treat him with great respect—to honor all of the soldiers who had died in the war and to remember him, since his family couldn't visit his grave, because they didn't know where he was.

The battle between good and evil has resulted in a lot of unknown soldiers buried all over the world. Many of them no one even remembers. *Foxe's Book of Martyrs* lists some, but often it just says things such as 21 people were put to death on such and such a date at such and such a time. We don't even know their names or if they had families. But God knew each one personally, and He has watched over their graves carefully and will treat them with the greatest honor someday. And even though no one remembers who or where they are right now, someday they will be great heroes and get even more honors and respect than the unknown soldiers in Arlington Cemetery.

Dear God, I'm glad we can count on You to remember each of Your soldiers. Amen.

320

SABBATH SCHOOL AND HAPPY HOUR

When I first learned to read, one of my favorite things was to watch the signs as we drove along and read what they said. A sign outside a lounge that we passed every day on the way to school said something about "happy hour." "What's happy hour?" I asked Mom.

She laughed. "That's the hour before the puking hour," she said.

My brother also laughed. He explained to me, "Happy hour is an hour around the time that people usually get off work when they can buy alcoholic drinks cheaper. They call it happy hour because people often drink too much and get pretty silly."

Now it made sense. I knew from some of the stories I had heard that drinking too much alcohol ended up making people throw up—which sounded a lot less happy to me.

On this day in 1745 the first "happy hour" took place in a local pub in Ireland.

Other things besides drinking too much can make a person happy. Listening to praise music and singing along can make you a whole lot happier, and they don't make you vomit afterward. Perhaps "happy hour" is a silly name for something that takes place in a bar. But maybe that's what we should call Sabbath school. It would make a lot more sense. So come on, try praising God. Get happy, and you won't even need Alka-Seltzer afterward.

God, You are able to make people really happy. Amen.

NOVEMBER 12

You always show me the path that leads to life. You will fill me with joy when I am with you. You will give me endless pleasures at your right hand.

Psalm 16:11.

321

THE BRAVEST OF THEM ALL

Blessed are those who wash their robes. They will have the right to come to the tree of life. They will be allowed to go through the gates into the city.

Revelation 22:14.

On this day in 1982 the United States dedicated the Vietnam Veterans' Memorial in Washington, D.C. When I was 5 years old my mom took me to see it.

At that age I was heavy into war heroes, but had a little trouble keeping my wars straight. My favorite hero was Stonewall Jackson. As we stood looking at the wall and watching all the mourners and tourists, I asked my mom, "Why are so many of them crying?"

"Every name on the wall is the name of somebody who died in this war. Lots of these people were families of the men who died, and they miss them." I noticed several people watching me and nodding as Mom talked. "These men died fighting for their country," Mom continued. "They were brave men."

"But the bravest of them all," I replied, pausing for dramatic effect, "was Stonewall Jackson!" Laughter rippled through the crowd. Even those snuffling into tissues stopped to chuckle. I could hear people repeating what I had said to those who hadn't caught it the first time, and then they laughed too. I was a little confused about my heroes.

Jesus has something even more special than a black marble slab planned to honor the veterans of the war between good and evil. He's going to give them a new home and a new life And the bravest of them all will be Jesus, our hero.

Dear God, I am looking forward to spending eternity with You in the handkerchief-free zone. Amen.

322

CELEBRATING CREATIVE GENIUS

NOVEMBER 14

So God created man in his own likeness. He created him in the likeness of God. He created them as male and female.

Genesis 1:27.

November has been designated as International Creative Child and Adult Month. Sponsored by the National Association for Creative Children and Adults, in Cincinnati, Ohio, its goal is to help people appreciate the importance of creativity.

I think creativity is vital too. When the Bible says that God created us in His own image, I believe that meant a whole lot more than just having a power of choice and some of the other things that we hear about in church. Preachers and Sabbath school teachers tell us about such characteristics of God as love and truth and power, but one of the things I find the neatest about God is His creativity.

Consider the imagination, as well as the sense of humor, it took to design a giraffe. He imagined all the physics that it takes to hang our world in space, creating just enough gravity and making our world rotate just fast enough for everything to work right.

I believe that when we express our creativity, whether we are strumming on a guitar, dabbling in oil paint, or doodling in a notebook we are expressing the part of us that God made in His image, for God is the ultimate creative person.

Today celebrate your creativity, for you are made in the image of God.

Thank You, God, for making me in Your image and allowing me to be creative. Amen.

323

APPRECIATING THE BEHIND-THE-SCENES PEOPLE

NOVEMBER 15

Give thanks no matter what happens. God wants you to thank him because you believe in Christ Jesus.

1 Thessalonians 5:18.

Today is National Education Support Personnel Day. Schools often have Teacher Appreciation days and things like that, but often many of the behind-the-scenes people don't get recognized or appreciated as they probably should. People such as the secretaries, bus drivers, cafeteria staff, maintenance personnel, and others, without whom our school just wouldn't work, often seem almost invisible to those of us who spend all our days in the classrooms with teachers.

Today is a time when we should recognize them and thank them for what they do to make our lives better. Mr. Ockenga runs the cafeteria at the school where I go. While it is terribly uncool to admit to liking cafeteria food, and I would never do such a thing (especially in print), I do have to admit that with a mother who is not particularly domestic, it is nice to be able to get the things Mr. Ockenga makes for my lunches.

I appreciate Mr. Little, without whom things like lightbulbs would never get changed at school, without whom the heat might not be turned on at the right time, and other important things like that.

Part of being a Christian is to develop an attitude of gratitude and give thanks and affirmation to the people who help us along the way. Everyone needs encouragement sometimes. As I grow more like Jesus I will learn to express appreciation to the people who make a difference in my life.

Dear God, help me keep an attitude of gratitude.

324 *Amen.*

GREAT AMERICAN SMOKEOUT

NOVEMBER 16

Dear friend, I know that your spiritual life is going well. I pray that you also may enjoy good health. And I pray that everything else may go well with you.

3 John 2.

The American Cancer Society has designated November as the Great American Smokeout Month. It especially encourages smokers this month to quit the habit. For those who can't do it for a whole month, it has the Great American Smokeout Day on the third Thursday of every November. On that day the American Cancer Society urges people to try quitting for just one day.

I have some friends who smoke. It baffles me why people do it, since it smells bad and it makes their teeth and their fingernails yellow. Often they get little holes burned in their clothes where the ashes have fallen. Besides that, it can stunt their growth, and it's hard to stop once you start.

Two of my friends *have* to smoke. If they don't have a cigarette, they begin getting the shakes and are really cranky. Why would anyone start doing something that would make them a prisoner to it and their lives miserable if they didn't do it every single day?

Apart from the diseases it can cause, smoking is just gross. I want the Holy Spirit to enjoy living in my body and not to sit in there fanning the air and coughing, and wishing He could see what was going on.

People who are going through withdrawal have a really hard time. This month give extra moral support to the smoker friends you know. Encourage them to join the Great American Smokeout, and be extra patient with them if they try to quit.

Dear God, I want my body to be a place where You like to live. Amen.

325

POLITICIANS AND PLAIN SPEAKING

The Lord hates those whose lips tell lies. But he is pleased with people who tell the truth.

Proverbs 12:22.

I read a riddle on the Internet that said, "What is the definition of politics?" The answer: "poly means many; ticks are nasty little blood-sucking insects; politics, therefore, is a large gathering of nasty little bloodsuckers." Politicians get made fun of almost as much as lawyers do, but they were the first ones who sprang to mind today as I looked at my calendar because . . .

Today is designated as "Doublespeak Day." Every year on this date a Doublespeak Award goes to American public figures who have used language that is so deceptive or evasive, euphemistic, confusing, or self-contradictory that they stand out from the others. The National Council of Teachers of English annual convention in Syracuse, New York, awards it.

Unfortunately, politicians and lawyers are not the only ones who have a little trouble with doublespeak sometimes. Let's face it—anything we say that is intended to give people the wrong impression, whether we are technically lying or not, is just not honest. God didn't mince any words in the Bible when He told us how He feels about dishonesty and lying.

As someone who loves Him and wants to please Him, I need to eliminate all doublespeak from my vocabulary. God's followers need to be honest and clear in what they say.

Dear God, please help keep me from doublespeak so my speech will always be acceptable to You. Amen.

GOD AND WILLIAM TELL

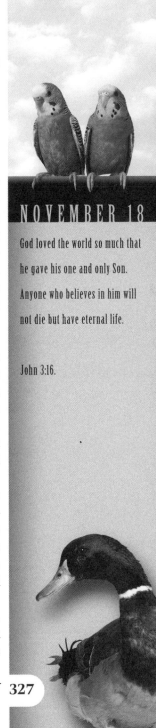

NOVEMBER 18

God loved the world so much that he gave his one and only Son. Anyone who believes in him will not die but have eternal life.

John 3:16.

One of my favorite cartoonists is Gary Larson. As a little kid I remember paging through the books of his cartoons that Mom often used in teaching her nursing classes at the hospital. I remember having to ask questions about one of them. It was a picture of a boy with a very big head and a tiny little apple on top of it. The caption was "William Tell's little-known first son." I didn't get it.

"Why is this one funny?" I asked her.

Mom told me the story of William Tell, a brave man who lived in the 1300s and fought for the freedom of his people in Switzerland. The Austrian bailiff, Gessler, set up a pole with a hat on it in the main square of the town of Altdorf. He ordered all the Swiss to bow to the hat. Tell refused, and Gessler arrested him. Knowing about Tell's skill with a crossbow, Gessler said that Tell could go free if he would shoot an apple off his son's head.

Tell had only one son. Back then crossbows were just coming into vogue. Most of them weren't very accurate. William Tell's son believed his father could do it, though. He had so much faith in his father that he stood perfectly still as his dad aimed toward the apple on his head and fired. William Tell hit the apple and eventually helped his people gain their freedom.

God risked His only Son to set His people free. How much He must have loved us! And how much His Son must have trusted Him to go along with the plan. Certainly we can trust Him too.

Dear God, thank You for giving Your only Son for my freedom. Amen.

BAD-HAIR DAYS

How terrible for you, teachers of the law and Pharisees! You pretenders! You are like tombs that are painted white. They look beautiful on the outside. But on the inside they are full of the bones of the dead. They are also full of other things that are not pure and clean.

Matthew 23:27.

Yesterday my mom produced a picture she thought would be a good one to go on the back of this book. It had me sound asleep in a chair in the living room with Miss Cinnamon, my cockatiel, sitting on top of my head, patiently waiting for me to wake up and play with her. She figured that I had mentioned Miss Cinnamon so many times in the book that it would be a great picture.

You will not see this picture on my book, because I was having a bad-hair day. I definitely do not want a photo of my hair cut that way on anything that might ever get published!

Some people get really upset with their bad-hair days. My mom used to. She would get so frustrated when her hair wouldn't do what she wanted it to until . . . she had to take some medicine that made a lot of her hair fall out. Once she got over being so upset about it, she purchased a T-shirt that said "A bad-hair day is better than no-hair day." Also she bought my friend Rachel, who was on chemotherapy at the time, a hat that declared, "No-hair day." That sort of puts my bad-hair days into perspective.

While God approves of our being as attractive as possible, I don't believe He wants us to spend a lot of time worrying and agonizing over how we look on the outside. What is most important to Him is who we are on the inside. To God, a bad-hair day is much less up-setting than a bad-heart day.

Dear God, thank You for giving me a good-heart day—and thank You for my hair, too! Amen.

PUNCHING THE TIME CLOCK

On this day in the year 1888 a man named William Bundy invented the time clock—the type you punch a time card in. I have become very familiar with one of them this past year. William Bundy developed his invention so that employees would get paid only for the actual hours and minutes they worked, ensuring that each person would receive only the money they actually deserved instead of everyone's getting the same amount no matter how many or how few hours they put in that day.

While this seems fair to most employers and employees, God doesn't work on the time-clock theory. When God rewards His people, He doesn't base it on how long they worked for Him or how much they did. Rather, He looks for whether they loved Him or not and whether they showed up.

Jesus told a parable about a man who recruited workers for His vineyard all through the day, and yet he gave them all the same wages at the end of the day. If that happened where I work after school, everyone would be up in arms and furious, except those who had worked only a very short time. Yet that is how God operates. Without a time clock we can just relax and love God. We do those things because we love Him and because we want to, not because we're trying to put in a certain number in order to get our reward.

Thank You, God, that You don't use time clocks when we work for You. You are very generous to us. Amen.

NOVEMBER 20

So it can't be said that anyone will be made right with God by keeping the law. Not at all! The law makes us more aware of our sin.

Romans 3:20.

329

REMEMBERING TOM

NOVEMBER 21

There are different kinds of gifts.
But they are all given
by the same Spirit.

1 Corinthians 12:4.

On this date in the year 1877 Thomas Edison announced the invention of the talking machine. Eventually people came to refer to it as the phonograph and still later, the record player. He actually invented it on July 18, but not until November 21 did he share it with the American public. By the time people our age have children, they probably won't even know what a record player is.

Without Thomas Edison's invention, the other talking machines, such as cassette players and my beloved CD player that I take everywhere with me, might never have come into being. As much as I like my CD player, that is not the reason I appreciate Thomas Edison the most. Why I have a really soft spot for him is that he had a hard time in school, just like me.

He was just one of countless people who proved that even with a learning problem you can still do awesome things with your life and make the world a better place because you were here.

Do you have a part of your life that you have trouble with—school or otherwise? Don't get discouraged. Every time you play your cassette or CD player, remember Thomas Edison and remember that no matter what you're having trouble with, you can still do awesome things.

Just ask Jesus to help you understand the areas you are gifted in. Concentrate on those and He will help you.

Dear God, thank You for reminding me about people like Thomas Edison, so I don't get discouraged. Amen.

JEWISH
BOOK MONTH

From November 18 to December 18 (the beginning of Hanukkah) is Jewish Book Month. It is sponsored by the J.W.B. Jewish Book Council in New York. During this month the organization encourages people to read books by Jewish authors and on Jewish interests.

The organization would approve of our family. My mom belongs to a Jewish book club and reads so many of their books that they probably think we *are* Jewish. For a year she even subscribed to a Jerusalem newspaper. My brother is into it too. His favorite Jewish author is Elie Wiesel, a Holocaust survivor who came to speak at our school one time.

Jewish history is fascinating, and the fact that it goes back to the time of Abraham makes it even more interesting to me. However, the Jewish book I'd like to recommend to you this month is the Bible. Most of the authors in the Bible were Jewish.

Since I became a writer, I have learned about royalties. Royalties are the money that writers get paid each year, based on how many of their books sold. Imagine what a wealthy nation Israel would be if it could collect royalties on the Bible! It's the all-time best-seller. Israelis wouldn't be receiving aid from the United States—we'd be asking them for some!

Fortunately the Bible belongs to everybody.

This month, read a Jewish book. Have a look at the Bible. It's the greatest book you'll ever read.

God, Your Book is the best—even better than Elie Wiesel! Amen.

NOVEMBER 22

You Samaritans worship what you do not know. We worship what we do know. Salvation comes from the Jews.

John 4:22.

PREACHERS AND PARACHUTE PACKERS

He says, "My flock does not have a shepherd. Many of my sheep have been stolen. They have become food for all the wild animals. My shepherds did not care for my sheep. They did not even search for them. Instead, they only took care of themselves. And that is just as sure as I am alive," announces the Lord and King.

Ezekiel 34:8.

Skydiving has always looked like fun to me—a whole lot more fun than bungee jumping! The idea of floating down through the sky beneath an unfurling parachute just exhilarates me. Whenever I talk about skydiving, my mom always makes jokes and advises me to get a job in a parachute packing plant instead. (Nobody ever comes back to complain about your competence.)

One thing about skydiving that is different than other pursuits is that *everything* is critically important. Your life depends on it! A newspaper in Warrenton, Virginia, printed this: "IMPORTANT NOTICE: If you are one of the hundreds of parachuting enthusiasts who bought our 'Easy Skydiving' book, please make the following correction: On page 8, line 7, the words 'state zip code' should have read 'pull rip cord.'" A significant oversight! I can just imagine hundreds of parachutists all plummeting toward the earth as they shout their zip codes!

God is pretty hard on people who make mistakes while instructing others on how to make life-threatening decisions. Ezekiel is full of God's opinion of His people's shepherds who took care of themselves but ignored their spiritual flocks or didn't search for His lost sheep. I wouldn't want to be in their shoes. It makes me stop to think how much God cares about each of His people.

Dear God, thank You for having strict guidelines, since preachers and other spiritual leaders are responsible for helping us with our spiritual parachute packing! Amen.

ORIGIN OF THE SPECIES

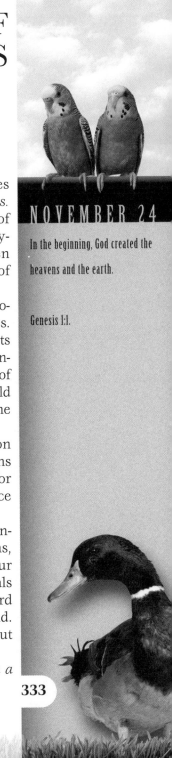

In the beginning, God created the heavens and the earth.

Genesis 1:1.

On this day in the year 1859 Charles Darwin published *The Origin of Species*. In his book he described his theory of evolution. Schools teach it everywhere. Evolution convinces children that humans came from a little primordial glob of slime that slowly evolved to what we are today.

This theory makes it understandable that some people still feel like slime or act like apes or even reptiles. After all, consider where they came from! Such concepts have been part of the curriculum for more than a hundred years, and now schools are having to do all kinds of work with kids suffering from poor self-esteem. Could part of it stem from the idea that they believe they came from a glob of slime and are going nowhere?

As Christians we believe that God placed us on this earth perfect, fresh from His hand, to be His sons and daughters. Each of us has a job to do, a plan for our lives, and a hope and a future. What a difference it makes!

Meanwhile, atheists and evolutionists will continue to struggle with self-esteem, but as Christians, we shouldn't have to. How different every part of our lives is because of this one theory! Even at funerals Christians find it a time of hope as they look forward to the resurrection. But to atheists death is the end. Darwin may have sold a lot of copies of his book, but he was still wrong. Aren't you glad?

Dear God, I would much rather be Your son than a monkey's great-grandson! Amen.

333

REAL FISHERS OF MEN

"Come. Follow me," Jesus said. "I will make you fishers of people."

Matthew 4:19.

An ad in the *Hendon Times,* in the United Kingdom, read: "Swimming teachers required for both children and adults, ASA qualified. Must be prepared to go into the water." While that sounds silly and we can't imagine someone actually teaching swimming without getting wet, sometimes we approach the things God calls us to do exactly that way.

I live out in the country on one of the forks of the Shenandoah River. Several of my friends like to go fishing—that is, they like to sit around with fishing poles on the bank of the river, goofing off, laughing, joking, and eating a lot of junk food. They don't actually catch fish. If they did, they probably wouldn't know what to do with them. No one would eat anything that came out of our little river anyway. It's pretty dirty. Yet they get together, have a good time, and call it fishing.

Jesus called us to be fishers of men. But getting together once a week to talk about it and sing about it and enjoy each other's company doesn't make us fishers. We actually have to catch fish to really count as fishers of men. Each of us actually has to get into the water. Jesus summoned us not just to sing and talk about it but to actually get something done. Let's do it. Be a real fisher.

Dear God, help me not to be a big talker but actually get involved in the fishing! Amen.

NEVER FORGOTTEN

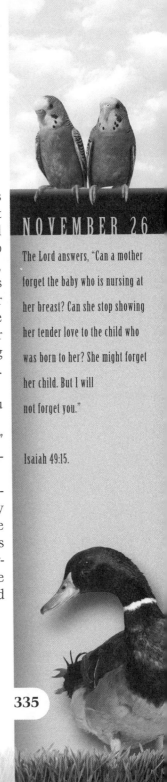

Being forgotten is no fun. During the years when my dad worked from an office at home and Mom labored in the hospital all day, he was the one who picked me up from school. My dad is a really smart guy, but he can be extremely absentminded. Many times we would be out there after school with all the other kids. Everyone else's parents would pull through the parking lot and pick them up. The group got smaller and smaller, and still my brother and I were standing there. Eventually we would be the only two kids left. We felt pretty terrible.

Sometimes we would have to call Dad. "Did you forget us?" I'd ask.

"Oh, dear," he'd reply. "I'll be there right away." And he was, but I still felt bad that he hadn't remembered us.

Sometimes it feels like that with God too, especially when He doesn't answer my prayers the way that I expect Him to. I feel as if God has forgotten me too. That's why I like this verse so much. It reminds me that no matter what happens, God will never forget me and will always be there for me. Even people who love us very much sometimes forget, but God never does. That's comforting to know.

Thank You, God, for never forgetting me. Amen.

NOVEMBER 26

The Lord answers, "Can a mother forget the baby who is nursing at her breast? Can she stop showing her tender love to the child who was born to her? She might forget her child. But I will not forget you."

Isaiah 49:15.

335

HOME-CARE HEROES

Give thanks as you enter the gates of his temple. Give thanks as you enter its courtyards. Give thanks to him and praise his name.

Psalm 100:4.

This is National Home Care Week, set aside to show appreciation to home-care providers. My mom was one back before I was born, but I never thought about it much.

But when I was in the fourth grade, my mom became terribly ill. Usually someone with her problems would have had to remain in the hospital for a long time. But instead Mom was able to stay home because of the home-care nurses.

Mom lived in a special chair in the living room, since she couldn't breathe if she lay down in a bed. The nurses slid a long tube up into her arm through a needle. I couldn't believe how long it was. The nurses hooked the tube in her arm up to a little pouch of medicine and a computerized pump. The computer made sure that she got a little bit through her tube every hour and a big dose every six hours. That way someone didn't have to wake up in the middle of the night to give her medicine.

The home-care nurses came every day to check on Mom and to put a new bag of medicine in the machine. My brother, my dad, and I all had a part in Mom's care.

Even though having mom so sick was hard for us, it would have been much worse to have had her in the hospital.

We greatly appreciated her home-care nurses. Even more, I appreciate Jesus, who was there with us and with Mom every day. I made sure not only to thank the nurses, but to thank Him too.

Dear God, thank You for being willing to help us **336** *wherever we are, however we are. Amen.*

GIRRAFIC PARK

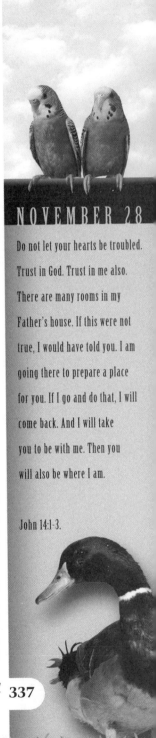

When I was little, my mom and my brother and I used to enjoy sitting around fantasizing about what our dream house would be. Not a house that we would buy or build some-day, but the one that we wanted in the new earth after we had spent 1,000 years in heaven with Jesus and had come back to the earth made new.

My brother always wanted a tree house, and his dream house got fancier and fancier as the years went on. Mom talked about having a house with a bubble room underwater where she could watch the fish and the sea animals. She is a marine-biology enthusiast.

I imagined my house somewhere on the new earth that resembled the plains of the Serengeti. All my life we've had pets—but none with fur. We've had birds, fish, and reptiles, but Mom has been allergic to the furry animals. My dream house in heaven will be somewhere where there are a lot of furry ones, and not just little ones. I'd like lions, zebras, elephants, and a large tribe of giraffes. I don't care what the house is like, but I want lots of animals there. I think I would call my spot "Girrafic Park."

Many people worry about whether or not they're going to be in heaven, but we don't need to do that, because Jesus has promised us that He will take away our sins if we will ask Him. And since I've asked Him, I'd rather spend time thinking about what life there will be like with Him. How about you?

Dear God, it is fun to imagine life in a perfect world with You. I hope it happens soon. Amen.

Do not let your hearts be troubled. Trust in God. Trust in me also. There are many rooms in my Father's house. If this were not true, I would have told you. I am going there to prepare a place for you. If I go and do that, I will come back. And I will take you to be with me. Then you will also be where I am.

John 14:1-3.

SECRET MESSAGES

NOVEMBER 29

Your word is like a lamp that shows me the way. It is like a light that guides me.

Psalm 119:105.

I think I would have liked Sir James Jay. Of course, I'll never know for sure, because he lived back in the 1700s, but he seems the kind of guy I would have had fun with. Sir James Jay invented invisible ink in 1775. His friend, Silas Deane, was the first person to actually use it. What fun they must have had!

Invisible ink has been useful not only for spies and those involved in espionage, but also for guys like me who just like to send secret notes to their friends. When I was little, my mom taught me how to make invisible ink out of lemon juice. She filled up her fountain pen that she had used when she was a little girl, and we wrote on paper. When it was dry, you couldn't even see it. To read the message, we would swipe a hot iron over it. Anyplace we had written with the lemon juice would show up brown, and we could read the message clearly.

We had a lot of fun doing that, and my brother and I sent each other lots of secret messages and pictures. But I'm really glad that when God inspired people to write the Bible, they didn't use invisible ink. Even though some of them, such as Jeremiah, got into a lot of trouble for the things they wrote, they wrote clearly so that we could all get the message.

God's Word is important to us, and He didn't make it hard to read or hard to find. He wants us to understand it. And if we do, it will make our lives better.

Dear God, I'm glad Your Word is not a secret. Amen.

338

TAKING THE BLAME

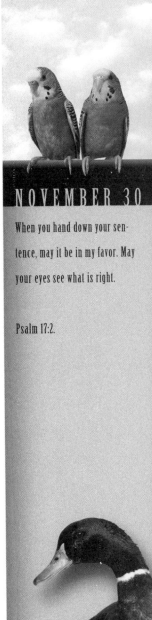

NOVEMBER 30

When you hand down your sentence, may it be in my favor. May your eyes see what is right.

Psalm 17:2.

One day someone wrote a whole lot of graffiti on the walls in the guys' bathroom at school. For some reason the principal got it in his head that I had done it or knew who had. Even though I told him I had nothing to do with it, he continued to question me about it. Nothing I could say seemed to make him believe me.

Now, I don't mind getting in trouble for things I did. It happens occasionally, and I'm usually willing to take responsibility for my own mistakes. But being blamed for someone else's deeds and not being able to convince the principal that I was telling the truth was frustrating. It made me angrier and angrier.

I like this text in Psalms because it helps me understand that I'm not the only person who ever went through this and felt upset.

David had similar feelings. When he wrote his psalms, he told God exactly how he felt. He didn't pretend or try to make things sound better than they were. I especially like reading the psalms in more modern words. As I read this psalm in one of those versions, it sounds just like something I might have said after spending the afternoon in the principal's office.

I'm glad that God protected David's psalms and the others through the centuries so that we could read them in the Bible today. It helps to know that someone else has felt this way before and that God understands.

Thank You, God, for understanding me. Amen.

339

THE ONLY HILL MY MOM CAN CLIMB

DECEMBER 1

Who can climb up to the temple on the hill of the Lord? Who can stand in his holy place? Anyone who has clean hands and a pure heart.

Psalm 24:3, 4.

My brother and I enjoy hiking. We really like the Appalachian Trail. However, since Mom became disabled we don't do as much hiking together as we used to. But we did discover one little stretch of the trail that she can walk. It's up on Skyline Drive, in the Blue Ridge Mountains. We found a place where we can park. The trail is mostly downhill. The bottom of the hill is not far from a road. Mom cuts across to the road, and my brother, Dad, and I hike back up the hill, get the car, and pick her up.

One time Mom saw a big eight-point buck as she sat there quietly next to the road waiting for us. It's her favorite hiking spot.

Mom likes this verse a lot, because the people who can climb the hill of the Lord are not just those who are in the best condition or those who have the lightest backpack or the strongest legs. They are those who have clean hands and a pure heart. The hill of the Lord may be the only hill my mom can climb. I'm glad that God has one she could make it up, and as far as hills go, it is by far the most important.

God, please give me a pure heart today. Amen.

SO YOU LIKE FROGS, EH?

I went through a period of life being interested in Egyptian history. It taught me a lot about ancient Egypt and its culture. Going back now and reading Exodus 10 convulses me with laughter. What a sense of humor God has! God took things that the Egyptians worshiped and pointed out to them how helpless and silly their gods were. The Egyptians thought the river Nile brought life to Egypt, so God turned it to blood. And Pharaoh, who was god on earth and in charge of the Nile, could do nothing about it.

They worshiped frogs and had little ponds and gardens in their homes and palaces dedicated to the frog goddess. God said, "Do you want to worship frogs? Here, I'll give you frogs." Suddenly they had the critters coming out of everywhere and getting into everything. They couldn't avoid stepping on a frog or lying on one or having one hop on their face. Now, I like frogs, but I don't think I could have stood that either.

God wasn't picking on the river or the frogs or any of the other things He used for the ten plagues. He was just pointing out that they directed their worship toward things that had no power. The God of Israel was showing them that He was the one with the power, the one whom they should worship.

After learning about Egypt, it helped me understand more about God. He has a sense of humor. Even more, I found that not only do I worship God because of His power, but I like Him too.

Thanks for humor, God. Amen.

If you do not let them go, I will send the full force of my plagues against you this time. They will strike your officials and your people. Then you will know that there is no one like me in the whole earth.

Exodus 9:14.

341

DISABLED MINDS THINK ALIKE

DECEMBER 3

I was like eyes for those who were blind. I was like feet for those who couldn't walk.

Job 29:15.

By the time I was in sixth grade, my mom was already disabled. A girl in my class had a disabled mother too, although her disabilities were a lot different than my mom's. When our class was planning our outdoor education trip, we felt kind of left out. The school invited other parents to come along, but neither of our moms wanted to go. Neither of them felt she could keep up with the group. And we knew they couldn't.

So Rachel and I plotted together. "Mom," I said, "Mrs. Antisdel would go if you would go."

At the same time Rachel told her mom, "Mrs. Dillon would go if you go."

We won. Both of our moms came. They didn't sleep on the gym floor at the local church school as we did. Instead, they stayed at a nearby hotel. Mr. Litten, our science teacher, arranged the afternoon activities to be in handicapped-accessible places, and they joined us for half a day each day. Rachel and I had a much better time, having our moms along like other kids did. The neatest thing about it was that Mom and Mrs. Antisdel got to be best friends and had the most wonderful time together at the motel.

Today, take time to look at a disabled person, not to stare at them but to see them as a real person. See what kind of things they would enjoy, and include them when you do those things. Disabled people have a life too. Jesus believed this and was friends with everyone who came to Him.

342

Dear God, help me to look past the outside things and see people as You do. Amen.

PRIORITIZE

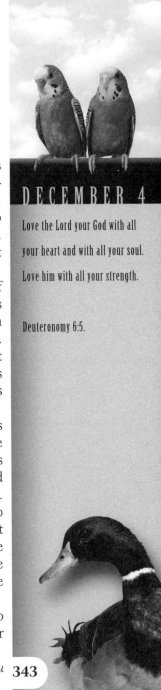

Sometimes life can get overwhelming. Things pile up, and everything seems absolutely important. I have chores, homework, and then, of course, this manuscript that I need to keep working on, or I won't be done in time. Sometimes I don't know where to start. It all just seems overwhelming, and I must set priorities.

Mom has taught me to sit down, make a list of everything I need to do, and then decide what is most important for today. Obviously, everything on the list is important, or it wouldn't be on the list. Therefore, I choose things that have the nearest deadline or that would produce the greatest penalties if I didn't accomplish them. Setting priorities makes life less overwhelming.

God knew that life would threaten to deluge us spiritually too. And so in the New Testament He gave us an outline of His priorities. Sometimes it seems as if God has too many rules, too many things we need to do. But here are His priorities to simplify things: 1. Love God totally. 2. Love others totally. There are no commandments greater than these, Jesus said. That means not rules about do's and don'ts or even the health rules about not smoking or having a beer. The highest priorities are to love God totally and to love others totally. It has helped me greatly.

Once I get my priorities set and I know what to focus on, I can put all my energy into that, and other things will then fall into perspective.

Dear God, I already love You—help me to love You totally *and learn to love others totally too. Amen.*

DECEMBER 4

Love the Lord your God with all your heart and with all your soul. Love him with all your strength.

Deuteronomy 6:5.

CONVERSION AND CHRISTIANS

DECEMBER 5

The law of the Lord is perfect. It gives us new strength. The laws of the Lord can be trusted. They make childish people wise.

Psalm 19:7.

I loved to look inside our big van and imagine what we could do with it, tearing the seats out, putting a bed in the back, maybe installing a little camping stove with a fridge and a counter and storage space underneath. My ideas were endless.

I was delighted when my dad finally bought a conversion van. It had the bed in the back that converted into a couch when Mom wasn't in it. Now we could go on longer trips. When Mom wore out, we could let the bed down and keep going while she took a nap. Our van had big comfy captain's chairs in it so that she could ride longer before she started complaining of joint pain. Outside it didn't look that much different than other vans, but inside it was cool.

Knowing Jesus does the same thing to us. We may not appear that different on the outside, but when Jesus converts us, He takes our empty interior, sometimes throws out the few things that He does find in there, and makes us all brand-new, filling us with beautiful things.

Sometimes the conversion process can be a little painful while it's going on, but the results are wonderful. Conversion is cool, and God's law and the Holy Spirit do it. I want to be a converted Christian made beautiful on the inside by Jesus. How about you?

Dear God, thank You for starting Your conversion process on me. Please help me to cooperate until You are finished and I am just the way You imagined when You first saw me. Amen.

344

GRANDMA TOM

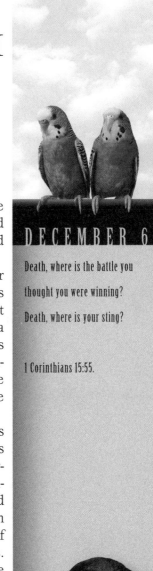

DECEMBER 6

Death, where is the battle you thought you were winning? Death, where is your sting?

1 Corinthians 15:55.

Funerals are generally sad times where everyone cries and remembers all the good things about the person who has died and tells everyone else about them.

We decided it would be a shame for Grandma Tadman to miss out on all the nice things people would say about her. The doctors told her that her cancer has come back and that she has only a short time to live. All of my mom's aunts and uncles and all of my aunts on Mom's side of the family gathered in Lynchburg for a weekend. They had a huge potluck, then spent Sabbath afternoon making the speeches that they might have given at the funeral.

Because it wasn't a funeral and because it was Mom's side of the family, they did it with large doses of laughing and giggling and reminiscing about hilarious and embarrassing events that occurred throughout Grandma's life. It was a blast. Many described how she had always loved them and accepted them through the hard times of their life, and some told of how she had shaped the way they understood Jesus. No matter what we shared, Grandma was there able to hear and enjoy it.

How neat to have a funeral *before* you die and to hear all those good things. How good it must be to be able to fall asleep in Jesus, knowing that you have followed Him, and that your life has brought the people around you closer to Him.

Dear God, please help my life to be that way too. Amen.

345

FORGET PEARL HARBOR

And when you stand praying, forgive anyone you have anything against. Then your Father in heaven will forgive your sins.

Mark 11:25, 26.

Timberville, the town where I live, has a used-car dealer. I notice him every time I drive by, not because of the cars he has out front (though sometimes he has some really cool ones), but because of the enormous billboard he has on his lot. It says in giant jagged red letters: "Remember Pearl Harbor."

In 1941 Japan bombed Pearl Harbor, the large naval base where the Pacific fleet of the U.S. Navy was based at the time. The Japanese wiped out most of the ships. It was the incident that pulled the United States into the Pacific part of World War II.

Many still remember December 7 as Pearl Harbor Day. This strikes me as major grudge holding. It seems that something that happened 59 years ago is something we should be able to forgive by now, especially since we have had a peace treaty between us and Japan for a long time, and the Japanese are one of our major economic trade partners.

Yet Christians can hold grudges as long as this or longer. Jesus told Peter we should forgive each other not just seven times but 70 times seven. Perhaps that applies even to grudges we hold on December 7. In the Lord's Prayer Jesus said that our heavenly Father would forgive us as we forgive others. I certainly have some things that I hope God will forgive me for, so it is important that I learn how to forgive other people too.

Dear God, help me to forgive and not hold grudges. I certainly need Your forgiveness, and I want to be like You. Amen.

346

PAYING A FAITHFUL TIDE

Joyce Meyer tells a story of obedience. She runs her ministry through seminars and on TV, so most of her parishioners write to her. Every month her office headquarters received a box of Tide laundry detergent. They were pretty sure it wasn't a sample from the company, yet could never figure out who sent it.

A couple years passed, then one day a woman called the ministry with a request for special prayer. The prayer counselor asked, "Do you know Jesus as your personal friend and Saviour?"

"Oh, yes," she replied. "I send Him a faithful Tide once a month."

It rang a bell in the mind of the prayer counselor, who asked, "Where do you send it?"

"To your office," the woman on the phone answered. "I send a box of Tide every month just like the preacher on television said to do."

The mystery was solved. The woman was living up to every bit of light she understood. She thought God wanted her to send a faithful Tide every month, and she did.

While we laugh at this story, perhaps we look like that to God sometimes. Yet here are the people God really wants in His family. They try their best to do everything they can to please Him. Then, when they find out something else, they do that too. I hope that God will look on me with the same favor as He did the woman who sent Him the faithful Tide every month.

Dear God, I want to obey You and to please You too. Amen.

DECEMBER 8

Abraham had faith. So he obeyed God. God called him to go to a place he would later receive as his own. So he went. He did it even though he didn't know where he was going. Because of his faith he made his home in the land God had promised him. He was like an outsider in a strange country. He lived there in tents. . . . Abraham was looking forward to the city that has foundations. He was waiting for the city that God planned and built.

Hebrews 11:8-10.

JOINING THE FLOCK

Then he will call his friends and neighbors together. He will say, "Be joyful with me. I have found my lost sheep."

Luke 15:6.

My latest clutch of new-born parakeets has two yellow babies and a white one in it. The oldest yellow infant came out today. She is sitting up on the valance of our miniblinds. Mr. Tasselhoff, who is actually her grandpa but who sort of adopts all the babies in the flock, has made several trips up there and fed her some predigested seeds. She'll have to come down to the feeding place to get the other kind. So far, she has figured out only how to climb *up*—not how to get back down. All the birds seem excited and curious about her. It's a celebration. Their flock has gained another bird.

This reminds me of the kind of celebrations that must go on in heaven when another person chooses to join the family of God. Just like baby birds, sometimes the new people are going to need extra support, extra feeding, not always from their own parents. Yet the smart babies will accept that instead of hissing, "You're not my mom," and starving up on the valance. I'm sure before the day is over, Mr. Kiwi, this baby's dad, will be up there nudging her off the edge. As she goes flopping down she'll either learn to fly or Mr. Kiwi will swoop down under her to break her fall, and then they will try again.

Being a new member of the flock isn't easy, but this baby will receive lots of support. Remember that in your church flock. When new members join, give them lots of support too.

Dear God, help me to be willing to accept help from other members of my spiritual flock, and help me to be willing to give it in turn too. Amen.

348

BLESSED ARE THE NONVIOLENT PEACEMAKERS

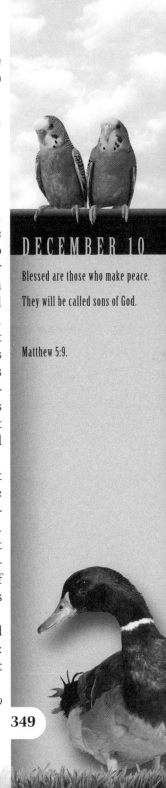

DECEMBER 10

Blessed are those who make peace.
They will be called sons of God.

Matthew 5:9.

O n this day in 1964 Martin Luther King, Jr., received the Nobel Peace Prize. He had worked hard to bring civil rights to the United States at a time when our country was embarrassingly slow in granting them. But unlike some of the other civil rights advocates during his time, such as Malcolm X, Martin Luther King believed in using nonviolent methods. He knew, just as Jesus did, that violence is only a temporary fix and that ultimately it just causes more fighting and resentment. Even though our government used force toward some of the people in his protests and even toward him, he still believed that nonviolence is the only way to achieve the rights and dignity that he and his people so badly wanted.

Even though Martin Luther King was not a perfect man, and some people have tried to make his private shortcomings public, he did show us a side of his character and provide leadership that reminds us of Jesus. Jesus too used only nonviolent means to bring about change in humans, and ultimately in world government. We can credit Martin Luther King for much of the progress made in our country against racism this century. An assassin killed him not long afterward.

All Christians should be peacemakers. We should also advocate nonviolent methods. The Bible says: "Blessed are the peacemakers" (even those without Nobel prizes).

Jesus, You are the ultimate peacemaker. Help me to be one too. Amen.

349

GOD'S NORTHERN LIGHTS

I will send the Friend to you from the Father. He is the Spirit of truth, who comes out from the Father. When the Friend comes to help you, he will give witness about me.

John 15:26.

O n this day in the year 1719 someone first wrote a description of the aurora borealis. We know it more commonly as the northern lights. The streams of light are visible only at night and best seen in the northern arctic regions.

My mom saw the aurora borealis once, but since she didn't know what it was, she didn't tell anybody. She didn't grow up in the United States. Her parents moved back to the United States when she was 16, leaving her heartbroken.

On the way from England their plane stopped in Reykjavik, Iceland, and Mom and her sister and their dad stayed there over the weekend before they went on to the United States. Mom said she cried most of that weekend, though her dad tried to make it fun and take them sightseeing. She remembers not being able to sleep at night and sitting at the window of the hotel looking out at the sky, tears rolling down her face as she told God how unhappy she was. Feeling as if her life were over, she thought that she would never have any friends again.

As she was praying she saw streams of light in the sky. Mom knew nothing about the aurora borealis. She thought that God was actually coming and being with her to comfort her and keep her company in that lonely hotel in Iceland in the middle of the night.

Our God loves us very much and comforts us when we hurt. How can we keep from loving Him back?

Thank You for Your love and Your lights. Amen.

SAINTS OR SUCKERS?

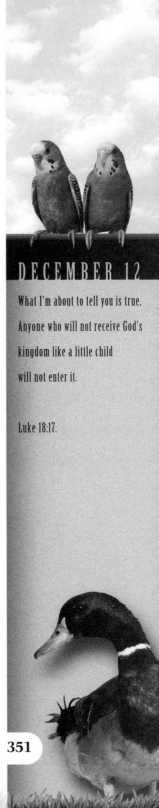

DECEMBER 12

What I'm about to tell you is true. Anyone who will not receive God's kingdom like a little child will not enter it.

Luke 18:17.

When my mom was younger, a little girl stayed at her house. One day they went to the beach when the girl tasted the sea water.

"Oh, it's so salty," the child said. "What made it so salty?"

My mom, who was always pulling someone's leg, told her, "Oh, we had several bags of salt in the trunk of the car and dumped them in one day to get rid of them, and this water has never been the same since."

That night the girl informed her family that it was all the Piersons' fault that the ocean was so salty.

Everyone laughed that the child was so gullible and that Mom had fooled someone *again*. Yet that quality in kids is one God really appreciates. As we get older we get kind of cynical. If things don't fit our picture of the future or what we think the world is like, we don't believe them. It can be a real problem in our spiritual life. Often God will promise things beyond our ability to grasp, and we have trouble believing Him.

The difference between believing tall tales from my mom when she's teasing and believing God is that God doesn't try to fool us. If He tells us something, He means it. It's not being gullible, but is called having faith.

God loved kids for many reasons, but this quality was special about them. As we learn more about being God's kids, this is something we need to acquire too. We must unlearn our cynical attitudes and begin to trust Him.

Dear God, help me realize I can trust You just as a little child can—and You will never pull my leg. Amen.

351

SAFE STOCK INVESTMENTS

Instead, put away riches for yourselves in heaven. There, moths and rust do not destroy them. There, thieves do not break in and steal them.

Matthew 6:20.

Money isn't worth much anymore, and it's worth less every day. A few days ago I was complaining about how low the minimum wage is and how little we get per hour. Mom started laughing when she told me how much she earned per hour when she got her first job. Minimum wage has more than tripled since Mom started working.

Are we richer now than she was then? No. The money is worth less, so we need more. Mom can remember when gas was 32 cents a gallon. Now we look for gas stations at which we can get it for less than a dollar.

I read in the book *Countdown to the Millennium* that a 1997 dollar will be worth only about 63 cents by the year 2010. As a result, either people will have to buy less or wages will have to go up. If money loses its value, it makes more sense to invest it in something that won't shrink in value than to just stash it away in banks. God invests in people and relationships. To be like Him, perhaps it makes more sense to put my money into other people.

My mom and dad have done that as my brother and I have been growing up. Last year we had another young person living in our home who was having trouble in life. Mom and Dad believe in investing in people. They know their value increases with time. I believe my parents are laying up treasure in heaven by doing it. It's a great idea, and I'm glad they bank there.

Dear God, help me to make wise investments too. Amen.

352

PEACE: A DYNAMITE IDEA

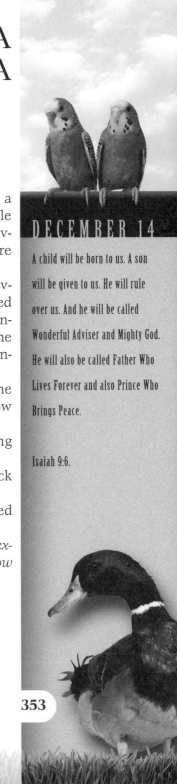

I've known for a long time, since my mom is a nurse, that nitroglycerin is a medicine people with chest pain use to help keep them from having a heart attack. What I didn't know until more recently was that it's a powerful explosive.

An Italian scientist named Ascanio Sobrero discovered it in 1847. Ascanio was a smart guy and realized its terribly destructive potential. In 1866 a Swedish inventor, an engineer named Alfred Nobel, used the compound to create dynamite. He became a millionaire. The Nobel Prize received its name from him.

It seems ironic to me that the Nobel Prize has the same name as a man who invented explosives. How odd that looks next to Jesus, the Prince of Peace!

Alfred Nobel made his money by blowing things up.

Jesus made His reputation by putting things back together—lives, ears, human hearts.

The Peace Prize may be named after Alfred Nobel, but the true Prince of Peace is Jesus.

Dear God, You are much more powerful than any explosive—yet You chose to be our Prince of Peace. How great You look to us! Amen.

DECEMBER 14

A child will be born to us. A son will be given to us. He will rule over us. And he will be called Wonderful Adviser and Mighty God. He will also be called Father Who Lives Forever and also Prince Who Brings Peace.

Isaiah 9:6.

PROUD TO BE AN UNDERDOG

But many who are first will be last.

And many who are last

will be first.

Matthew 19:30.

Today has been designated as Underdog Day. It's the day to salute the second bananas of history and literature.

Jesus was always a patron of the underdog. It wasn't the rich and the famous that He spent most of His time working with and encouraging. Rather, it was those who people thought were poor, or stupid, or sick. He knew what many other wise people have found out—that underdogs, given enough time and encouragement, can end up highly successful people.

Consider these underdogs: Peter J. Daniel's teacher told him in the fourth grade, "You're no good, you're a bad apple, and you're never going to amount to anything." For a while he believed his teacher and remained totally illiterate until he was 26 years old.

One day a friend hung out with him and read him a copy of *Think and Grow Rich.* They had to stay up all night to finish the book. However, he now owns the street corners he used to fight on. He has just published his latest book titled *Mrs. Phillips, You Were Wrong.*

Beethoven's teacher labeled him hopeless as a composer. Awkward with the violin, Beethoven preferred to play his own compositions instead of working on his music lessons. Yet he went on to become one of the world's greatest composers.

Today, go out of your way to be supportive to an underdog. Who knows? They might be your boss someday.

354

Dear God, it is comforting to know that You are the champion of underdogs! Amen.

NO CHRISTIAN COSTUME PARTIES

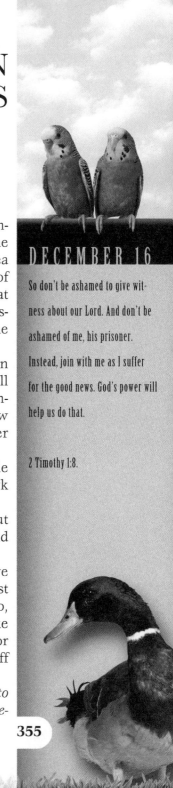

DECEMBER 16

So don't be ashamed to give witness about our Lord. And don't be ashamed of me, his prisoner. Instead, join with me as I suffer for the good news. God's power will help us do that.

2 Timothy 1:8.

Recently I heard on the radio that scientists have tested the water from the Boston Harbor and found traces of tea in it. Probably it reflects the amount of tea that people in Boston drink that eventually winds up in the harbor from the sewer systems rather than what might be left over from the Boston Tea Party.

The Boston Tea Party took place in 1773 when American colonists, angry about the tax on tea as well as other taxes, and unhappy with the British government, boarded a ship to cause trouble. They threw 342 chests of tea into the harbor. They would rather live without tea than have to pay taxes.

What I thought was kind of slimy about the whole deal was that the colonists, dressed up as Mohawk Indians to do their dirty work.

If they wanted to rebel, that was one thing. But dressing up as Indians made it look as if they would be perfectly willing to let the Indians take the rap.

Taking a stand in their own name would have made more sense. In life you have the right to protest some things that you feel are unfair. When you do, however, don't be a tea partyer. If you're going to take a stand, do it as yourself. Be willing to be counted for what you believe. As God's kid, you're a lot better off just being yourself.

Dear God, help me to have the fearless courage to stand up for what I believe and not pretend to be someone or something else than what I really am. Amen.

355

SUICIDE IS NOT A SOLUTION

But I will bless any man who trusts in me. I will show my favor to the one who depends on me.

Jeremiah 17:7.

Suicide is an ugly thing. It's something we don't talk about very much, although it is a major cause of death among people our age. Many people get discouraged and feel suicidal at some point in their life. My mom tried to commit suicide when she was a teenager. She had problems in her love life (one could interpret it as lack of love life).

Even in the Bible, Elijah was so discouraged after his big day on Mount Carmel that he asked God to let him die. It happens. The sad thing is that when people commit suicide, their lives are over. Many of them could have gone on to have had wonderful experiences, but they missed it all by giving up. If my mom had been successful in her suicide attempt, she would have lost out on all the fun and the neat things she has done in her life (like getting to live with me).

Elijah would have not performed a bunch of miracles and ridden to heaven in a fiery chariot and then hung out with God face-to-face.

We all get discouraged, but when we do, we must remember that there's still very much ahead of us. No matter what's going on, you can usually count on things changing in the future. God plans to give us both a future and a hope. Even more than that, I hope to join God in heaven without ever dying, just like Elijah, and hanging out with Him face-to-face. Who wants to miss that? Not me. Take courage, get help. Talk to someone, talk to God.

Dear God, help me to remember to turn to You when I get discouraged. Amen.

FAREWELL TO SLAVERY

So if the Son of Man sets you free, you will really be free.

John 8:36.

I n 1865 the United States abolished slavery, when our Congress adopted the Thirteenth Amendment to the Constitution. But we were among the last of the major Western nations to give it up. (Brazil passed a law freeing its slaves in 1888.) Britain and Europe had ended slavery long before we thought of it. In fact, Britain had been campaigning against slavery before America started using slaves in large numbers. Yet our country gave up slavery in 1865, kicking and screaming all the way and only because of the Civil War, which had cost the lives of thousands and thousands of men and boys, some of them younger than me.

I have gone through museums and seen some of the artifacts from slavery. It horrifies me to imagine that such things went on all around me here in Virginia and that people considered such abuse as normal. Even people who loved God and considered themselves good Christians kept slaves. What is even worse is to know that forms of slavery continue in our world today.

I'm eagerly looking forward to the day Jesus returns and sets all the slaves free. For it won't really be until we live in heaven with Him that we can honestly sing that we are in the land of the free and the home of the brave. "Even so, come, Lord Jesus" (Revelation. 22:20, KJV).

God, You are the key to real freedom. Amen.

"CHRISTIAN" KILLERS

Blessed are you when people make fun of you and hurt you because of me. You are also blessed when they tell all kinds of evil lies about you because of me.

Matthew 5:11.

As I was listening to the news last night I heard that another doctor who worked at an abortion clinic had been shot through the window of his home. I don't believe in abortion in most cases, but I think that killing a human being in order to protest his destruction of other human beings makes no sense.

Since most antiabortionists are Christians, the bad press that goes with whoever shot the doctor gives all of those who are against abortion a bad name. But it isn't a new problem.

Martin Luther had similar trouble during the sixteenth century. Some good people led the early Protestants as they originated in Germany, Holland, and Switzerland. However, some very strange people also claimed to be a part of the Protestant Reformation. One was named Jan Beukelzoon.

In 1534 he established himself as the king of New Zion and expected his Protestant followers to worship him. His rule included polygamy (multiple wives), communal property, and a lot of shocking sexual behavior. Many Christians who might have accepted Protestantism found themselves turned off by radicals like him.

In spite of the counterfeits, God will win in the end. And though they may cause confusion and persecution in the meantime, don't get distracted by them. Just keep your eyes on Jesus.

Dear God, help me keep my eyes on You and not get distracted and discouraged by what other people who claim to be Your friends do. Amen.

358

COCKATOO CONSCIENCE

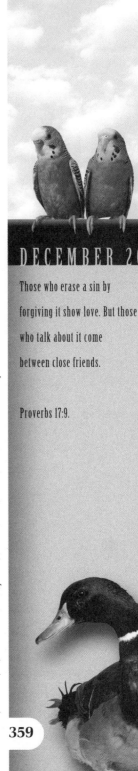

As I am writing this, Skippy, my lesser sulphur-crested cockatoo, is shouting "No! No! Bad bird! Bad baby!" It means that either he has done something naughty or he's yelling at Puff, my pet iguana.

Since Skippy rarely berates himself after doing something naughty unless someone else initiates it, a logical conclusion would be that Puff has wandered from his home in the living room into Mom's office, which Skippy considers his domain. Probably Puff climbed up to look out the window and has knocked some papers down.

Skippy loves to tattle on other people's (or pets') wrongs. Perhaps it's because he gets into trouble for naughty behavior so often that it feels good to point out when someone else is misbehaving.

How much like Skippy humans can be! It's funny when he does it, but how often a reprimanded person responds by saying "Well, so-and-so does it" or "He did it first"! It just makes us feel better to know that perhaps someone else is worse than we are.

As children of God, we need to develop a sense of humility and a sense of responsibility. That means being willing to admit when we've made a mistake, without pointing out the mistakes of other people. Cockatoos generally develop a mental and an emotional age of a 3-year-old human. That's as far as they get. What's your excuse?

Dear God, help me not to be like Skippy but to concentrate on taking responsibility for my own behavior. Amen.

DECEMBER 20

Those who erase a sin by forgiving it show love. But those who talk about it come between close friends.

Proverbs 17:9.

GETTING OFF THE BOAT . . .

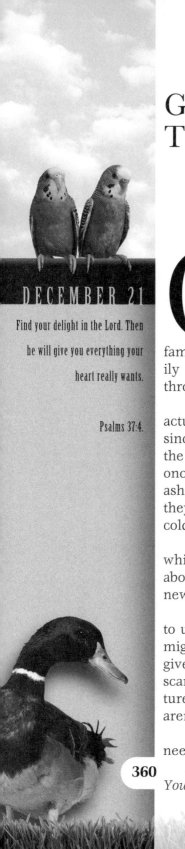

Find your delight in the Lord. Then

he will give you everything your

heart really wants.

Psalms 37:4.

On this date in 1620 the Pilgrims set foot on American soil for the first time. I have found learning about them a lot more interesting since I discovered that I was descended from one of the families who came over on the *Mayflower*. Their family name was Soule. And I am related to them through my mom's side of the family.

Taking a closer look, I found that the Pilgrims had actually been anchored off the coast near Cape Cod since November 11. Even though they had come to the land that they had asked God to help them find, once they got here they were too frightened to go ashore and check it out. They stayed on the ship until they ran out of food and water, the weather became cold, and more of them began getting sick.

They had spent two months in that tiny space while crossing the Atlantic, and yet they sat there for about 40 days off the coast, scared to set foot on the new land.

While at first that might seem a little hard for us to understand, if we took a close look at ourselves it might not be. How often do we pray and ask God to give us something, yet when He does we are too scared to reach out and take it? Perhaps human nature hasn't changed much over the years, and we aren't that different from the Pilgrims.

God is good. He's given you many gifts. You just need to get off the boat and take them.

Dear God, help me not to be afraid to accept the gifts You've given me. Amen.

360

DO AS I SAY . . .

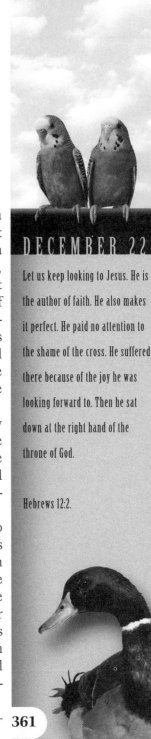

Doesn't it bug you when people tell you to do as they say and not as they do? It never made sense to me when I was a little guy. My mom would say, "No, sweetie, don't drink that—caffeine's not good for you," as she chugged away on her bottle of Diet Coke. Of course, I didn't take it into consideration at the time that she worked night shift and was trying to stay awake long enough to get me to school that morning. All I saw was that she was telling me not to drink caffeine as she gulped it down in large quantities. It just didn't make sense.

Thomas Jefferson fought against slavery as they developed the Declaration of Independence, the Constitution, and the laws of our new country. Yet he refused to free his own slaves because of his financial status. Jefferson was never very effective as an abolitionist—perhaps because of his own example.

Fortunately Jesus didn't do that. He asked us to love everyone and forgive everyone, but He lived as one of us and did exactly as He told us to do. We can trust Him never to ask us to do something that He Himself wouldn't do. His words and His example are compatible. They agree. Because of that, Jesus is our only true role model. Other humans may teach us good things, but ultimately we will see weaknesses in them. Yet when you keep your eyes on Jesus, you'll find that He'll never let you down, He'll never disappoint you. Jesus is awesome!

Dear God, please help my own example to be consistent with what I say I believe in. Amen.

DECEMBER 22

Let us keep looking to Jesus. He is the author of faith. He also makes it perfect. He paid no attention to the shame of the cross. He suffered there because of the joy he was looking forward to. Then he sat down at the right hand of the throne of God.

Hebrews 12:2.

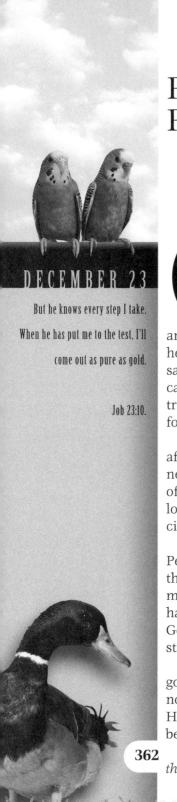

But he knows every step I take.
When he has put me to the test, I'll
come out as pure as gold.

Job 23:10.

PAINFUL PERSPECTIVES

On the TV show *Home Improvement* Tim's neighbor Wilson often quoted the German philosopher Nietzsche. Friedrich Wilhelm Nietzsche was one of Germany's most important writers and philosophers of the mid-to-late 1800s. However, he had some rather Kevorkian attitudes. Once he said: "The sick man is a parasite of society. In certain cases it is indecent to go on living." It sounds extremely harsh to me. My mom is a sick person, and I, for one, am very glad that she is still alive.

In 1889 Nietzsche suffered a mental breakdown after producing some of his most notable writings. He never recovered. For 11 years he could not take care of himself, and his mother, and later his sister, had to look after him. Apparently Friedrich Nietzsche decided that going on living wasn't so bad after all.

Often pain can change a person's point of view. Perhaps that is why God allows some of the difficult things to happen in our lives. Without them we too might make some pretty sweeping statements and have rigid, unbending attitudes toward other people. Going through hard times makes us more understanding of others who are still struggling.

God is good, and whether you are going through good times or hard ones, you can thank Him, because no matter what's happening in your life, you can trust Him to be allowing only those things that will help you be stronger or better or more like Him in the long run.

Dear God, thank You for sticking by me as I go through good times and hard ones. Amen.

MOUNT RUSHMORE, THE ARK, AND THE GREAT COMMISSION

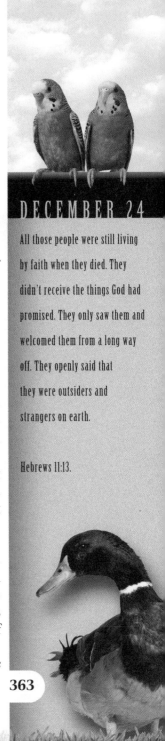

DECEMBER 24

All those people were still living by faith when they died. They didn't receive the things God had promised. They only saw them and welcomed them from a long way off. They openly said that they were outsiders and strangers on earth.

Hebrews 11:13.

When I think of South Dakota, the first thing that springs to mind is Mount Rushmore, the huge national memorial with the faces of presidents Washington, Jefferson, Lincoln, and Teddy Roosevelt. Each one is carved into the side of the rocks of the Black Hills. They are between 50 and 70 feet high.

The memorial was the brainchild of sculptor Gutzon Borglum. He worked for years with his dynamite and pneumatic hammer, carving out one piece of rock at a time. As it took shape the tourists who came to see it began to understand his idea. Unfortunately, Gutzon Borglum died before he finished the job. His son, Lincoln Borglum, finally completed the work. Today you can go to South Dakota and visit the memorial. It is just awesome.

Methuselah helped work on the ark. Believing that God was going to destroy the world, he assisted with the preaching, the building, and the getting ready. He died before the Flood actually came.

As we help get our world ready for Jesus to come, not everyone will make it to the end. Some people will die before our task is finished. No matter which part of the job we end up doing, the beginning or the end, God has promised rewards. All we have to do is buckle down and work on it, and He will take care of everything else.

Dear God, I'm looking forward to meeting You there too. Amen.

363

HAPPY BIRTHDAY, JESUS!

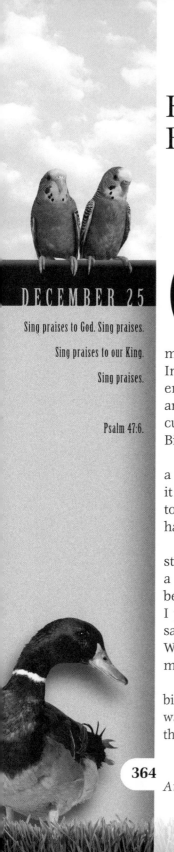

Sing praises to God. Sing praises.

Sing praises to our King.

Sing praises.

Psalm 47:6.

One of my most memorable Christmases happened when I was little. We attended the Takoma Park, Maryland, church, where my mother and father ran a children's church service once a month. That year Christmas Day fell on Sabbath. Instead of the usual children's church program, my parents had a party. Mom brought a helium tank, and Dad and I filled more than 200 balloons. Mom made 150 cupcakes and got finger cramps from writing "Happy Birthday, Jesus" in frosting on the top of each one.

While some people regarded a party atmosphere as a little inappropriate for Sabbath and church, I thought it was one of the greatest Christmas celebrations I ever took part in. We sang "Happy Birthday" to Jesus and had cake. Then we each gave Him a present.

At our little tables we received paper, scissors, stickers, glitter, and glue. Making a card for Jesus with a heart in the middle, an eye on one side, and a number two on the other, I meant to say "I love You too." I painstakingly decorated it. Mom passed out bags of satin bows, and I carefully stuck my bow on the top. When the time came, each of us approached the manger and put our presents for Jesus in front of it.

It was the first time I had ever thought of giving a birthday present to Jesus. Until then Christmas had always meant presents for me. I'm older now and have been through many more Christmases, but I still like that idea.

What will you give Him this year?

Dear Jesus, I give You myself for another year. Amen.

NATIONAL WHINER'S DAY

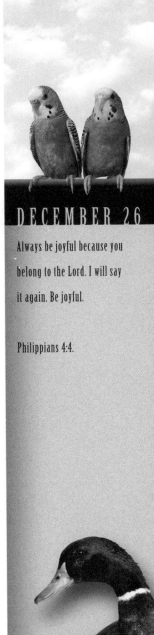

DECEMBER 26

Always be joyful because you belong to the Lord. I will say it again. Be joyful.

Philippians 4:4.

Today is known as National Whiner's Day for all those who complain about their Christmas presents while they exchange them at the store for something else. Some people we knew when my family lived in Illinois *always* asked for the receipt from your gift so they could exchange it for something they liked better. My brother watched all this silently.

Then when I was born, he was not sure how he felt about me. After I had been home from the hospital for about two days, he asked my mom, "When are we going to take Michael back to the hospital?"

"We aren't taking Michael back," Mom replied. "We are keeping him. He is going to be part of our family and live here just like you and me and Daddy."

"Why?" Donnie persisted. "Did you lose the receipt?" (Apparently they did, for they did keep me after all.)

In Great Britain, where my mom lived as a teenager, people call today Boxing Day. On it they give gifts to the support people in their lives—servants, if they have any; the mail carriers; the people who deliver their paper; and those who bring their milk.

The day after a big celebration everyone has been looking forward to can sometimes feel like a letdown, but we have a choice in how we celebrate. Just like every other day, we can choose to have fun and give to others, thus making their day good too, or we can whine and wallow in self-pity and complain.

Dear God, I choose to celebrate. Thank You for everything! Amen.

365

TEMPERATE WITNESSING

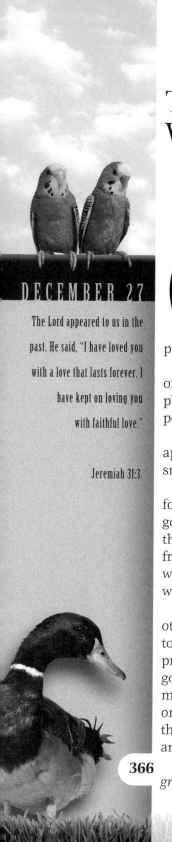

The Lord appeared to us in the past. He said, "I have loved you with a love that lasts forever. I have kept on loving you with faithful love."

Jeremiah 31:3.

On this date in 1900 Carry Nation staged her first saloon raid in Wichita, Kansas. She and her followers broke into the saloon, smashing all the bottles within reach. Carrie Nation was a prohibitionist who violently opposed alcohol.

Ellen White was also a prohibitionist who did a lot of public speaking during that time. In fact, in some places she was more well known for her work as a temperance advocate than she was as a spiritual leader.

Both of them strongly opposed alcohol, but one appealed to people's sense of choice while the other smashed their bottles with axes.

Was Carrie Nation right? In my opinion, using force even in support of something that is right is ungodly. God respected our freedom of choice so much that He was willing to let His Son die to restore our freedom. He wasn't sending His Son to die so that we would all automatically follow Him but so that we would have a choice again.

If I want to be like God in the ways that I deal with other people, then I believe that it's important for me to respect their freedom of choice. Certainly it's appropriate for me to express my opinions and set a good example for the way of life that I'm recommending to them, but I don't believe that beating anyone up or destroying their things is going to convert them to Jesus. Jesus gently convinces us that His love and His peace are much better. I want to be like Him.

366

Dear Jesus, I want to be like You. Please help me grow that way. Amen.

QUESTIONS AND KWANZA

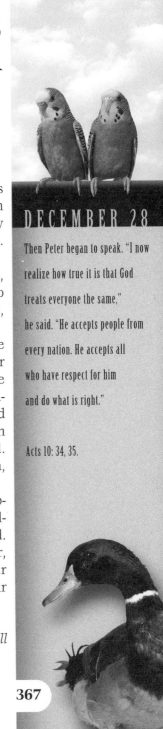

Today is the third day of Kwanza. Kwanza is a seven-day holiday that celebrates African and African-American heritage. Each day people think about a single virtue or idea. Kwanza is a cool celebration.

My mom lived in Africa when she was a little girl, and she loves African culture and history. She sees no reason why our family, which happens to be White, can't celebrate Kwanza too.

My mom taught me that Africa was by far a more culturally advanced continent than Europe, Asia, or the Americas at one time. The greatest library in the world was in Alexandria, and people living there considered the European cultures to be barbaric. And they were. Mom even taught me how to play an African game she learned when she was a little girl. You can buy it in this country now. Called Mancalla, it's lots of fun.

During the seven days of Kwanza, take the opportunity to learn a little bit more about another culture. After all, we're part of one big family of God. The more we know about and appreciate each other, the closer our family will be and the happier our Father will be, since dads always appreciate their children getting along.

Happy Kwanza!

Dear God, You are the center of my culture and all my celebrations. Amen.

HE SAID WHAT?

Then Jesus said to them, "Give to Caesar what belongs to Caesar. And give to God what belongs to God." They were amazed at him.

Mark 12:17.

The book *The 365 Stupidest Things Ever Said* includes a lot of quotes from politicians such as Jim Scheibel, a former mayor of St. Paul, Minnesota: "I'm not indecisive. Am I indecisive?"

Or Charles Peacock, the ex-director of Madison Guarantee, justifying his writing a check to Clinton's reelection campaign: "I'm a politician, and as a politician I have the prerogative to lie whenever I want."

Or the many quotes from former vice president Dan Quayle, such as "I haven't been to Michigan since the last time I was there" or "It's time for the human race to enter the solar system." (What does he think we've been a part of all this time?) Or his attempt to explain the difference between the House of Representatives and the Senate: "There are lots more people in the House. I don't know how many exactly—I never counted—but at least a couple hundred." Or "a low voter turnout is an indication of fewer people going to the polls."

All of these quotes sound pretty silly. And all of them come from political leaders. Even though it is easy to make fun of them, the Bible tells us that we need to respect our leaders because of their position of authority.

As a follower of Christ, I need to do that. It also applies to other authority figures such as principals and parents and pastors, especially when they upset us. As one of God's kids, even though I may struggle with it, it is something I will learn to do.

Dear God, help me to remember to treat my leaders with respect—even when I feel more like making fun of them. Amen.

HAPPY ENDINGS

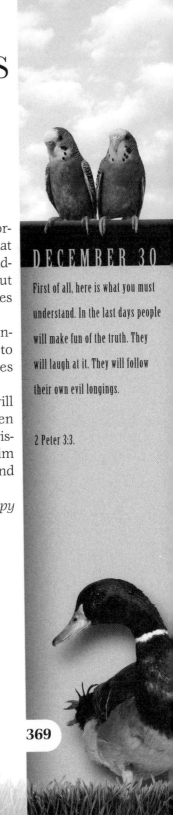

Geoffrey Fieger, who once was Jack Kevorkian's attorney, told the Detroit *News* that "the world will end when hell stops sending us its rejects or when Elvis comes out of the Holiday Inn in Kalamazoo and sees his shadow, whichever comes first."

Mr. Fieger was making fun of those who constantly predict the end of the world. Yet he's going to need his sense of humor when Jesus actually does come and the world does end.

The Bible predicts that in these days people will ridicule our message. Whether they laugh, throw rotten tomatoes, or make fun of us won't matter as we're rising through the air to meet Jesus and to live with Him for ever and ever. We won't care. It will be all over. And it will have ended just as Jesus promised it would.

Dear God, thank You for Your promise of a happy ending! Amen.

DECEMBER 30

First of all, here is what you must understand. In the last days people will make fun of the truth. They will laugh at it. They will follow their own evil longings.

2 Peter 3:3.

FAREWELL, FRIENDS!

Well, there you have it. I'm Mike, and this has been my world. I'm just a kid, not a role model. Not perfect, I make mistakes. I get frustrated with the people that I know and love. I get frustrated with my church. Sometimes I get mad at God. I sin and do all kinds of things wrong. But I love God and am drawing closer to Him every day. And to me that's what's really important.

Just like Paul, I end up doing some of the things that I hate doing and that I hate seeing other people do. Some of the good things that I plan to do I don't always end up doing. And just as the case with Paul, God is very patient with me and loves me, and He appreciates me, forgiving me every time I screw up. And He'll do the same for you, too. All you have to do is ask Him.

So join me in the incredible journey of getting closer to God and getting to know Him and letting Him get to know you. You'll have the time of your life.

Thank You for being my Friend. Amen.